PN
1998.3
.R35
A25
1989

Rainer, Yvonne

The films of Yvonne
Rainer

The Films of **Yvonne Rainer**

D1003299

THEORIES OF REPRESENTATION AND DIFFERENCE

General Editor: Teresa de Lauretis

The Films of
Yvonne Rainer

Yvonne Rainer

with contributions by

B. Ruby Rich
Bérénice Reynaud
Mitchell Rosenbaum
Patricia White

INDIANA UNIVERSITY PRESS ● BLOOMINGTON AND INDIANAPOLIS

Watkins College
of Art & Design

© 1989 by Indiana University Press

All rights reserved

No part of this book may be reproduced or utilized in any form or by any means, electronic or mechanical, including photocopying and recording, or by any information storage and retrieval system, without permission in writing from the publisher. The Association of American University Presses' Resolution on Permissions constitutes the only exception to this prohibition.

Manufactured in the United States of America

Library of Congress Cataloging-in-Publication Data

Rainer, Yvonne
  The films of Yvonne Rainer / Yvonne Rainer with contributions by
B. Ruby Rich . . . [et al.].
    p. cm. — (Theories of representation and difference)
  Bibliography: p.
  Filmography: p.
  ISBN 0-253-34906-0. — ISBN 0-253-20542-5 (pbk.)
  1. Rainer, Yvonne—Criticism and interpretation. 2. Experimental
films—History and criticism. 3. Feminist motion pictures—History and
criticism. I. Title. II. Series.
PN1998.3.R35A25 1989
791.43'0233'0924—dc19   88-46035
                                                            CIP

1   2   3   4   5   93   92   91   90   89

Contents

Foreword

The films of Yvonne Rainer are a distinguished exemplar of contemporary American art. Produced at the intersection of creative and critical practices—the avant-garde and the women's movement, filmmaking and theories of representation and spectatorship, performance art and psychoanalysis, autobiographical writing and the critical study of culture—her films situate themselves in the figural space between text and discourse, in a sustained exploration of the material, political relations of subjectivity to sociality.

The scripts of her films are far more than a notation of the dialogues or the verbal support of the cinematic images; they are artistic and critical texts in their own right, as intensely and deliberately *written* as the essays of Virginia Woolf or the "writerly" texts of Roland Barthes may be said to be. They are so rich in speculative insights and intertextual allusions, meditations on art and life, political commentary and quotations from other cultural texts, that even several viewings of the films do not suffice for one to grasp the texture of excess that characterizes Rainer's creative imagination, her critical art.

Hence the idea of this book, bringing together Rainer's film scripts to date in a carefully edited version, complemented by a comprehensive introduction to her earlier and recent films, and an up-to-date bibliography, is to make her work available for serious study as well as greater appreciation by anyone concerned with the visual arts, women's cinema, aesthetics, and cultural criticism. The introductory essay by B. Ruby Rich, first published as a monograph on Rainer, covers her films up to 1980 (*Journeys from Berlin/1971*), while Bérénice Reynaud's reading of *The Man Who Envied Women* and the 1988 interview by Mitchell Rosenbaum address Rainer's most recent work and current concerns with social criticism and film theory, feminism, narrative, and of course the economics and politics of independent filmmaking. The bibliography compiled by Patricia White includes all the critical writings both by Rainer herself and about her work, with the exception of reviews in daily or weekly newspapers.

The unusual format of the book, halfway between the single-author work and the multi-authored collection, is intended to provide a valuable resource for students and scholars of film, as well as the record of a singular, highly original film practice and artistic achievement.

TERESA DE LAURETIS
January 1989

The Films of **Yvonne Rainer**

Yvonne Rainer: An Introduction

B. Ruby Rich

THE START of a new decade is an auspicious moment at which to survey Yvonne Rainer's work in cinema over the past eight years. Rainer had begun the Seventies as an established and celebrated performer, a dancer/choreographer credited with the wholesale re-invention of dance within a modernist lexicon. Now she has begun the Eighties as an established filmmaker, a key force in the re-invention of narrative, thereby contributing to the course of avant-garde cinema through this past decade. Of her dance work, it was said that she worked at "tearing away the facade of ar-tificiality" and suggested that "no one who has ever been exposed to her work can again succumb to theatrical illusion with quite the same innocence."[1] The same might be said of her work in cinema, where this theme of innocence forever-lost has been a constant thread, linking Rainer's frustration of narrative continuity with her jabs at character identification and her landmining of emotional terrains. Initially conceived within the context of the performance world, Rainer's films have grown in complexity and assurance, reaching a climax of synthesis in her fourth and latest film, *Journeys from Berlin/1971*. In titling the film with that particular date, Rainer has provided a clue to the necessary starting point for any examination of her filmmaking career. As arbitrary as the choice of any particular date will inevitably appear, the year 1971 is, nevertheless, a persuasive index to Rainer's development.

In retrospect, 1971 is a crucial year for a number of reasons pertinent to Rainer as dancer, filmmaker, woman, and traveller.

1971 marks the ten-year point in Rainer's career as a dancer, which formally began with her performance of "Three Satie Spoons" at the Living Theater in 1961. Her work in dance was characterized by a hostility to artifice, an insistence upon granting the everyday movement of the ordinary body the status of dance, a con-centration on pure movement unencumbered by metaphor, a will to make the body stand for nothing but itself. During the days of the Judson Church performances, a complaint often levelled at Rainer and company was: Why are they so dead set on being themselves? When reviewing the history of dance in this period at the Walker Art Center, Rainer in a recent lecture commented on the similarity between this dance

© 1981 by Walker Art Center. Reprinted with permission.

emphasis and the parallel art-world commitment to "unadorned, uninflected, sculptural objects" but admitted that bodies in space could never attain the level of abstraction that a painting or sculpture could. It is precisely this limitation of the body which, transferred to film, became Rainer's greatest strength.

Rainer made the move from dance to film for a number of reasons. Struggling with her attraction/repulsion to authority, Rainer had disbanded her own company and formed a new collective group under the name of the Grand Union. The collective was calculated to maximize improvisation, decentralize decision-making, combat the dance world's notorious star system, and democratize its processes. Doubtless its formation was intended to solve Rainer's dilemma of 1969: "The weight and ascendancy of my own authority have come to oppress me."[2] Yet, once formed, the company's very anarchy came to exercise its own form of oppression upon the now-incipient director: "There was no way of my getting back in control. . . . When there's no boss, there are new problems."[3] Such individualist anarchy was no doubt an attractive model for Rainer, judging by an exercise sheet distributed at a dance workshop she conducted at roughly the same period, which includes in its exhaustive list of possibilities the seductive number 18: "Do anything you want (at your own risk)." Certainly the new situation quickly became riskiest for Rainer, who found the old oppression of authority replaced by a new, more equitable one: competition. "It wasn't the right atmosphere for me," she recently acknowledged.[4] The way out appeared in the unlikely form of a travel grant awarded to Rainer by the Experiments in Art and Technology.

Under its auspices, Yvonne Rainer spent the beginning of 1971 in India, where the impact of the music and theatre events which the still-minimalist-inclined New Yorker attended took root, tapping into the desire for character and narrative that had already begun to appear in her performance work. In the future, this brief India sojourn would have a major effect on the shape of Rainer's creativity. Its immediate effect, though, was a culture-shock negative: "I went into a deep funk, was flooded with contemptuous feelings toward my culture and my place therein, entertained fantasies of giving up my profession because I no longer had anything meaningful to say. . . ."[5] As these feelings of contempt and inadequacy were played out during the low days of 1971, Rainer presented a new performance.

Grand Union Dreams, perhaps the pivotal work in moving her concerns wholly out of performance into film, was presented on May 16, 1971. Autonomous, it was the last of its kind (after May, all performance work was linked to the film meant to incorporate it). It was also the first of her performance pieces to emphasize individual characters and fictional plot strategies, showing the Indian legacy. At the same time, however, the masquerade of *Grand Union Dreams* as performance belied the fact that it was already the seed of a film. The film would be *Lives of Performers,* in which both rehearsals for and audience response to the performance would play a part.

Rainer's own writings from the summer of 1971 (in Vancouver) make it clear that film as future was already forming in her mind.[6] She writes on her dissatisfaction with mixed media (the bits of film she had used as backdrop in her performances before) and of her determination either to stop making films or do it right. Her plans revolved around her antagonism to voyeurism as a cinematic component and her attraction to the theme of human relationships. In a letter published after the premiere of *Lives of Performers,* in fact, she stresses that the need to deal more specifically with emotion was a prime motivation behind her move from dance to film.[7]

In 1971, film must have looked like an art in its ascendancy. The Anthology Film Archives had opened its doors just before the New Year, with an energy that could not have failed to impress the inflated art-world spirit of the time. 1971 was a key year for avant-garde cinema, witnessing the release of a score of works that by now constitute its orthodoxy (such as Michael Snow's *La Region Centrale,* George Landow's *Remedial Reading Comprehension,* and the first half of Hollis Frampton's *Hapax Legomena).* There could hardly have been a body of work, though, more foreign to most of Rainer's intentions: the avoidance of emotion, psychology, even character, a purity of expression and damn the consequences, an emphasis on the materiality of the film screen/frame/grain/splice/flicker/camera, an antipathy to narrative and cinematic representation. Except for some of the Frampton work (like *Critical Mass* and *Poetic Justice,* which appealed to Rainer), there was quite a line of demarcation between the dominant avant-garde direction and the sort of emotional and procedural investigations that Rainer was pursuing. Probably more pertinent influences lay elsewhere. "Martha Graham and Jean-Luc Godard were as responsible for my leaving the circus as anybody."[8] The first influenced her dance, the second her films. While Rainer's work takes up some of the same issues raised by Godard, particularly regarding the autonomy of the director and the inviolability of the audience within the system of cinema, her point of view is quite different.

An accounting of Rainer's development in film (particularly her attention to issues of sexuality, power, and emotion) cannot bypass the emergence of a vital women's movement in this same period.[9] Rainer had always been "political." Her father was an anarchist, leaving that persuasive influence to color her childhood. Her own performances during the time of the anti-war movement were aimed variously against the Vietnam War, flag jingoism, and the invasion of Cambodia. By 1971, though, the war was coming to an end, flags would soon be a bitter reminder packed away, and the unified counter-culture audience was splintering. A new politics was growing in its wake, developed alongside the recognition that "the personal was the political" and extended to the same themes now occupying Rainer: the power politics of interpersonal relations, male-female dichotomies, the ambiguity of power, and, in terms of media, a critique of dominant modes of production and representation. In the performance *Inner Appearances,* Rainer worked through and reworked the implications of having either a man or a woman perform the primary activity that comprised the piece (vacuuming the performance space), weighing the audience response that seemed to adjust meaning according to gender. In the performances, and even more so in the scripts of the new films, Rainer began to present material clearly attuned to the feminist culture then coming of age.

Simon and Schuster published, in 1971, the screenplay to G. W. Pabst's classic *Pandora's Box (Lulu),* which would become the closing coda to *Lives of Performers,* which Rainer subtitled parenthetically "a melodrama." This film, essentially a series of exercises coming to terms with a series of problems, lays out the basic terms upon which Rainer would proceed in her three succeeding films. Here, however, she is still dogged by the world of performance. The disarrayed scrapbook of stills and script instructions littered across the frame at the film's beginning reveal a cartoonish figure at frame left. It is a cut-out photo of Rainer herself, suspended in space apart from the clustered groups of dancers in the other photographs, with a handwritten comic-strip balloon labelling her: "director." However ambivalently, she has again taken up that role.

The title evidences what is to come. While the performances of the preceding years had often been rehearsals for themselves, enacted on stage before an audience, the film offers, in place of such a rehearsal of a performance, rather a performance of a rehearsal. Rainer plays off that deception on the soundtrack, as the characters' voices challenge the illusory spontaneity of her dialogue with: "Yvonne, were you reading those questions?" Her response introduces the problem of directorial authority (which cinema can so smoothly mask). The title also questions the autonomy of art from daily life, by mixing modes in its very phrasing (of the "lives" as "melodrama") and by keeping the performers' names and seeming identities as the data for the characters as well. If the performer could not be separated from the performance, nor the performance (with its "ordinary" movement) from daily life, then how to sort the dancer from the dance? Thus rehearsal time was now screen time, the private now public, and emotion—so long off-limits for ascetic modernists—now itself a form of melodrama, expressed via a vocabulary of cliche and banality in place of drama. The unity of the film derives from its constant themes of artifice and deception, as variously manifested in dance or film, product or process, story or image, male or female, art or life. The "melodrama" of daily life and artistic process is still very much with Rainer, and with us.

The film's first sequence presents a quotation from the *Walk, She Said* performance world: a rehearsal space, with the bodies moving but the sound, at least initially, removed. The voice of the director does intercede, after much exploration by both camera and performers, leading to the second, discursive section. Here, a cast of voices appears to improvise reminiscences off the photographs of past performances laid out before our eyes. The voices continually interrogate both the material and the director who has assembled it, quarrelling over past history and present process. When Rainer objects to a particularly over-romantic remembrance with a "Bullshit" she is admonished: "Oh come on, Yvonne, get with it," followed on the soundtrack by a burst of canned laughter (that was actually canned live at a previous performance). As this section winds to its conclusion, a particularly crucial exchange is included. There is an objection to Rainer's inclusion of the words of Jung, which she tries to defend self-deprecatingly: "Well, you know, Shirley, that I have always had a weakness for the sweeping revelations of great men." They constitute a form of authority already being questioned throughout the film, leading to an audience reception of this line as entirely comic. It is, furthermore, an indictment of those who, as Shirley contends, exhibit "a tone of self-congratulation or complacency" common to one who "has had a revelation and is laying it out," a response that might have been familiar to many an audience member at the mythopo-etic or structural film screenings of the time.

Scenes of purportedly fictive narratives constitute a third section, with a sound-track constantly shifting from instruction to reaction, prediction to afterthought. Variation is the password. Intertitles frequently supply motivation to the ambiguous representations on screen. The camera runs through (as though provisionally) visual approaches to the woman's and man's body. When one woman speaks, face front to the audience, it is another woman's voice that summarizes for us what she might be saying. Corrections and contradictions abound.

If the sense (and dread) of women's interchangeability surfaces throughout this third section of the film, then its central sequence[10] acknowledges the possibility and examines the consequences. It is an intertitle that gets the ball rolling. "I remember that movie. It's about all these small betrayals, isn't it?" Valda proceeds to run through the variants of a triangle composed of one man, woman no. 1 and woman no. 2, as all three on screen enact a primitive choreography entitled "story." The possibilities are legion, the visual enactment crushingly skeletal, until Shirley is permitted the film's first sound-synch line in order to interrupt: "Which woman is the director most sympathetic to?" Valda guesses that it might be the woman no. 1, but wagers that might be only because she appeared first. Such is, indeed, the nature of perception and of cinematic power politics. (And not just in film. Perhaps the man stays with no. 1 simply because *she* appeared first.) As Rainer becomes increasingly concerned with the politics of visual representation, such "screen tests" become increasingly crucial.

As the narrative devices of the third section continue, time passes, if only fictively. "One week later." The scene seems suddenly to compose itself into the familiar outlines of an age-old story, as Valda opens the letter from The Other Woman and begins to read, revealing that the familiarity was an error. Valda herself is the "Other Woman" (if, as Rainer suggests, that means simply the one who appears second) and this letter, far away from Hollywood convention, has a new message. Complaining of the two little boxes "he" has stuck both of them into, the writer goes on to reject her half of that false equation and, handing over the reins to power, wishes Valda good luck: "I just wanted to tell you that I like you and I wish you'd take him away from me right now." The letter is a transitional document, carrying as it does a new perspective on an old pattern, as though "sisterhood" at that time carried all the burden of a feminist consciousness focused upon older still-oppressive behavior. Women could empathize with each other, but could find no way out of the old roles. Tradition still prevailed, standing despite its cracks—a paradox which the balance of the film reflects.

The narrative takes the shape of a series of tableaux, varying the shots and the characters in an effort to gauge the variables of viewer response in a reasonably controlled manner. Just as Fernando is about to leave in search of cigarettes, though, Rainer shifts modes to present "Valda's solo," which in actuality was filmed at a Whitney Museum performance, a fact which supplies the elegance of parquet floors and the purity of museum-white walls in contrast to the rougher environs of the preceding action. The solo is similarly high in the register of expression. Dressed in a black evening gown, traced by a hand-held spotlight, Valda Setterfield moves between the classicism of the Cunningham style (in whose company she was a dancer) and the exaggerated expressionism of Nazimova in the silent film *Salome*, which, according to Rainer, inspired her choreography here. The performance is a Greek vase in the midst of an industrial age. The shadow etched on the wall becomes a throwback to another age of cinema as well, a simple shadow-play keyed to our imagination. She freezes into certain positions, providing a pun on "silhouette" as the shadow mimics the black paper cut-outs that long ago served as portraits. Her audience is unimpressed: "he has seen it a hundred times" and despite the claim to difference "it looks the same to him." It is a judgment that cuts in two directions, both as a critique of male insensitivity and of the arch-subtlety of minimalist work.

As the film winds to a close, Rainer pulls no punches. Indeed, the intertitle that appears in the midst of this fourth section (which again quotes from the *Walk, She Said* rehearsals) charts the course of much of her work since and refocuses our attention within this one: "Emotional relationships are relationships of desire, tainted by coercion and constraint. . . ." The performers are moving about their central prop, a box, calling inevitably to mind the "little boxes" alluded to in the letter from one woman to the other. Though Valda is now in functional overalls, the shadow of the black evening dress is still upon her. Valda and Fernando are in the box together; by the end of the intertitle's warning she is outside the box, apart from all four other characters inside. By the scene's conclusion, all have emerged, yet the spectre of the box remains in the background, with its symbolism intact.

Lives of Performers concludes with the performance of the end of a life: the sequence of stills, reenacted, from Pabst's *Lulu*, terminating with the death of Lulu at the hands of Jack the Ripper. During the course of that film, the sexual power of the femme fatale becomes transformed, first into the powerless sexuality of the prostitute and last, into the terminal victimization of murder. In a technique that would be explored further in *Film About a Woman Who . . .* , the characters are made to simulate photographs by holding stasis for periods of time, lending an edge of tension and artificiality to an otherwise straightforward scene and punning visually off the word "still" used in the movie biz. In a stagy replica of the 1928 melodrama, the four characters get to exhibit extremes of emotion never displayed in the preceding footage. Lest the viewer, however, thereby assume that the emotions themselves were not in evidence (albeit devoid of the matching acting style), Rainer slyly matches the last three minutes of the "stills" to the Rolling Stones song "No Expectations," of yet another affair of the heart gone wrong. What might, then, have been a swan song to a lost era becomes instead a reminder to what extent the present conceals the past, intact within it. The theme of woman as victim is one Rainer has just begun to consider.

If *Lives of Performers* is a compendium of possibilities, then *Film About a Woman Who . . .* is their fruition. Again in black and white, again photographed by Babette Mangolte, this film pushes even further Rainer's initial thoughts on representation, narrative, sexual relationships, and the politics of personal power manipulations. The effect of feminist thinking becomes even clearer in this work, especially as reflected in hindsight by Rainer's own remarks (in 1973) on the attraction of film over dance: that since "rage, terror, desire, conflict et al" were not unique to her experience in the way that her body had always been, now she "could feel much more connected to my audience, and that gives me great comfort."[11] It was during this period, in fact, that a whole new audience was opening up for the work of women filmmakers, and an equally new context for their work. No longer was it sufficient to bring the brunt of film history to bear upon each individual work; new values were at stake. What Rainer was up to, after all, was the reinvention of melodrama as a genre, accented for the contemporary psyche.

> This is the poetically licensed story of a woman who finds it difficult to reconcile certain external facts with her image of her own perfection. It is also the same woman's story if we say she can't reconcile these facts with her image of her own deformity. . . . Not that it's a matter of victims and oppressors. She simply can't find alternatives to being inside with her fear or standing in the rain with her self-contempt.

Contradiction is the basic grammar of *Film About a Woman Who . . .* , dialectic its movement, cliché frequently its vocabulary. As always, the title is a significant indicator, for the various characters on the soundtrack are identified only as "he" or "she" while the screen offers us the actions and words of a cast of characters we can match up or discount at will. From the first opening scene, Rainer plays upon audience expectation of filmic tradition and foils its fulfillment. Even as the credits are rolling, the soundtrack sets us up with violent thunder, the cinematic code for horror-movie suspense or emotional revelation, in sardonic counterpoint to the list of names on screen. When an image does appear, it initiates a further dupe of preconditioned senses: expecting to find the film up there, we find instead another audience watching their own show, which appears to be slides on a screen judging from the light flashing with the light-dark rhythm of the carousel apparatus (just as ours, at this moment, must be reflecting the 24-frame-a-second rhythm of the sound-film projector). Continuing the hall of mirrors, Rainer transforms our screen into theirs, which is filled with a second level of images: snapshots and slides of a life heretofore unidentified. Lest the viewer try for the easy way out, and identify with the on-screen audience, the image switches to another locus altogether: a moving sound-and-image ocean, the archetypal movie set. The switch signals, as well, Rainer's own successful cross-over from dance to the vocabulary of cinema. While *Lives of Performers* may have been more self-reflective, it is *Film About a Woman Who . . .* that exhibits the assurance of a director dealing with known materials.

The effect can be seen, for example, in Rainer's new points about the cinema-to-audience relationship. The soundtrack, as always, concentrates upon charged reminiscences dealing with self-image, intimacy, sexuality, and human interaction as performance, until interrupted by an intertitle: "Social interactions seem to be mostly about seduction." Like most of Rainer's wry statements of "fact" this one reverberates at several levels. In terms of the narrative, it offers a missing piece to assemble the fragmented characters on view. In terms of the audience, it sets up a conduit carrying the narrative directly into play with our own experiences. And last, it offers a coded comment upon cinema itself. If "social interactions" stand as well for the "movies" that depict them, then a shift in the locus of "seduction" from the sphere of the bedrooms illuminated on the screen to the sphere of the viewers couched in darkness would suggest a seduction of the audience by the filmmaker through the medium of the text, the film itself. "Who is the victim here?" is asked. The question echoes the point made earlier (in *Lives of Performers*) about woman no. 1 versus no. 2. Now, Rainer has collapsed the distance separating character from viewer, removing our protective spectatorship through her intertitle's direct recognition of our in-process manipulation. The hypnotism of cinema and the concurrent need to free the audience from its enthralment to the cinematic apparatus were both hot topics of discussion in theoretical circles at the time of this film; yet Rainer is able to construct an object lesson far more persuasive than any text by fusing the moment of our realization with that of our participation in the very system we come to identify.

As a woman filmmaker, Rainer is particularly aware of the function which women's victimization has served within the narrative structure. If the death of Louise Brooks in *Pandora's Box* provided a fitting climax for the previous film, then the death of Janet Leigh at the start of *Psycho* offers an even more fitting middle to this one. As before, Rainer is playing with the notion of "stills" by using, this time, actual stills frozen out of an earlier film's footage and now, rehydrated, incorporated into her own film text for a different purpose: no longer a murder, the stills this time around are an autopsy. The stills detail the famous 45-second sequence in which Marion Crane (Janet Leigh) is stabbed to death in the shower. The scene provoked a furor of attention, not so much for its since-recognized brilliance of editing as for its violation of a treasured principle of the suspense genre: i.e., that the "star" is guaranteed survival through to the end of the picture, both because of the studio's financial investment and the audience's emotional investment. Hitchcock's transgression in killing off the high-salaried idol so early in the film paid off in shock value at the time, while Rainer's quotation of the famed sequence redefines its significance. In fixing on a moment which, historically, marks an undermining of narrative convention by Hollywood's own hand, Rainer manages to annex the traditional movie-making to her own enterprise, a feat of revision that makes film history supportive of her own terms.

The feat is not an idle one; woman's fate is inextricably caught up in the balance, as the choice of the *Psycho* material should indicate. "An Emotional Accretion in 48 Steps," the tour-de-force central section of the film, employs a range of narrative strategies in order to elucidate a particular, albeit typical, male-female interaction. Rainer avoids any one stylistic choice, overturning every possible variation of presentation in the effort to dissect the subjective emotions of an affair going awry. Setting on a single mode of communication would have placed the film within a prevailing convention, as Rainer lists them: "the *acting* of the narrative film, the *inter-titles* of the silent movie, the *sub-titles* and *dubbing* of the foreign-language film, the *voice-over* of the documentary and the flash-back, and the *face-front-to-camera* delivery of Godard."[12]

The *Psycho* stills in the middle of *Film About a Woman Who . . .* numbered 40;

Rainer's psychic stills in the "Emotional Accretion" number 48. The disjunctions between sound and image, between text and voice-over, correspond to the alienation separating "he" and "she," to the contradictions between how "she" feels and how "she" acts. At points, she seems to be dubbing her own behavior, substituting the authentic gestures with conciliatory translations. The movie remembered for all its "small betrayals" in *Lives of Performers* has been consolidated into one crucial moment in which the woman asks the man to hold her. "Somehow she had betrayed herself," reads step 46. It seems she hadn't really wanted to be held. "She had wanted to bash his fucking face in."

The section dedicated to the emotional accretions presents a story in rather the same sense that the choreographed "story" did in earlier film. Its coherent narrative may well be a precis for the film's overall fragmentation of narrative causality, while its climax in emotional resolution points to the central theme, indeed the genre definition, of the film as a whole. To be sure, the elipsis of time, the flat nonemotive voice, non-naturalistic "stagy" movement, verbal cliché, tableaux vivants, and unidentified pronouns, all combine to engage the spectator in the shaping of the film. At the same time, however, it is evident that these techniques precipitate a complete abstraction of the narrative. The only constant left to the film, finally, is emotion itself. It is the narrative structures of *Film About a Woman Who* . . . that advance the emotions instead of the usual model of emotion advancing a superimposed plot. In preserving the customary elements while inverting their relationship, Rainer has created a meeting-ground for the sort of formal and psychological concerns that, prior to her work, were frequently dismissed as mutually exclusive. In so doing, Rainer has arrived at a redefinition of melodrama for our times.

One of the major contributions of feminism to the arts has been an insistence on the inclusion of emotion as a primary value. For women, whose emotions and instincts have so long been denied as fraudulent or unrepresentative, the revival of emotion as a proper subject of artistic concern is a crucial issue. In the area of film, the revival and legitimization of the "woman's film" genre, previously despised as matinee weepies worthy of extinction, is significant. Simone de Beauvoir, in an argument pointed at annexing Stendhal to the feminist cause, once cited his upholding of the life of the heart as the worthy equal of the life of physical adventure. Molly Haskell has applied that standard to the screen, suggesting that the very qualities which provoked denigration in the past (i.e., the emphasis on emotion and sentiment) were proto-feminist values.[13] Melodrama, and by extension soap opera, deal in the drama of emotional involvement, substituting the risks of emotional commitment for the risks of physical danger. A provisional set of elements can be identified as intrinsic to the "woman's film" melodramas, indeed so implicit as to require a feminist attention. Such a set includes: the presence of a woman at the center of the film; a domestic setting, usually the site of domestic conflict; an ellipsis of time to allow for the development of emotion, always central to the drama; extreme verbalization, which replaces physical action as the means of communication for the now-interior movement; and finally, the woman's ultimate decision to release her emotions.[14]

While Haskell's work has been concerned primarily with analyzing this pattern as found in Hollywood films of a particular period, it can be traced as well throughout *Film About a Woman Who . . .* (and other Rainer films). In such a context, the very aspects of the films that appear most offensive to traditional movie-making and so scrupulously modernist in source (the use of texts, one-room staging, lack of physical activity, atemporality) may be viewed as the most natural, indeed requisite, characteristics of traditional melodrama. In turn, Rainer's fidelity to such a wide range of melodramatic conventions throws into sharp relief her flagrant departure from its codes in her handling of narrative and audience expectation. Retaining the still-valid emphasis of the genre, Rainer has reshaped them to fit specifically contemporary concerns—a formal complexity to match overwrought sensibility. *Lives of Performers,* despite its titular claim to being a "melodrama," was too much of a *roman à clef* to allow for that wider interpretation. It took Rainer until the next work, *Film About a Woman Who . . . ,* to develop the mechanisms by which the materials of autobiography could be successfully combined with those of fictional and documentary materials to form a unified, personal text.

> "When I woke up he expounded his ideas about education. Victimized once more victimized once more victimized once more. . . . No, it wasn't a breeze."[15]

Though excised from the text before the final filming, this passage points directly at one of the central themes of *Film About a Woman Who . . .* (and much of Rainer's other work as well). If women seemed to be victims of relational triangles or the machinations of art in Rainer's first film, then now the more pernicious mechanisms of society enter into the picture. For example, a long scene detailing one woman's sexual fantasy transpires within a theatrical, uninflected space, in which she is undressed by a couple ministering to her needs. Slowed down and prolonged, the scene bears witness to her disrobing via sculptural camerawork that accents the dreamlike quality. Yet, lest the viewer fall for this vision of sexuality self-controlled and removed from society, Rainer follows with herself in pasties: not the literal pasties of a strip-tease, but rather the pasted-on bits of newspaper which, originally a public testament, now adorn Rainer's own face. These patches of newsprint carry the words of Angela Davis to George Jackson, letters of affection that were used by the press to undermine and negate Davis's political work and strength. Thus is Rainer able to convey to what an extent women are still victimized through the exercise of emotional rights or powers. Furthermore, the closing performance in the film (*pas de deux* with ball) is choreographed in accordance with 20 poses derived from photographs and drawings of Isadora Duncan. In citing these two legendary women (Davis and Duncan) from the worlds of dance and politics, Rainer is making the first step toward an identification with other women (apart from film stars) that would lead, eventually, to her very different handling of identification and distanciation in *Journeys from Berlin/1971*. First, the notion of victim would have to be broadened through the strategies of *Kristina Talking Pictures,* the film which also initiates Rainer's first extended use of color (alternating, at this point still, with black and white).

Kristina Talking Pictures opens with the same theme of emotional risk established in its predecessor, but eventually moves to a broader consideration of more global, less individual, crisis. At the film's center is one Kristina (actually, several, as the character is represented by various women), a lady lion tamer from near Budapest who comes to New York to become a choreographer, and one Raoul, her seaman lover who leaves her at the film's beginning, only to return to join the dance and leave once more. The image of the lady lion tamer is a charged one, crying out to us immediately on the level of metaphor: the lady in a cage, the woman in danger, Daniella in the lion's den. She's the supreme embodiment of the paradox of the public persona: invulnerability endangered. Her scanty sequined costume reinforces the paradox. Allegedly symbolic of her skill, power, and mastery of the elements at hand (presumably the lions), the costume yet produces an effect of exposure, vulnerability, a body prone to danger. The paradox is that of femininity itself. And whence the danger? Following her introductory cast of characters, a get-acquainted section featuring lion-taming footage and Kristina stand-ins from the circus past, Rainer presents a scene that explicates the lion-tamer myth as yet another performance, with the circus now taking the place of the dance world in her first film.

The scene is actually a remake of a similar scene in *Lives of Performers,* in which a roving hand-held camera focused in on a woman in what seemed to be her bedroom, moved across her bed, onto the floor, surveying a sheet of paper with a quotation about "cliché," charted her body and eventually the body of the nearby man, and concluded with her resolution of ambivalence: "she starts to leave, then changes her mind, and rejoins him." By the time of *Kristina Talking Pictures,* Rainer has a different scene in mind.

Kristina and the camera both roam the bedroom, their points of intersection allowing us a view of her movements. Otherwise, we are free to explore the room, clearly 70's SoHo, at leisure. Again, there is a sheet of paper lying on the floor, but it's a letter this time instead of a critique, an embodiment of cliche rather than a treatise on the subject. Also in the room, prominently visible to us for its iconic significance, is a green-glittered costume lying atop the radiator. Kristina misses both. After brushing her teeth, getting dressed, packing her bag, hailing a taxi for LaGuardia Airport, yelling "Stop" . . . only then does Kristina rush back into the room for her costume, notice the letter, and collapse on the bed. "To hell with it" she says (or rather, doesn't say, since little of the film is sound-synch and voices bear no necessary relevance to the faces occupying the same screen time). The letter is by now an obligatory object for a Rainer film (cf. the Other Woman's letter to Valda, Angela Davis's letter to George Jackson). This one from Raoul, with the usual narrative omniscience of movie letters, says that he's left her, to please forgive him, etc. The reaction shot of Kristina, shot from above, finds her lying on the bed with the sequined costume in place atop her street clothes, like a body laid out for a wake gone wrong.

This crucial scene, like Kristina's body, is layered with meaning. The emotional content of the letter and her reaction immediately supply a corrective to any notions of the lion tamer as invincible. Though Kristina has tamed the wild beasts, her conquest of the physical world cannot help her escape a woman's fate of emotional risk. The lesson posed by the Beauty and the Beast fable is an enduring one: danger may be disguised as a lion but will be revealed as a man. Thus, Rainer incorporates the metaphor of the circus into her continuing preoccupation with the contradictions between the public and private persona, particularly as that split afflicts the woman artist.

By privileging the emotional struggles of Kristina over her animal-training skills as a sphere of investigation, Rainer is recommitting her work to the territory of melodrama as cited above for the centrality of emotion as authentic experience. That point was underlined sardonically in the last film by the choice of "the 48 steps" in conjunction with a quotation from *Psycho,* as though Rainer were pointedly challenging Hitchcock's priorization of physical suspense and skill, in films like his *39 Steps,* with her own drama of emotional accretions that required a full nine steps more to reach its goal.

> The sensitive intellectual or artist agonizing over the nature of his existence in the face of world poverty, over-population, pollution, and the depletion of natural resources. . . . But when it comes to women all he can think about is tits and ass.

The formal disjunctions of image, text, continuity, framing, all lend a textural codification to the disjunctions between the private and public politics of daily life. The tone may be ironic, but the contradictions are everpresent. Moving between memory and history, sexuality and world politics, Rainer assiduously removes all mock-naturalistic cues, flattening the acting, disinflecting the voices, even blocking any escape hatch into history or nostalgia by conflating past with present and background with foreground. Ironically one character opts out with "Oh, let's forget about it and go to the movies" as though there could be at least a film-within-a-film immune from ideology. "The Return of Raoul" is announced on plain lined yellow paper, its arrival on screen accompanied by a silent-movie musical flourish.

In a sense, the scene is reminiscent of a very different boy-remeets-girl scene in an equally different film, Joseph Von Sternberg's *Shanghai Express.* Meeting up with Shanghai Lily again, Doc recounts his adventures and physical exploits of the intervening years to an unimpressed Lily, who responds only: "Sounds like a lonely life, Doc," a judgment from which he does not dissent. Thus Shanghai Lily succeeds in imposing the standards of the "woman's film" (emotional richness) upon the material of the male action script, devaluing his acts of valor on the basis of their emotionally barren nature. While Rainer does not affix any hierarchy to the testimonies which she has Kristina and Raoul present, the polarity is clearly etched.

Kristina (enacted by Rainer herself) and Raoul (her brother Ivan) sit together in bed in an asexual intimacy reminiscent of the Hayes-Act movie bedrooms of the 50's. Strange pillow talk, though: Raoul speaks texts on the mechanics of crude oil carriers (based on Noel Mostert's *Supership*), Kristina speaks texts on the mating habits of lions. The obvious phallic significance of the supertanker, gliding silently across the screen, reinforces a sense of its male world of mechanization; Kristina, despite her lion-taming, concerns herself with the domestic sphere of her beasts' sexuality and procreation. The scene is played straight by the two actors, with stiff elocution-class delivery, but is broken up in the editing by words that skip and circle back on themselves, by gestures that command instant replays and looped repetitions, by camera movements that abandon the characters entirely to climb the walls, spying out the pictures there. This long, difficult scene stands at the heart of the film, epitomizing as it does a duality of focus: the emotional battlefield of alienated affections between men and women, on the one hand, and the worldwide battlefield of past and future holocaust, on the other.

The pictures on the wall offer one key to this duality. "Talking pictures," they are enigmatic souvenirs of different times and places. One looks to come from a circus, some emblem of Kristina's past. Others speak of war, ration lines, interrogation, slaughtered bodies piled up in anonymity. There is a profound feeling of alienation and loss that suffuses more than sexuality, encompassing history and infecting the present. Just as Rainer has superimposed the story of the Budapestian upon the '76 SoHo milieu, and the persona of the lion-tamer upon that of the dancer/filmmaker, so has she layered the politics of the 70's with the moral crisis of the Third Reich. There's a broader focus in terms of character, as well. Unlike the first two films, which concentrate almost exclusively upon the high-art banter of SoHo liaisons, there are other personae here, ranging from James Cagney to an old shopping-bag-lady with a German accent who's invited in off the stoop (to talk about menstruation, Marlon Brando, and the anxieties of sexuality).

In the background of many scenes, shadowy figures move about in shades of grey performing an ongoing nightmare of human suffering. Their presence sparks memories of concentration camps that are reinforced by key remarks in conversation, such as the analysis of a Yiddish joke that dominates a dinner party. As the need for a Yiddish-accented punchline is questioned, the scene begins to shift registers like so many Berlitz accents: clothing switches from shot to shot; voices change in mid-sentence from one speaker to another; remarks begun in one location conclude in another; cuts move from color to black-and-white; the scene becomes a continuity nightmare, at once challenging the illusionism of "realistic" *mise-en-scène* and defying the audience to catch the punchline without the "accent" of traditional cinematic codes. "The theater has gone out of it," the jokester concludes.

In fact, it is no longer a simple world in any realm. Raoul's bed-time conversation laid out our alienation from the earth itself, as represented by the creation of monster supertankers that destroyed the life of one sailor and may destroy all life on the planet in the event of accident. The old models of behavior and belief don't hold. If women no longer want to fill the roles previously imposed, well, men no longer have much left in the way of traditional roles to fill. Raoul laments the passing of the sailor's life (quoting at one point from Melville in despair) and its degeneration into the sterile world of the modern tanker that no one would dream of calling "she." That world of glamor and adventure, the life of the seaman, is no more. Raoul can no longer be a sailor, nor Kristina a lion-tamer. If simple roles are nowhere to be found, neither is simple representation. The camerawork reinforces the breakdown, splitting both Kristina and Raoul with the frame line, isolating portions of their bodies, mis-matching one's face with another's voice. Just as the old ways of living are dead, so are the old forms, in politics, literature, dance, film. Our ways of perceiving and our modes of illusion are equally dead.

Death, in fact, is a frequent theme in the film. At one point, Kristina breaks up a roomful of chairs, tossing them into the air and crashing them to the ground in a dreamlike slow-motion explosion of grief as the soundtrack relates, "Max, I heard you died." As the memory of Max unfolds, we realize that the mourning is not for Max alone but for an entire way of life that has passed on as surely as he (Cocteau, Chinese rugs, "soignee young men who spoke of axiology"), as well as for Kristina's own past (the chairs, after all, are the lion-tamer's tools of trade). A voice recalls, "Mama, I heard you died last night" and makes reference, at another point, to a daughter's death. Throughout, ever present, is the reference to the death of the six million in a Germany past our memory, muted by time but still speaking in pictures on the wall or texts that issue unexpectedly, ventriloquist-like, from characters' mouths. Most chillingly, near the end of the film, when its most elegant personage (Valda) consults her arm for Kristina's telephone number, it is with newly-learned horror that we perceive the concentration-camp tatoo inked onto her forearm; and with newly-felt relief that the seven digits become a Bell-Tel joke. In the spectre of eco-death raised by the supertankers, death is a less humorous threat, lurking almost unimaginably in the shadow of *Supership* disaster, where the plankton are merely the first of us to go.

If this summary begins to resemble a dirge, rightly so. *Film About a Woman Who . . .* might have been laying the final touches to the reworking of melodrama begun in autobiographical researches of *Lives of Performers,* but *Kristina Talking Pictures* presents another genre altogether. Consider Kinsley writing on Burns in the *Oxford English Dictionary:*

> The poet descends from . . . the dramatic domain of song, into the subjective and reflective one of elegy.

Melodrama was *melos* (song) plus drama. In pre-release references, the title of the film was described initially as *An Opera* and then as *For a Novella,* finally on screen becoming *Kristina Talking Pictures.* "We think there is a sure road. But that would be the road of death," spoke the Jungian text in Grand Union Dreams and Rainer's first film. Elegy is prompted by death, at least insofar as death touches and is incorporated into the spirit of the filmmaker (or, as above, the poet). In *Kristina Talking Pictures,* it may be said, melodrama met elegy and was consumed.

The film is an elegy, not only for the characters delineated above, but also for periods, roles, styles, forms, solutions (even Final Solutions) that have passed on. In the earlier works, the references to death were specific and individualized (*Lulu, Psycho*). Here, the deaths are broadened, the blow encompassing more victims, just as the character of Kristina now encompasses more performers. References that before were cinematic here are historical.

Yet the personal has not been forsaken. Elegy permits, indeed demands, a probing into one's own life and feelings, easily suiting Rainer's own penchant for including the details of her life in her fictions. When Kristina gripes that "I'm fucking around in more ways than one," we can find her sentence in Rainer's own journals. When the line of figures files hands-up through the SoHo streets, a precedent is visible in Rainer's own performance in the same streets at the time of the invasion of Cambodia. Such references proliferate throughout the film. More than the previous works, however, this film insists on pushing past the circle of private lives and loves into the wider arena of public action, concentrating our gaze on the points of intersection between the two, and laying the foundations for the more intensive mining of this same intersection in *Journeys from Berlin/1971*.

Kristina Talking Pictures, moreover, may be seen as elegy even at the fundamental level of form. The title itself harkens back to an antiquated moment in moviemaking, that era in which film "progressed" from the golden age of silent film to the much-heralded future of synchronized sound. Rainer turns her back on any such notion of "progress" by ignoring even that future in her de-synchronized sound-image combinations throughout the film. While there has been much talk, in this year particularly, concerning where the medium of film went "wrong" in its development since the days of so-called primitive cinema, and how avant-garde film practice might present a remedy to a misguidedly narrow path of technological orchestration, Rainer does not herself seem to be calling for any return to basics. Rather, by pursuing the logic of disjunctions, refusing to pander to our voyeurism, she has pushed the classic forms to the very point of disintegration, i.e., death. In this film, in particular, she has made a frontal attack upon the intelligibility of narrative, pushed disjunction past the point of illustration, defeated temporality with simultaneity of tense and ellipsis of action, and beat illusionism on its own ground.

The tone of elegy, despite the implication of mourning, need not be a somber one; there is nothing dirge-like about *Kristina Talking Pictures*. In a program note to her *North East Passing* of 1968, Rainer cited a definition of "to pass" as "to undergo, live during, discharge from the body . . . undergo transition . . . come to an end, die, depart, go by, move onward."[16] The various elements of the film are neatly marshalled under these definitions: to undergo World War II, to live during an era of impending annihilation, to discharge blood as in the old woman's menstrual memories, to undergo transition from lion-tamer to dancer (or sailor to supertankster); to come to an end (as a film) or die (as a person) or move onward (as a form). Committed, as always, to her future work, Rainer ends the film with the words "to go on." Form, as workable entity or possible ideal, no longer holds. By coming to terms with the death of the old forms and passing through our ritual of nostalgic grief, *Kristina Talking Pictures* prepares us for the future, and incidentally, for Rainer's next film. If it seems less accessible, less immediately pleasing, than the other films, it is precisely because of its determination to take a step forward in the evolution of new film languages and inflections. If its theme, as I have suggested, is one of elegy, then it is above all an elegy in the spirit of one who believes in resurrection.

Rainer, indeed, is here moving toward an acceptance of polarities, a move beyond the either/or confrontation of contradiction that toned the earlier work. Kristina's departure from the circus suggests her affinity with another cinematic figure, Leni Peickert (in Alexander Kluge's *Artistes under the Big Top*), who tried to transform the circus from an arena of physical expertise into a carnival of the imagination, but in vain. If Peickert's dedication to the circus clearly paralleled Kluge's own in terms of cinema, surely Kristina is a similar stand-in for Rainer, the circus itself a metaphor of the theatrical illusion she rejected. But how, then, to break with that need for the utopia of the circus, that clear enactment of ideal fantasies intermixed with fears and hopes? In the *Grand Union Dreams* performance, Rainer divided her cast into heroes and mortals, thereby allowing our daily life its failure to be mythic. By the time of *Kristina Talking Pictures,* however, a detente has been achieved. The introductory narration defends the characters to come: "For after all . . . they are . . . in a sense . . . if nothing else . . . nothing less than heroes." If we are not in the circus, we are nonetheless performers. If we do not walk the high-wire, we nevertheless survive.

Rainer could have ended the film on its blackboard lesson, bearing the "faint and cold" words from Samuel Beckett's *The End.* Instead, she follows his story of despair with Valda's reading of a very different letter from the one which opened the film, this one, a letter full of pain, longing, love, and above all, consolation. It is only then, after this text has been spoken, that the camera can return to the hopeful last two words which, as I've just pointed out, close the film: "to go on." The camera pans from the blackboard to the white wall. (A black and white case?) The screen goes white. The texts have been exhausted, the forms cracked open. *Kristina Talking Pictures* has passed on, leaving the task of transformation to *Journeys from Berlin/1971.*

> I was pretty happy doing the lion act for a while. But I'm afraid Emma Goldman and Virginia Woolf ruined me for the circus. Dominating brute beasts . . . how can that compare to what they did?

Feminism, anarchism. The swaying of public opinion, the organizing of popular action. Two women, furthermore, whose private and public lives were fused as one and entered into the log of history as a unity. How to justify her own taming of the wild beasts of creativity and imagination with what they did? is the question posed by Kristina and answered, at last, by Rainer in the next film, *Journeys from Berlin/ 1971.* Building upon and diverging from the researches of the past works, this film is Rainer's culminating deep-sea dive into the wreck of the psyche and the violence of history.

If *Kristina Talking Pictures* can be compared to an elegy as phrased by a resurrectionist, then *Journeys from Berlin/1971* must be the consequential next step, the phoenix arisen from the ashes. The spirit is uncannily akin to that discerned by John Berger in his critique of Soviet artist Ernst Neizvestny, whose sculpture treats some of the same subjects (the body as metaphor, the contradictions of the political being, the responsibility of the individual) that have concerned Rainer:

> It would be wrong to conclude that [he] is obsessed by death. I spoke of a polarity. Death for him is a starting point rather than an end. It is *from* death that he measures, instead of toward it. [17]

The analogy may be applied to Rainer's latest film thematically and stylistically, for here she has reshaped both her past material and her formal trajectory. She has transgressed the provincial boundaries of SoHo's art-world mentality geographically and artistically, as evidenced in her Berlin locus and in her new use of rolling titles to communicate certain information free of ambiguity. *Journeys from Berlin/1971* is without a doubt the most ambitious, most risk-taking work of Rainer's cinematic career.

The film is constructed out of a variety of filmic and literary materials. Its two major sections involve a psychoanalysis session, which occupies much of the screen time, and a kitchen conversation, which resembles a radio drama that we hear but never visually witness. The disjunction between the public and the private, always a central focus of Rainer's work, here is made wider and more explicit through the counterpoint set up between the analysis session and the conversation about terrorism: the one an excavation of innermost fantasies and emotional traumas within an impersonal space, the other a debate of pressing social issues enacted as table-top repartee. The counterpoint weaves in and out of that tricky terrain wherein the individual psyche connects up to the historical body politic.

The motif of the psychoanalysis session dominates the film visually and metaphorically. Certainly some of its strength derives from the inspired casting of Annette Michelson as the patient. While her physical presence, age, stature, and sheer acting ability must have determined Michelson as Rainer's choice, there is also a hidden irony. Writing about *Lives of Performers,* Michelson had astutely characterized its discourse as "that idiom of somewhat manic autoanalysis which characterizes life and love in a therapeutically oriented culture . . . there is really one single mode of intellectual discourse . . . that of psychoanalysis. . . ."[18] Rainer has cast Michelson into precisely the arena that she herself had first detected as the subtext of Rainer's work. And yet, perversely, Rainer has removed the sign that once prompted the diagnosis: the analytic language. Michelson's character speaks often in non-sequiturs, shifting sense and direction in a blink of the eye, traversing her subject in a stream-of-consciousness flow, sounding at times as though an editor has been hacking away at her words in some non-existent post-production phase of the film; but no, she is simply speaking, as Rainer puts it, "in tongues." The synch-sound strategy shifts attention away from the film's construction and onto its constructed: the patient and her text. With the emphasis on printed texts, subtitles, and visual addenda stripped away, the psychoanalysis-session portion of the film invests meaning in the soundtrack more intensely than any previous Rainer work, using that intensity in turn to re-invest layers of meaning into the comparably static image.

The mere use of a psychoanalysis session, of course, is redolent with formal implications. Given Rainer's standing interest in narrative, the psychoanalytic monologue inevitably becomes a model of narrative possibility. Roy Schafer, in a paper analyzing the psychoanalysis patient's history as a kind of narrative, has established a persuasive correspondence between the two. He sees the patient's testimony as "a series of tellings and retellings in the terms of self and others and the events in which they have played a role." As to the structure of these tellings, and a propos of the film under our consideration, Schafer observes: "The telling of that history is achieved in a circular fashion, the present questioning and informing the past and vice versa," in other words, an approach identical to Rainer's own handling of temporality. In conclusion, Schafer explicitly identifies "transference and resistance . . . as narrative structures," in which "the analysand shows and tells, shows by telling and tells by showing, as in 'acting out.' The analysand is a certain kind of unreliable narrator. . . ."[19] The device of the psychoanalysis session, in *Journeys from Berlin/1971,* thus integrates with precision Rainer's dedication to narrative experiment and her attachment to mediated autobiography. The two are joined in that most intimate of performances, psychoanalysis, which yet, like dance and the circus, battles still with illusion and theatricality. Schafer's critique centers on aspects of oral history and physical presentation, but the nature of cinema suggests a further extension, into the area of representation.

Throughout the footage of the psychoanalysis session, Rainer has slyly positioned her camera behind the back of the therapist in a reference to that prevailing film theory which sees the entire filmic enterprise as a voyeuristic endeavor. If all films pander to the voyeurism of the audience, then Rainer at least underlines the institutionalization of the peeping by assigning her audience the place of society's other privileged voyeur, the psychiatrist. Lest the viewer become comfortable in that role, however, Rainer pulls the rug out from under such a system of identification by recasting her doctor at unpredictable intervals. Whether a function of transference, resistance, or directorial design, the doctor appears variously as a woman, a bearded man, and a nine-year-old boy who barks. The visual perspective shifts in accordance with the hierarchy of power, the specially-built wedge-shaped set tilting for our line of vision to tilt *down* on the patient as the man, *up* as the boy, or with the possibility of equality, as the woman. There are interruptions. The patient's monologues are mixed with readings from Rainer's own adolescent journals altering the scene's chronology. Obscene phone calls disturb the air of security. A rug literally is rolled out in the background, a space peopled by a shadowy cast of characters not unlike the extras moving through *Kristina Talking Pictures.* Sometimes they form a silent chorus, other times a proper crew. This is no realistic psychoanalysis session, which after all, is simply a new way of getting to the bottom of the private/public split underlying art-making in general. Its counterpart, its alter ego perhaps, is the other part of the film: the table-top conversation between two SoHo types (played by the voices of Amy Taubin and Vito Acconci) idly talking politics while preparing dinner. Their conversation offers an initial connection between the two segments:

He: "Did you ever read Emma Goldman on political violence?"
She: "No. I have a collection of her essays, but all I've read is her autobiography."

These two characters embody the contradictory, self-absorbed view of political violence held by a fair share of artists and other mortals of the U.S. cultural establishment. Their vision of past anarchists is idealized and, therefore, prone to excessive criticism. They debate a succession of points, bolstering their positions (and our knowledge) by reading aloud not only from Goldman but also from accounts of women nihilists fighting against the czar and from writings by Ulrike Meinhof. Their voices animate a host of historical figures: Angelica Balabanoff, Olga Liubatovich, Elizaveta Kovalskaia, Vera Figner, Vera Zasulich. The models are both defended and attacked.

Rainer does not restrict our view to the studio-like space enclosing the psychoanalytic session. Much of the voice-over accompanies shots out train windows or through the windows of various flats and lofts of Berlin, New York, London. Film as a window on the world? A train of thought? Other tracking shots reveal a mantelpiece in perpetual displacement and rearrangement, cluttered with objects culled from the patient's narrative. Bread, knives, shells, steaming pasta, all appear at one time or another to break the spell of the soundtrack, provide comic relief, or literalize with cutting irony a number of seemingly serious philosophical points. The irreality of the shifting sequence parallels the patient's own leaps of logic.

Other interpolated footage is more systematic. Rainer includes two symbolic sets of aerial footage, one circular and one linear. The first shows Stonehenge, mute mysterious witness to pre-history, interpreted sardonically as standing for "flight, romantic agony, futility of effort, history as impenetrable." The second, man-made, is the Berlin Wall. Not one unified structure at all, but a series of barriers laid end to end across rural and urban landscapes, dividing the natural terrain with political rigor. The circle of stones is an analogue for the psychoanalytic session, that circling and probing of essential mysteries removed from time, space, and social context. The wall dividing east and west, in turn, is an analogue for the march of history as embodied in the terrorist debate and, more graphically, in the rolling titles detailing the history of state repression in Germany. The mantelpiece and the train tracks shuttle us visually back and forth between these symbolic terrains. The counterpoint moves closer and closer to resolution as the film progresses. The human psyche must somehow relate to the social body politic. Psychoanalysis must be made to acknowledge history. Berlin becomes, for Rainer, their meeting ground.

The combination of psychological and political reflections is an explosive one. How easy to go wrong, linking suicide and violence together, to equate political action with neurosis. It is to Rainer's credit that no such wrong step is taken. A corrupted psychoanalytic practice becomes the state's method for making (helping) its individuals adapt, while political violence becomes the individual's attempt to make the state change. Rainer sifts through the two with infinite care.

If the word "suicide" is repeatedly blipped off the soundtrack record of Michelson's speech, perhaps that is another sign that Rainer has moved beyond the Jungian notions of death that inflected her earlier work. One scene does stand out from the rest of the psychoanalysis session, though, offering the key to some of the film's innermost meanings. The scene opens with a bucket of water being thrown across the frame in slow motion, just after the patient has raged that "my cunt is *not* a castrated cock" in a rejection of fashionable Lacanian film theory. Amidst the phone's ringing, the therapist rapidly shifts from woman to little boy and back again. Meanwhile, a rowboat has appeared; in it, the patient, wearing slinky glasses. It's a radical displacement, landing us in an unexpected homage halfway between Tallulah Bankhead in *Lifeboat* and Maya Deren in *Meshes of the Afternoon*. A ship of fools? The boat as life?

The strange glasses call to mind the similarly odd headgear of Deren in *Meshes,* which she wears precisely at the moment of traversing the universe with a knife directed ultimately at her own sleeping body. "What I meant when I planned that four-stride sequence was that you have to come a long way—from the very beginning of time—to kill yourself, like the first life emerging from the primeval waters."[20] What Deren made explicit, here takes a different shape. The texts surrounding the boating interlude deal with the dilemma of woman's existence. While a crank telephone caller bemoans the distance between this untried soul and the brave movie women who always fought the good fight, the patient realizes that "it isn't as though I haven't been through pain." She is recalling her surgery, though the obscene phone calls stand for the other, less physically direct kinds of pain inflicted on women far more often. The patient takes out a comb and fixes her hair. When she tries to brush off her clothes, the sound of birds beating their wings in attempted flight fill the soundtrack. She is still, after all, a woman: combing her hair, virtuously maintaining the shape of her vulnerability (which is horrifyingly acted out, at scene's end, by a dummy auto crash).

In a sense, then, *Journeys from Berlin/1971* does not break from the refitted "woman's film" genre of its predecessors. In fact, it rather fits one type: "Haskell identifies a category of 'affliction' which particularizes in certain films the genre's general tendency to center on the suffering of its female characters. The 'affliction' films make this tendency manifest in their portrayal of woman as middle-class, female, Job."[21] Woman is indeed at the center of this film, both in the person of the patient and that of the historical anarchists and nihilists. On one level, the film seems to be acknowledging woman's location as a member of an oppressed class. Women needn't look elsewhere for victims to liberate. Woman as the victim has always been a figure in Rainer's cinema . . . and yet, here there's a change. *Is* the personal the political? Is the political merely the personal? Is the personal always political? Surely there's a difference between this woman, talking to her analyst, and Ulrike Meinhof, in prison. A difference, surely, between the power struggles of patient/analyst (or woman/man) and class struggle. A sure difference between the politics of art-making and the global politics of nations and peoples. Rainer is aiming for a more rigorous demarcation of the political, eschewing none of the complexities to signify her route. Contradictions are not swept under the rug. The motivations of revolutionaries are examined as intently as those of noncombatants. Nothing is automatic, simple, taken for granted.

Journeys from Berlin/1971 was begun when Rainer was living in West Berlin on a D.A.A.D. grant. It was a chaotic time in the Federal Republic. The woman whose apartment Rainer had rented was forced, by the *Berufsverbot* (blacklist), to leave the country in order to find work. The degree of repression attending everyday life for West Germans rarely finds its way into the subject matter of the celebrated New

German Cinema, but as an outsider Rainer apparently found it hard to ignore the spirit of her locus of production. She has credited Sebastian Cobler's *Law, Order, and Politics in West Germany* with providing her a veritable dossier on the history of state repression, and its historical antecedents to the terrorist actions used often as its justification. The dossier of facts and figures found its way into this film as the rolling titles that Rainer has affixed to the start and finish. Crucially, the need to accommodate such new material led to a marked shift in style.

Journeys from Berlin/1971 is the least self-reflective of her four films. While traces of her penchant for formal exercises, or ambiguity for its own pleasure, do remain (in the form of the characters pacing in front of an ornate church, or the recorder lesson, or the boy with a dog and an invention), they are no longer emphasized. While she is still concerned with codes of power, no longer is power a question only of visual manipulation or cinematic theory. While her own power was a source of considerable preoccupation in *Lives of Performers,* by now it is the powerlessness of others that bears scrutiny. When Rainer stands in for the patient in a last, videotaped monologue, she is no longer the go-between, the one who must wear another's words (like the Davis texts) to qualify. Tearfully facing the camera, half tourist and half daughter, she recounts her shock at seeing a film of lost Berlin, the city before the war. Rainer has dared to enter into the zones of ambiguity, breaking with the codes of infinite play of meanings long required of avant-garde film, and has been willing to fix meanings within her delicate balance of contradictions.

> A new style in art evolves—if it is not artificially stimulated—to meet the problem of treating new content born of social change.[22]

While a style might appear unrestrictive and ever-open, its very unity of form and (older) content mitigates against any new material. To continue with Berger's analysis:

> The further new content then demands a further new style. But this new style does not necessarily render the former one obsolete . . . its initial opposition may start a process which leads to the liberation of the former style from its latter-day formalism . . . (leading to) more complex expression in a liberated version of the former style.[23]

Such a process certainly seems to be operative in Rainer's expansion of her former strategies for *Journeys from Berlin/1971.* She has sacrificed neither grace nor substance in her broadening of permissible styles (for example, the inclusion of fixed roles, like "patient" and "therapist"). She has worked through a number of minimalist concerns, solving the formal problems and, by now, exhausting the aesthetic pleasures. Melodrama has reached its most naked mirror in the authorized confessional of psychoanalysis. Even the battle of the sexes has been displaced from stage center, to be replaced by a woman struggling, perhaps, with the same eternal issues, but now confronting directly the woman in the form of the therapist and the woman in the form of the mother to whom the videotape of Rainer is addressed. The SoHo pundits and the dance-world bodies are still very much present, but no longer are they the heart of the matter. The exercise of compassion and the acceptance of personal responsibility shape a demand for (not obviation of) condemnation. At last statement, a clear drawing of the lines, is a necessary finale.

Were the film to end on the psychoanalysis session, or within the unsettled debate on the ethics of political violence, it could remain on too individual a plane. Were it to end on the recorder lesson in the comfortable apartment, it could end without struggle. Or on the videotape confession, in which case the soul of the artist would provide the classical finish. But, no. The rolling titles bear the weight of history, transporting its traces past our vision. It is precisely the uncompromising end title, quoting the sinister words of H. Herold, head of the Federal Criminal Investigation Bureau, which confirms the target of Rainer's new trajectory. It is an uncompromisingly political ending, one which places *Journeys from Berlin/1971* into an unambivalent, courageous focus. The political deliberations which characterized Rainer's thinking throughout the making of *Journeys from Berlin/1971* have not ceased with its completion. In private correspondence with me recently, Rainer laid out the thoughts which form the core of the film and must inflect any interpretation of it, as of her work in general. With her permission, then, I let Yvonne Rainer have the last word:

> It is only when the patient stops believing in the absoluteness of her powerlessness in relation to others—men and women—that she can confront her suicide attempt. The feelings of powerlessness have been manifested in her projections and evasions, or "resistance." The signification of the therapist can be extended to include the power of the parent, of authority, of the state, of men. But in each case, one's personal, *actual* power is available, to however limited a degree, and must be confronted, or acknowledged, in some fashion. The patient takes responsibility for her own destructiveness— and stops struggling with the shrink. She assumes responsibility for her own life. This is truly the sphere of psychoanalysis—and the personal. What one does here would not be appropriate or possible in an extermination camp. It is obviously not the same case—to maintain (or resist) the values of the oppressive culture when other options are open, as in a relationship with a reliable shrink (or lover, or friend), or to maintain (or resist) them when no other options are open. I don't mean to underestimate the limits of the psychiatric ideal in our own culture where notions of freedom and self-determination everywhere obfuscate the needs of minorities, middle-aged women, the aged, and problems of illness, labor, and pleasure. Although the differences between personal autonomy in a prison and in the streets of the democracy are substantive, an analogy can be made. The patient's situation in *Journeys from Berlin/1971* can be seen as analogous to Meinhof's. The former, in her limited personal sphere, has taken her first faltering steps out of the imaginary dimension of her powerlessness. Meinhof, on the other hand, has died a victim, never having figured out where her powerlessness ended or real power began. Both ended at the hands of the police, or "state apparatus." She could have anticipated that from the beginning and weighed possible losses in the balance. And both began in her womanhood, and, as such, were more significant than she ever knew. Or so I suspect. If she had been able to see her oppression as *sexually* conditioned and generated rather than equivalent to the oppression of men at the hands of the state, who knows what the outcome would have been? The personal and the

political are not synonymous. They overlap and intertwine. And one must struggle constantly to assess one's power, or lack of it, in every sphere of one's life. This is all very general. Approaching from a somewhat different angle: I find it necessary to question the relationship of my personal frustrations to my social criticism. When am I justified in explaining the former in terms of the latter? Social criticism may not be disqualified by personal interest, but then neither do social formations always account for my private frustrations.

NOTES

1. Don McDonagh, *The Rise and Fall and Rise of Modern Dance* (New York: Outerbridge and Dienstfrey, 1970), p. 144.

2. Yvonne Rainer, *Work: 1961–73* (Halifax: Nova Scotia College of Art and Design, 1974); other quotations from here unless otherwise identified.

3. Yvonne Rainer, in Sally Banes, *Terpsichore in Sneakers: Post-Modern Dance* (Boston: Houghton Mifflin, 1980), pp. 224, 229.

4. Ibid.

5. Rainer, *Work,* p. 189.

6. Ibid., p. 209.

7. Ibid., p. 238.

8. Script to *Kristina Talking Pictures.*

9. See Lucy Lippard, *From the Center: Feminist Essays on Women's Art* (New York: Dutton, 1976), pp. 266–67.

10. According to Rainer's script notation in *Work*: shots nos. 9a–23.

11. Rainer, *Work,* p. 238.

12. Ibid., p. 278.

13. Molly Haskell, "Madame de: A Musical Passage," in *Favorite Movies,* edited by Philip Nobile (New York: Macmillan, 1973).

14. This definition was formulated together with Sharon Russell.

15. Rainer, *Work,* p. 263, from the performance "This is the story of a woman who. . . ."

16. Ibid., p. 117.

17. John Berger, *Art and Revolution* (New York: Pantheon, 1969), p. 98.

18. Annette Michelson, "Yvonne Rainer, Part Two: 'Lives of Performers,' " *Artforum,* February 1974, p. 32.

19. Roy Schafer, "Abstract: Narration in the Psychoanalytic Dialogue," program of "Narrative: The Illusion of Sequence," conference held at The University of Chicago Extension, October 1979.

20. Maya Deren, "Letter to James Card," in *Women and the Cinema: A Critical Anthology,* edited by Gerald Peary and Karyn Kay (New York: Dutton, 1977).

21. Molly Haskell as cited in Alan L. Williams, *Max Ophuls and the Cinema of Desire: A Critical Study of Six Films, 1948–1955* (New York: Arno Press, 1980), pp. 66–67.

22. Berger, p. 138.

23. Ibid.

Impossible Projections

Bérénice Reynaud

YVONNE RAINER'S 1980 FILM, *Journeys from Berlin/1971,* revolved around scenes of psychoanalytic sessions which, quite elegantly, demonstrated the impossibility of cinematically *representing* the psychoanalytical act (an important element in our civilisation's sexual apparatus, as Foucault has shown in his *History of Sexuality*). A middle-aged blonde woman, imposing, with an impeccable, rather theatrical delivery (cinema scholar Annette Michelson), is seated at a table, facing the camera, and addressing a character visible only from the back: the analyst. An oblique line extends to the patient's eyes from the analyst's hidden face (such that it becomes, more or less, one of the faces of God, "God's hidden face upheld by feminine *jouissance,*" as mentioned by Lacan[1]), and continues behind the patient's body to reach, in classic Renaissance perspective,[2] a "vanishing point" that defines a space behind her, a "vanishing space." And in this space, which appears as separated from that of the analytic session as if it were a back projection—like the landscapes running behind the car windows in Hollywood classics[3]—various actions take place: a carpet is unrolled, a vertically placed bed is lowered, etc., as in Rainer's choreographies for the Judson Church Theater in the '60s, in which she made casually dressed people do very simple and mundane things on stage. Also, as if to balance this special brand of "incongruous realism," the artificial quality of the background in *Journeys from Berlin/1971* is enhanced by the intrusion of quasi-surrealistic events: the back wall vanishes, and the street traffic becomes visible.

None of this has, of course, anything to do with the words uttered during the session, with the nature of the exchange between patient and analyst. It establishes a visual counterpoint to the *real* vanishing point of the image constituted by the *figure* of the analyst (in the double meaning this word has in French: face, and configuration of elements within an ensemble). Rainer emphasises this point by assigning the part of the "supposed subject of knowing"[4] (the analyst) to three different people (who, and this is no coincidence, represent the three figures of the Oedipal triad: a man, a woman and a young boy[5]). Thus, the analytical situation is represented by Rainer in

Copyright © 1987, Bérénice Reynaud. Copyright © 1987, David Jacobson and Bérénice Reynaud for the English translation. Reprinted, with permission, from *Screen,* vol. 28, no. 4 (Autumn 1987), pp. 40–52.

the form of an ellipse, with two vanishing points: one in the patient's "background" (in all senses of the term), and the other in the analyst's "field," continuing in the imaginary space off-screen.

The Man Who Envied Women radically changes this perspective, flattening the cinematic space even further. The two imaginary, quasi-anamorphic[6] protrusions are eliminated: the analyst disappears, swallowed by the off-screen space (which means that he/she ends up literally on the spectator's lap,[7] unless it is the spectator who has become the analyst—i.e., the idiot who does not know anything but whose ignorance assumes all possible knowledges). On the other hand, the space of the subject's "background" is replaced by a film screen, the flat surface par excellence onto which are projected excerpts of *noir* movies (*Clash by Night, Dangerous, Dead Reckoning, Gilda, In a Lonely Place*), classic melodramas (*Caught, Dark Victory*), and various "independent" or "art" movies (*Un Chien Andalou, Night of the Living Dead*, Hollis Frampton's *Otherwise Unexplained Fires* and Babette Mangolte and Trisha Brown's *Watermotor*). Squeezed between these two non-existent spaces, and always seated in front of the camera, a man is speaking. Delivering the opening line of the film, he says: "Doctor, I'll tell you all you want to know about my sex life." *To whom* does he speak? And *about whom?* Those are the two vanishing points, no longer governed by the rules of classical perspective, to be found within his discourse.

His discourse, however, is not the only one to be developed in the film. Rainer, who had already subverted the classic form of the frontal interview by making the interviewer a silent and sexually indeterminate psychoanalyst, adds another "cliché": the voice "off" of an invisible character, that of dancer/choreographer Trisha Brown, a friend and colleague of hers since the days of the Judson Church Theater.

It is the alternation of these two voices that will weave the first network of oppositions behind *The Man Who Envied Women*. From the outset, they fail to mesh. The man's "I'll tell you all . . ." is followed by the woman's first line: "It was a hard week. I split up with my husband and moved into my studio." When he talks, the man occupies the foreground. His speech is confident, slightly complacent. What is more, he is in a position where he is paying to be able to speak, to be listened to with the proverbially benign professional neutrality, to have the right to say it "all" about his sex life.[8] What he says, with a touching monotony (the text of his monologue is a compilation of the rather obsessive letters written by Raymond Chandler in his last years), is that he knows "nearly too much" about women. This "nearly too much" has to come out, be emitted. Visibly. From his very lips. It is what, in an article published in 1977 in *Cahiers du Cinéma*, Serge Daney calls, the *voice out* (as opposed to the *voice off*—for example, a commentary superimposed over the images—and the *voice in*—a voice coming from off-screen but impinging on the image, the interviewer's voice, for example).

> The *voice out* is an emission, a spurt, refuse: one of these objects the body expels (along with the gaze, blood, vomit, semen, etc. . .). [It] partakes of pornography in that it allows the moment of emission to be fetished. Porn cinema is likewise entirely centred on the spectacle of the orgasm seen on the male, that is to say on *the most visible,* end of things (coitus interruptus, ejaculation).[9]

Rainer both stresses and subverts the self-satisfied position of the male ejaculating words. She does so by naming her hero Jack Deller. Deller for "tell her." The male's discourse is always addressed, ultimately, to women, to a woman, even though, to be able to utter this discourse, he often needs to intimidate, eliminate, reduce her to silence, slavery, submission, to make her disappear from the screen. And why "Jack"? someone asks in the movie. First, because Jack has a "male" sound; it resounds as cock, dick, prick and pecker: and also because of "good Anglo-Saxon rhymes," such as "The House that Jack Built."

The film-maker, however, subverts this position by cutting the speaker short (or up) from time to time, by leaving the image without sound or the sound without image, by dividing the character of Jack between two actors[10] (William Raymond, of the experimental theatre troup Mabou Mines, and Larry Loonin), and, during the mix, by processing and distorting the hero's voice when he lectures to his students on literary and psychoanalytic theory. (His discourse, pointedly pedantic, is a collage of utterances made by New York academics.) This sequence, which some spectators wrongly take in a literal sense, is in fact a profound reflexion on the violence certain forms of seduction exert, and the "stupidity of the signifier," of which more below.

So much for the man. The woman is not seen, or rather is seen only in the guise of shadows, duplications, images, simulacra, traces. *Her* voice is never synchronic—never *out,* never confident. It is rather discreet, confused, sometimes enraged. She comments, asks questions, doubts. Her position is exactly the reverse of Deller's. In Daney's terms, her voice is *off,* defining an "imaginary space," with the man's *voice out,* on the contrary, "the flat image gives an illusion of depth . . . [and] what we have is an illusory space, the space of the lure."[11] We have returned here to the figure of anamorphosis, which Lacan views as a metaphor for erection:[12] when a man speaks on screen, it is to assert his manly potency. But what does a woman assert when she speaks?

Rainer laid the premises for *The Man Who Envied Women* not only by reading the feminist theories of the last ten years about the way the cinematic gaze "exploits and controls women's bodies,"[13] but also by reflecting upon *Comment Ca Va* (1976) by Jean-Luc Godard and Anne-Marie Miéville (a film whose main conflict is represented by the discussion between a "traditional" trade union militant, shot from the front, and a woman working in the same factory, shot from the back, who forces him to re-examine some of his positions): "The heroine's face is kept in the shadows. She is the 'teacher,' and she has the power. *She has the power because she does not appear.*"[14] According to Michel Chion's splendid book, *La Voix au Cinéma,*[15] it is possible to say that the absence of Trisha Brown's body makes her voice an "acousticometer" (*acoustimetre* in French), that is to say, the voice of someone who is not seen:

> . . . even the most harmless of acousticomatic voices, once it has impinged on the image, is invested with magical powers, mostly maleficent, rarely tutelary. [A typical case is that of the invisible Dr. Mabuse.] Its impingement upon the image means that it does not speak solely as an observer, but that its relation to the image is one of a possible inclusion, of power and possession capable of functioning in both ways.[16]

This is exactly the case of Trisha, whose image, as we'll see, is constantly at the edge of the screen, always on the verge of entering it.

Chion connects the acousticometer to "the apparatus of the Freudian cure, where the analysand does not see his analyst who does not look at him."[17] That is to say that one has two stylised representations of the psychoanalytic act in *The Man Who Envied Women:* a male version, which provides a visual equivalent; and a female version, which provides an aural equivalent, wherein a space of lure is opposed to an imaginary space—in psychoanalytic terms, the lure is a component of male sexuality. This is an issue tackled by Rainer in one of the "erotic" confessions made by the analysand in *Journeys from Berlin/1971:*[18] erection may "lure" the woman who believes it is addressed to her while it is addressed to what causes desire, the *objet petit a,* which in her is not her, but rather the lost object that the man hallucinates while looking at her.[19] The imaginary, on the other hand, at its formation during the mirror stage, is defined in relation to the mother's body.

Chion traces the genesis of the acousticometer, and the mythology it brings about, to the most primitive of all situations: that of the foetus, whose sense of hearing is the first to develop, who is literally immersed in the sound of its mother's voice. He traces it also in the situation of the baby whose mother "incessantly plays hide-and-seek in his field of vision. . . . But the olfactory and vocal continuum, and possibly the tactile contact as well, maintain the presence of the mother when she is no longer seen. . . . These appearances/disappearances, dramatic as they are for the child, are somehow transposed, or reduced, by some of the ways cinema plays with the off-screen (hiding a character by keeping him perceptible through the sound)."[20] The power Rainer alludes to, investing the invisible woman, is thus that of the mother, whose voice engulfs, scolds and consoles the helpless child. If men have for ever tried to dominate women, to control them, to "keep them in their place," and even, eventually, to demean and humiliate them, if, in contrast, they assign themselves the "mission to rule the world," it is, according to Dorothy Dinnerstein's book, to which Rainer refers, because "All of us, female as well as male, fear the will of woman. Man's dominion over what we think of as the world rests on a terror that we all feel: the terror of sinking back wholly into the helplessness of infancy."[21] At some point, Trisha notices: "The trauma for the infant having to give up that first sense of harmony is much greater for the male than for the female and results in both the mother-whore syndrome and the H-bomb. Men spend their lives alternating between punishing and seeking mothering from women and carrying their rage and terror out of the family realm and into the public." This analysis enables Rainer not only to develop a vision of "sexual impasse," but also to connect it to political concerns: men's hunger for control is exerted not only over women, but also in the realm of economic competition, in real estate speculation, in war, against peasants in Latin America. . . .

The acousticometer, however, is omniscient and omnipotent only in the eyes of those who are afraid of it (woman's power as a reproduction of the Primitive Mother is a masculine fantasy enabling men to justify their desire for power, and not a reality). In fact, especially when it translates female voices, non-authoritative voices,

voices searching for their own voices (as in Marguerite Duras's films), the acousticometer is a voice "roaming the surface, *both within and without,* in search of a resting place."[22] It is exactly the position of Trisha in the film. First, as a woman, she does not really have a resting place in a capitalistic and patrilocal society; in addition, the day her husband's chronic infidelity makes her decide to leave his bourgeois loft, she receives an eviction notice for her own studio. As an artist, she is a victim of New York's unbridled real estate speculation. When she then registers in a programme called Housing for Artists, designed to allow people in her situation to be allotted a space to restore in a run-down building, she realises that such a programme *de facto* contributes to gentrification and expulsion of the ethnic minorities in the Lower East Side. In conflict over her need for space and her political consciousness, she is, literally, "between a rock and a hard place."

Trisha's presence and her voice, nonetheless, are scattered throughout the entire movie. We get a glimpse at her body once, at the moment when she leaves Jack. (Or do we? What we see is the body of a young woman, from the back, which the editing matches up with Trisha Brown's voice, as if body were producing voice.) On the other hand, when Trisha's real body does become visible, it is lost among a gallery of portraits including Barbara Bel Geddes, Bette Davis, Gloria Grahame, Rita Hayworth, Lizabeth Scott, Barbara Stanwyck—all the heroines of these *films noirs* being played in Jack Deller's fantasy theatre, fictions projected behind his back that demonstrate how, in our cultural past, "real men" knew how to handle women. In the midst of these images, light, aerial, incongruous, the figure of Trisha Brown in her beautiful solo, *Watermotor,* appears, as shot by Babette Mangolte. At the same moment, Jack, without seeing her (the apparatus has been designed to produce this effect), talks about his marriage with her and his compulsive philandering.

Besides these two occurrences, Trisha's missing presence pervades the entire movie. It constitutes the "holes" in Deller's (often ridiculous) discourse. It appears in the form of traces left by the woman on the walls of her husband's loft, her "art," pinned to the wall, consisting of a collage of clippings from the *New York Times Magazine, Mother Jones* and pharmaceutical journals: a cigar ad showing a businessman celebrating his first million; corpses beheaded by the Death Squads in El Salvador; an excerpt of an article on the "new male sensitivity"; publicity for a new hormone medicine designed to treat menopausal problems. These images, these texts, are submitted to New York intellectuals who are then asked to respond to them. Their commentaries, except for that of video artist Martha Rosler which is presented in its original form, have been transcribed and re-created in the film by the voices of Trisha Brown, William Raymond and Yvonne Rainer. Brown's and Raymond's voices play yet another part in the movie. They function as one of the signifiers (as the quasi-unique signifier in Trisha's case) through which the two main fictional characters are constituted. And there is no overlapping between the disembodied voices, uttering these commentaries on the image and the fictional characters (Jack, Trisha), "embodied" by the same voices at other moments of the films. Here we have an instance of what Chion calls "a voice depossessed of a place, a position, to be used as 'all-purpose acousticometer,' . . . a fine symptom for the blurred positions of some in relation to others."[23]

There is a third voice in these commentaries, because there is a third presence, which doubles that of Trisha Brown (just as Larry Loonin's presence doubles that of William Raymond): the presence of the film-maker. Yvonne Rainer appears towards the middle of the film, in an incongruous shot that occurs as one of many breaks within the narrative structure of the film. This happens in Deller's loft, when he is just coming back from the university: he empties his briefcase, listens to his answering machine, flips through *Playboy,* etc. . . . Suddenly Yvonne Rainer enters the field, bends her head sideways in front of the camera, takes off her glasses, says: "Will all menstruating women please leave the theater?" and leaves. This sentence is echoed by Trisha's remarks immediately after, that men, with their castration complex, are both fascinated and repelled by women's periods, and that, in our culture, causes post-menopausal women to be denied sexual powers.

Just before this "apparition," Rainer's voice has been heard on Deller's answering machine, playing the part of the "other woman," or, rather, of one of the other women, leaving the hero with an erotically ambiguous message.

These multiple aspects are synthesised in the dream sequence, again commented upon by the film-maker's voice—which constitutes yet another break, since this sequence, narrated in the first person, is supposed to represent Trisha's dream. The image of Yvonne Rainer's body represents alternately the character of Trisha (when wearing a rough paper mask hiding her features) and that of Trisha's mother (without the mask), who finds herself in a situation of sexual rivalry with her own daughter. Being married to Jack, she discovers him in bed with Trisha, but claims that she "does not mind one bit," for she and Jack "stopped having sex ten years ago."

Finally, Trisha's presence is multiplied on another level, that of Jack's desire. In the movie, as discussed earlier, she is an acousticometer, that is to say, a vocal presence engulfing the listener, and whose source is invisible. And Jack will endeavour to look everywhere for the body emitting the voice he is fascinated by—for it reproduces for him the primordial voice of the Mother. Here is the origin of his philandering (the famous aria celebrating *Don Giovanni*'s "mille e tre" sexual conquests, brilliantly expounded by Lacan in his 1973 seminar *Encore*). Here is the promised "envy" of the film's title. Here is also the explanation of the hero's strange "perversion" (an inversion of the Peeping Tom syndrome, in which ears replace eyes). Hidden behind the head-set of a walkman, walking in the streets or sitting in coffee-shops, Jack overhears, eavesdrops on women talking among themselves. And what do they talk about? Sometimes with humour, sometimes with rage, brilliance, naiveté, revolt, or stupidity, they comment on the difficulties of their relationships with men.

The purpose of *The Man Who Envied Women,* in this respect, is to set up an *apparatus* to translate the sexual impasse into cinematic terms. Male and female discourses do not overlap, do not communicate. They reveal the loneliness of beings trapped in their respective sexual identities, structurally incapable of crossing the gap that divides one sex from the other. *He* talks to an invisible psychoanalyst, while *she* talks without being seen. When he talks to her and/or when he talks about her (which amounts to the same thing), he does not see her: he covets a multitude of female objects, of representations of the female sex, shreds of femininity that he seizes on wherever possible, on movie screens, in the street, in his classroom, on his living-room sofa. And when she tries to talk to him, her absence from the screen, her absence from the scene and from his life negates her as the subject of her own discourse, of her own desire.

All of Rainer's movies have dealt with the question of the sexual impasse. In *Lives of Performers* (1972), the dilemma of a man who can't choose between two women and makes them both suffer is expressed in choreographic and performance art terms. There is also a scene of emotional and sexual disagreement at the core of *Film about a Woman Who* (1974). A man and a woman are lying side by side on a bed (actually, a large table). The woman, unable to express an obscure resentment against the man, decides instead to "demand his affection." They make love, and she "participates with pleasure, but something is still bugging her." The morning after, she realises that she has somehow "betrayed" herself, and that it is preventing her from experiencing her real feelings (rage as well as love) towards the man.[24] Except for one or two lines, the scene is silent: it is composed of short sequences intercut with typed out dialogues or commentaries on the action.

In *Kristina Talking Pictures* (1976), the heroine (Yvonne Rainer), a lion tamer, is in bed (a real bed, this time), with her lover, the sailor Raoul (played by the film-maker's own brother). Again, there are two bodies, two parallel discourses that do not meet. Kristina tries to explain to Raoul the petty acts of cowardice and betrayal she has been guilty of. He wants to tell her the story of his travels. The scene is shot frontally, but in a fragmented manner, with very short shots, taken from slightly different points of view, and edited to heighten their artificiality (jump cuts, inter-rupted gestures, etc.). From time to time a panning shot slides against the walls surrounding the bed, and scrutinises the pictures that are pinned on it, including a sign saying "photo of erection or penis entering vagina": the symbol of the master-signifier present in this scene. The day after, Raoul has gone.

In *Journeys from Berlin/1971* the presentation of the central couple is made through a new choreography of bodies and editing, a new connection between the image and the soundtrack. We see an anonymous man and woman, who will not touch or speak to one another, shot in black-and-white in the midst of colour sequences. They stand near the porch of a German church, walk toward each other, then move further away. . . . Their respective positions are abruptly permutated through editing, which creates a tension, an expectation that will not be fulfilled. The same shots, the same elements, the same permutations are repeated during the entire sequence, while the soundtrack tells a very different story: that of two New York intellectuals, a man and a woman, *whom the spectator never sees,* who meet to cook and discuss politics together. At the moment of the black-and-white sequence, they read to each other excerpts from the memoirs of Vera Zasulich and Alexander Berkman, each describing an attempted political assassination, in the name of the "cause." The vividness and excitement of the soundtrack contrasts with the formal, quiet, discreet and faintly elegiac aspect of the image. Rainer comments:

> At the visual level, nothing is consummated. And, at the level of discourse, it is entirely about consummation. There is in me a refusal, a resistance to *show* things happening . . . a refusal to let the characters connect with each other. . . .[25]

Such a refusal, which Rainer links artistically with the tradition of American avant-garde cinema, is prompted by the fact that, no more than the act of analysis in its essence, *the sexual relation cannot be represented*. It is only possible to find metaphors for it, equivalences, metonymies (for example, porn cinema, eminently metonymic, which thinks it can represent the sexual relation by close-ups of organs more or less in motion; its relevant feature is the repeated use of the male sex ejaculating *outside the body of the woman,* that is to say at the moment when intercourse has been interrupted). As Lacan argued in *Encore,* the reason for such an impossibility, for this gap in representation, is that "the sexual relation does not exist." For Lacan, the failure, the "missed encounter" is at the core of "the sexual relation," and of "the analytic relation" as well. According to him, there are not only one, but two ways of "failing" the sexual relation. A "male" way, and then "another." The specifically male failure is defined along phallic lines. For the phallus is nothing but "the conscientious objection one of the two sexed beings makes against service to the other. . . . Phallic *jouissance* is the obstacle preventing man . . . from experiencing *jouissance* of the woman's body, precisely because what he then experiences, is *jouissance* of the organ."[26] The other way of failing the sexual relation is the feminine way of being "not-whole" in relation to the phallic function, in relation to language. Lacan adds: "This failure is the only form of realisation of this relation, if, as I posit it, there is no sexual relation."[27] And this impossibility is, from the outset, related to issues pertaining to discourse, hence to representation. "The sexual relation cannot be written. Everything that is written is based on the fact that it will be forever impossible to write the sexual relation as such. This gives way to a certain effect of discourse called *écriture.*"[28]

Similarly, one may say that, since its impure and popular origin as nickelodeon, the very existence of cinema displays an effort to represent the unrepresentable, namely, the sexual relation. The situation of the scopic drive, however, differs from that of the desire to write, since it corresponds to the desire to repeat an event that has already happened, on a real or fantasmatic level: the primal scene, whereby the child has supposedly witnessed intercourse between its parents. What is remarkable in the primal scene is not only that the subject figures in it as an unwanted third party, but also that he understands only imperfectly what is happening, so that, years later, he will dream, for example, of white wolves with long furry tails gazing at him through an open window—all of this to deny the terrifying reality, glimpsed during the scene, of the Mother's lack of penis.[29] There is, then, in the primal scene, always a blind spot, something that the subject *cannot* see, *wants* not to see.

The *mise-en-scène* of *The Man Who Envied Women* is organised around this blind spot, and the strength of the movies lies in the fact that, instead of being used to "fill up" the image, to "narrate" the story of the relationship between the characters invisible on the screen to "furnish" the empty space between them, language functions to express this blind spot, this hole. Not only does language have holes; language bores holes in the image. It is no longer the image, specular fascination, which functions to halt narration, as in classical narrative cinema, but language which "de-narrativises" the story—and this in spite of the dense and at times unbearable quality of the text. This density expresses its vacuity. In *The Man Who*

Envied Women people talk because they do not communicate anything (or rather, because they communicate *nothing*).

The dialogue is composed for the most part of "found texts" used as found or reworked. There is an important documentary aspect in the film that should not be overlooked. Some sequences, shot in Super-8 or in video—whose grainy aspect, a bit "fuzzy," a bit "clumsy," contrasts with Mark Daniels' elegant, accomplished cinematography in the 16mm sequences—document political events involving part of the New York intelligentsia (and Yvonne Rainer in particular, which constitutes the autobiographical element of the film): the hearing opposing the supporters of the Artists Housing Project to the ethnic minorities of the Lower East Side; the preparatory meetings for the Artists Call protests against U.S. intervention in Latin America. The texts reworked by the director function also as documents on some New York *mores:* the role played by theories, more or less well assimilated; the omnipresence of the media; the role played by feminist controversy in social intercourse; a certain "well-meaning" liberalism; and, finally, the "current ideology" made up of sincere indignation, bits of popular wisdom, vast naiveté, stupidity, and, sometimes, viciousness. Such is the patchwork of phrases picked up by Rainer in the course of her social life, her reading, which she scatters throughout her film, on a street corner, at a coffeeshop table, at a party full of leftist intellectuals: "Women don't get hassled on the streets of Managua." "A feminist is a man who's found a new way to meet broads." "I'm not trying to pin him down or anything . . . just get him into bed. . . ." "Just because I like to look at pictures of erections doesn't mean I'm homosexual." "The bottom line is, women really *do* want to devour men." "In the universal mind nothing is ever lost. And sure enough, on retracing my steps, I found my glasses." "He said he doubted if most women would mind being raped. And *then* he said, after all, the vagina is only an orifice like any other." "Christianity demands that while living or thinking of herself as a virgin impregnated by the Word, [woman] lives and thinks of herself as a male homosexual."

One cannot help thinking of the look cast by Woody Allen in *Manhattan* or *Annie Hall* on a certain class of New York intellectuals, but Rainer's project is, more deeply, akin to that of Flaubert in *Bouvard and Pécuchet*. Here, too, the project is to make a statement on the stupidity which, in a society, accompanies the assimilation of scraps of science, theory, reading and half-knowledge in circulation. Flaubert's anti-heroes, however, are two middle-aged men, while it is within the heterosexual couple, and in particular in its female component, that Rainer encounters the stumbling-block of language. Something fails to be processed. It is the signifier which is "the cause of *jouissance*. Without the signifier, how could we even grasp this part of the body?" However, "in so far as it is the term of *jouissance*, the signifier is also what brings it to a stop."[30] It is because it is always askew in relation to *jouissance* that the signifier is "stupid." And, consequently, that "the subject is, properly speaking, he whom we [psychoanalysts] urge not to say everything, as we tell him to seduce him—one cannot say everything—but to say stupidities, that's it."[31] Just like Jack Deller, who fancies that he is going to "tell all she [if one accepts our interpretation that his analyst is, finally, a woman] wants to know," to pour out his overflow of knowledge on her, and who ends up, precisely, making stupid statements about women.

The situation described by Rainer, that of our modernity, is that the more we talk, the more we utter stupidities, and the less we experience *jouissance*. Yet, if we did not talk, we would experience *jouissance* even less. So, the end of the movie presents two versions of the impossibility of the couple. Trisha is compelled to coin a new word for her incapability to have satisfying relationships with men. "I cannot live without men, but I can live without a man. . . . I know there will sometimes be excruciating sadness. But I also know something is different now. Something in the direction of *unwomanliness*. Not a new woman, not a non-woman or misanthrope or anti-woman, not a non-practicing lesbian. Maybe *unwoman* is also the wrong term. *A-woman* is closer. *A-womanly. A-womanliness.*"

The second version of the couple is more comical; it deals with the violence of verbal seduction and triggers a sort of infernal ballet, a *danse macabre*. Before, we had seen Jack Deller seducing his young assistant by making use of his intellectual authority, while the lighting gradually transformed this banal scene by bathing it in a *noir*ish atmosphere. At the end of the movie, Deller goes to a party where he meets an ex-girlfriend, Jackie (Jackie Raynal), a French intellectual, feminist and post-marxist. They find themselves squeezed in a corridor that, ironically, leads to the bathroom, and, like all the couples in Rainer's previous movies, get closer without touching each other, entwine without embracing, ogle each other provocatively, perform a whole ritual of posturing, sexual thrusts and parries, while exchanging, like so many attacks, bits of theory. He quotes Foucault about the pervasiveness of centres of power, and looks at her as if he wants both to kiss and slap her. She answers him with a very funny text by the Australian feminist Meaghan Morris, and a demure look that could mean "He's a cute kid, but he's pulling my leg." The battle of the sexes, removed from the bedroom (*Woman Who . . .* , *Kristina . . .*) and the kitchen (*Journeys . . .*) now opens out in the theoretical arena (who is the matador, who is the bull?). But is there fair play here either, aren't the dice loaded? As Jackie says: "If a girl takes her eyes off Lacan and Derrida long enough to look, she may discover she is the invisible man."[32]

NOTES

1. See in particular the chapter "Dieu et la Jouissance de la Femme," in Jacques Lacan, *Encore* (Paris: Editions du Seuil, 1975), pp. 61–71. (For an English translation of part of this essay, see Juliet Mitchell and Jacqueline Rose, eds., *Feminine Sexuality: Jacques Lacan and the école Freudienne* [London: Macmillan, 1982], pp. 137–48. All translations in this article are by David Jacobson and Bérénice Reynaud.)

2. Here I must acknowledge my theoretical debt to French art historian Vanina Costa, who pointed out to me the "pictorial" aspect of the cinematic space in Yvonne Rainer's movies, when I introduced a retrospective of her films at the Festival d'Automne in Paris in December 1984.

3. In fact, to achieve this effect, Rainer simply changed the camera angle.

4. I prefer the translation "supposed subject of knowing"—coined by Stuart Schneiderman in his *Returning to Freud—Clinical Psychoanalysis and the School of Lacan* (New Haven: Yale University Press, 1980), p. vii—to the "subject supposed to know" used by Alan Sheridan. As Schneiderman puts it, what is supposed is the subject, not the knowledge.

5. A young boy and not a little girl, even though the patient is a woman. The Oedipus complex is a structure organised around a subject marked as "masculine," and this is why it is more difficult for women to find their place in it.

6. "Anamorphosis": "a figure enlarged and distorted according to the lines of what may be called a perspective" (Lacan); for example, the skull in Holbein's painting *The Ambassadors,* which, seen from a certain angle, is merely a set of flat lines, and, from another, "bursts out in space" to reconstitute itself in three dimensions. See Jacques Lacan, *The Four Fundamental Concepts of Psychoanalysis,* translated by Alan Sheridan (New York: Norton, 1978), pp. 85–89.

7. Since first writing this piece in French in January 1986, I have changed my mind about this specific point. First, art historian Elizabeth Lebovici suggested at the 1986 Women's International Film Festival in Créteil that in the scene in which the camera moves away from Jack Deller to enter another space (that of a movie theatre where *The Night of the Living Dead* is projected), the position of Deller's invisible analyst does not coincide entirely with that of the spectator. Deller's gaze defines an oblique line in the off-screen space, and his analyst is slightly *to the side of* the spectator. Secondly, in Jean-Pierre Oudart's seminal "Cinema and Suture," *Screen,* vol. 18, no. 4 (Winter 1977/78), pp. 35–47, he explains that the spectator is *not* a substitute for the Absent One constructed by the subject's imaginary in the missing field. In other words, Jack Deller's analyst does not occupy the spectator's seat, is not exactly seated on his lap, but is probably at an angle to him.

8. About the similarity of this situation to that of prostitution (the patient as "client"), see Daniel Schmidt's film *L'Ombre des Anges* (the prostitute is paid to listen). See also the final sequence of Mike Nichols's *Carnal Knowledge.*

9. Serge Daney, "L'orgue et l'aspirateur," *Cahiers du Cinéma,* nos. 278–79 (August–September 1977). An excerpt of this article has been reprinted in the appendix of Michel Chion, *La Voix au Cinéma* (Paris: Editions de l'Etoile, 1982).

10. Yvonne Rainer has consistently relied on the device of dividing one character among several performers.

11. Daney, "L'orgue et l'aspirateur."

12. Lacan, *Four Fundamental Concepts.*

13. Bérénice Reynaud, "Interview avec Yvonne Rainer," *Cahiers du Cinéma,* no. 369 (March 1985), pp. 43–45.

14. Ibid.

15. Chion, *La Voix.*

16. Ibid., p. 28.

17. Ibid., p. 27.

18. "That very night he . . . got such an enormous erection as I had never seen the likes of. It scared me half to death. What in God's name had turned him on like that? *It couldn't have been me*" (italics mine).

19. Men, who spend a great deal of time comparing (literally or metaphorically) their sex organs, nonetheless fancy that they can *lure* women and keep them in the dark about the identity of their penises. See, for example, the myth of Amphitryon, wherein Jupiter takes on the features of the king to discreetly make love (and a baby) with the latter's (faithful) wife. And for a masochistic variation, see Edmond Rostand's play *Cyrano de Bergerac.*

20. Chion, p. 25.

21. Dorothy Dinnerstein, *The Mermaid and the Minotaur* (New York: Harper and Row, 1977), p. 161.

22. Chion, p. 28.

23. Ibid., p. 52. Here Chion is alluding more specifically to a movie by Claude Lelouch, *Les Uns et les autres,* where this strategy is also used.

24. The script of *Film About a Woman Who* . . . was published in *October,* no. 2 (Summer 1976), pp. 39–67.

25. Reynaud, "Interview avec Yvonne Rainer."

26. Lacan, *Encore,* p. 13.

27. Ibid., p. 54.

28. Ibid., pp. 34–35.

29. Sigmund Freud, "The Wolf Man," in *Three Case Histories* (New York: Collier, 1963), pp. 187–315, in particular the chapter "The Dream and the Primal Scene," pp. 213–34.

30. Lacan, *Encore,* p. 27.

31. Ibid., p. 25.

32. Meaghan Morris, "The Pirate's Fiancée," in Meaghan Morris and Paul Patton, eds., *Michel Foucault: Power, Truth, Strategy* (Sydney: Feral Publications, 1979).

Interview with Yvonne Rainer

Mitchell Rosenbaum

A DECADE AFTER Yvonne Rainer established herself as a central figure in the avant-garde dance community of New York, the desire to explore the possibilities of narrative led her to the medium of film during the Seventies. Her work in film consists of five features: *Lives of Performers* (1972), *Film About a Woman Who . . .* (1974), *Kristina Talking Pictures* (1976), *Journeys from Berlin/1971* (1980), and *The Man Who Envied Women* (1985). These films, although apparently narrative in structure, are more formally complex, rigorous, and intellectually demanding than even most independent films. They are concerned with such issues as: the often oppressive manipulation of an audience by a fiction; the problems of imaging women in film; and the limitations of narrative codes. Rather than take a dogmatic stance on any of these issues, Rainer opts for a diffuse plurality of positions over a reductive unification.

Rainer's concerns about content and form usually position her works as avant garde in comparison to independent films that exhibit more interest in traditional narrative structures. However, like other independent filmmakers, she is reliant on government subsidies, foundation money, and financing from the private sector. But where financers of more traditional independent films are more likely to be interested in investment profits and losses, her donors are more likely to be interested in the arts.

Rainer's most recent film, *The Man Who Envied Women,* was not only included in the 1987 Whitney Biennial but was also shown at the Thalia, a New York repertory theater that occasionally exhibits new films. However, it enjoyed relatively few screenings, even in New York, where the filmmaker is based. Because Rainer is well aware of her limited audience, she attempts to confront this select segment in an effort not to preach to, but to "harangue" the converted. The film can be seen as a catalog of the ideas and debates percolating among the intellectual Left of the Eighties with its emphasis on conflicts between theory and practice, love and power, and New York real estate interests.

I spoke with Yvonne Rainer in August 1986 in Woodstock, New York.

Reprinted, with permission, from *Persistence of Vision*, no. 6 (Summer 1988), pp. 101–108.

Mitchell Rosenbaum: *You disbanded your dance company, The Grand Union, in 1971 . . .*

Yvonne Rainer: I never really had a dance company—they were people I worked with who were also choreographers who had come out of the Cunningham/Cage milieu, and I never considered them my company. I didn't like that proprietary, careerist kind of structure, and this led to making it into an improvisatory group, The Grand Union. That was the beginning of the end of my work with this group. Democratizing it was a way of easing myself out of it, although I wasn't conscious of this until later.

You found that was oppressive as well.

I found that I couldn't do my own work and I couldn't stand the pressures and rigors of improvisatory work.

You said at that point that not having a boss creates new problems.

Right. Also, having to be creative on the spot, which is what that group became. They did incredible work, but I only lasted about two years. By 1972 I was out of it, and my first film was made at that time.

Now, after five features, how do you feel about the potentially oppressive role of the director, a theme which you dealt with in your first feature, Lives of Performers?

Well, I guess I've changed my attitude about that. But also the hierarchies of filmmaking are at this point so ordered according to skills that you couldn't make a movie without this kind of hierarchy, unless you do it all yourself, as some people do.

So you've made peace with all that.

Yeah. I mean not that I like it any better, but I like the end product. I don't like production probably for that reason. I like the editing, and I like the scripting. But I don't like the actual shooting, I think, partly because the pressures of low-budget shooting are so extreme. You're on a murderous schedule and always going over budget. So there are those pressures that make it unpleasant in some ways. I just don't like to work under that kind of pressure. Some people thrive on it.

Lately, some critics have been comparing your work to that of Woody Allen. How do you feel about that?

It's not very accurate. Maybe superficially. *The Man Who Envied Women* is a very New York–based film with a lot of funny intellectual repartee which is of course Allen's forte. But the rest of the film is so different from anything he would do that I'm kind of put off by that comparison. It doesn't go very far. Jim Hoberman pointed out that the New York I show in this film with dilapidated lofts and slums is very different from Woody Allen's sleek New York of *Hannah and Her Sisters*, with its beautiful people and Upper West Side apartments. I have to admit I wanted a fancy apartment for the party sequence, but by the time I was shooting, that scene was consigned to just the hallway outside of a closed door through which you heard voices. If I had had more money, I might have used some kind of luxury space. But in a way I'm glad I didn't because that really wasn't the point. The constricted space of the corridor was a much richer metaphor.

How do you feel about Jean-Luc Godard's recent work?

Oh . . . I don't like his recent work. I don't like his obsession with nubile maidens and exploiting their sexuality. I think Godard can still do things that are just plain daring. Those last shots in *Hail Mary* of nature are just so astounding. I keep up with what he is doing and he still does things in his own way; I admire all that, but I think his really meaningful work was done in the late 1960s and early 1970s. He's an amazing, creative genius. I hate to use that term, but it may still be useful in talking about a kind of prolific and politically incisive imagination.

Would you say films like Numero Deux *and* Wind from the East *moved and inspired you?*

I can't say they inspired me. I have been slow as a filmmaker to appreciate Godard, or I came to him sideways through his writing. I just appreciated him as a force. People have compared the way I make movies to his, but my way of making movies came out of my particular modernist art-world milieu and not from the French New Wave.

I must have misunderstood something you once said about Godard.

Perhaps in a film. You can't believe anything I say in the first person in my films. I set up the heroine in *Kristina Talking Pictures* as someone who was inspired by Martha Graham, Godard, and Virginia Woolf. I can't say any of these were prime movers for me at the time I started making film. The statement was for its rhetorical and theatrical effect. I would say Andy Warhol was more influential on my ideas on film than Godard at that moment when I ventured into narrative film.

What do you think of Jacques Rivette?

The only film of Rivette's I like is *L'Amour fou*. He gives much too much permission to actors, and I don't find what actors do on their own very interesting. But the layering in *L'Amour fou* with the 16-mm. and the 35-mm. and the Racine play and the director's life I found utterly fascinating and beautiful.

But for you acting is secondary to language and structure and you prefer actors to be completely flat oracles of the word.

Not necessarily. What you see in *L'Amour fou* is the actors going about their task of rehearsal for a classic; you see them at work, and the director directing them. But when the illusion of a Rivette film is that the actors are creating the film or you actually sense that he's given over a lot of his directorial control to them in some kind of utopian gesture, it doesn't work. I mean Godard did that in *Wind from the East* but with a totally different effect.

Some people have a problem with the flatness of the acting in your films. For example, the narrators of your films are quite monotone and without affect. However, this can be seen as a very natural kind of acting because it's the way people talk in ordinary conversation, or as non-acting.

Well, that's a style I have cultivated.

Of course some people take that for inexperienced or bad acting.

I have trouble with so-called "bad acting" where nothing in the film tells you that the artifice of the illusion is supposed to be revealed. That's where bad acting interferes. In *Journeys from Berlin*, where the text is very non-naturalistic and it's obviously a surreal kind of recitation, then Annette Michelson's non-naturalistic performance is totally appropriate. The setting tells you this is not a realistic film so you are going for something other than totally credible, believable acting. Still, a character is built. That is the amazing thing about film. Just the framing and focus on a person speaking creates this bond with the spectator, and it's that illusion that builds the character. I mean it's a two-way thing: the audience in identifying is already constructing the character. It's a much more immediate process than the stage, which always requires the suspension of disbelief. The suspension of disbelief is there *a priori* in the cinema, with the dark room. It's this very atavistic kind of relationship to an image which some theorists liken to the earliest experience of the infant at the mother's breast watching shadows on the surface of the mother's skin.

Or as in a dream. But given the over-determined quality of your images, don't you agree that you've taken the work out for those same theorists who might examine your films? As opposed to a more intuitive filmmaker, you are probably the best analyst of your own work.

But I don't necessarily know the end effect. That is one by-product of collage. Ambiguity is something that is my stock in trade, and sometimes I'm sure of what an interpretation should be; sometimes I'm not and yet retain a particular configuration because I'm fascinated by the ambiguity of it. I like the Stonehenge image in *Journeys from Berlin*. I can't say definitively what I intended. I accepted the ambiguity and the possibility for multiple readings that it offered and let it remain. I knew there was no way, without forcing, to push that metaphor or direct it, so I left it open-ended.

Sure. You could say that about Journeys from Berlin, *but not necessarily about this last film,* The Man Who Envied Women.

Right. That is the result of having much more politicized intentions.

In this film you seem to have confronted the problem facing political filmmakers: that is, you don't so much preach to the converted, as scold them.

Harangue them.

Nobody on the Left gets away without a jab. In particular, artists—a group you're certainly counted among—take quite a beating.

Artists are seen as being in very compromised positions in the urban setting and yet, in other areas, are trying to work in a progressive way. Which I think is the true state of things with New York–based artists today. I had to approach this problem from many different angles: political activism, housing, and feminism.

So what about feminism at this point? In this last film you seem to both praise and lampoon the current state of feminism. This is exemplified by the Jackie Raynal character—a femme fatale *whose dialogue consists of poststructuralist feminist text.*

Well, there again it's hard. You are expressing this question about what my position is on some of that material which is very multifaceted. Nothing is resolved. I follow the debates on sexual difference and Women Against Pornography. I am personally committed to the abortion rights movement. What is expressed in *The Man Who Envied Women* is exactly what Jackie recites, this Meaghan Morris essay which points out where feminism makes these confusions between right-to-life and abortion rights. It's very complicated. I deliberately make the male character a feminist to show how a seemingly progressive position can be used for aggrandizement all over again. Just as I'm now reading about the history of the medical and scientific attitudes about women's orgasm and reproduction, how social theorists used to view women's organs as simply a version of the man's, like an inverted penis. Then when this was disputed around the turn of the century, and people like Havelock Ellis began to say women were biologically different, this recognition was used simply to say that women's place was in the home and to reproduce. So, theoretical debates are all very well but can be used in repressive ways. Maybe that's reactionary. I've been called a combat-liberal by Maoists at some point but I thought it was pertinent to these current debates which rage on in this academic realm and are very pertinent to problems of representation. Who in the film is uttering these kinds of doubts? It is a woman who is presented as a *femme fatale.* It seemed very appropriate that these debates, whatever they are, be keyed to these notions of imaging and sexual difference, or projections of male castration-fear, to open up one of the most pervasive and pernicious examples of female stereotyping in cinema history.

At a screening of a Peter Gidal film in the 1970s, which opened with an unendurably long shot of a corner of a room, you remarked to critic Jonathan Rosenbaum that the filmmaker had backed himself into a corner. Do you think that kind of pure structuralist film has reached its limit?

I think there's still a need for what in some quarters is called optical research, and it's very valuable this playing with the photographic optical materiality of film. Probably it's an avenue that's been exhausted by now. Unless you go into video, and then you get a whole other kind of imagery that's possible with electronics.

Can you talk about the way in which you used footage from other filmmakers, including structuralist filmmakers like Michael Snow?

I think I've shown another use for images that other people have made, including 1940s movies, Michael Snow, and Hollis Frampton. Snow was quite pleased with the way I used his footage. Annette Michelson wrote an essay on *Wavelength* many years ago that talked about the subtext of the film that is this abandoned piece of real estate that the film refers to and takes place in. So here I was talking about the change in use and exploitation by the real estate market and this classic piece of footage seemed eminently appropriate to use along with the other kinds of footage that I specifically shot to demonstrate this problem. So I'm interested in a certain kind of documentary that can incorporate previous treatments of the same material that originally had an aesthetically transgressive purpose. There's one part of me that will always have my roots in this approach to art-making. But it's become one possibility among more important ones, such as social implications in terms of domination and mystification that attend an image. But I like very much the idea of combining in one shot different levels of meaning, and references that are both aesthetically and socially historical. So I was very excited to explore this use of the Snow material in a new context.

How do you respond to those critics of the New American Cinema who have pointed out that this new kind of narrative form, which turns to the filmmaker for its text, merely relocates many of the central aspects of traditional narrative filmmaking and its form of identification to a different plane?

Feminist theorists like Mulvey and Kaplan have pointed out that melodrama, even soap opera, is a place where women's dilemmas are played out in a very visible way. So this offers the avant-garde filmmaker a formal arena in which to make the tensions and dilemmas of women living in a patriarchy accessible and visible. That's the way I pretty much feel about these forms now. It's not very productive to dismiss them outright. Gidal had fenced himself into a corner as of the mid-70s in some kind of material purity and didn't say much to anyone but a small coterie of filmmakers.

This business of something being narrative or not very much depends on what angle of entry you're coming from. For a Hollywood director I'm not making narrative. For me it doesn't matter if it's narrative or not. What matters is how you engage the audience and then lead them to participate in some other way than narrative melodrama usually demands of them, rather than making a narrative with a closure so people can have some sort of Aristotelian response of completeness and life goes on despite the murder and destruction and everything returns to order. I think narrative film conventions offer a way to engage people or give them entry into this familiar realm of identification and recognition, but then, I don't feel I have to be bound to it. So as far as I'm concerned, I can only get better at narrative forms. I'm constantly amazed at how little it takes to hook the audience. Like the way people responded to Annette Michelson's character in *Journeys from Berlin*. I thought I had made something so obviously artificial and constructed no one could possibly identify with or be repelled by her. It just didn't operate that way. People talk about her as though she is a real person.

I worked a little harder, or differently, to establish my "man who envied women" as a semblance of a "real person." The first scene in the film is the one where you follow a chronology of events. Most other scenes involved simply setting up a situation dominated by the camera or by extra-diegetic material, or an "idea," in locations that could be infused, at least initially, with fictive credibility, such as the "lecture hall," the "therapist's office," the "coffee shop," etc. As far as narrative goes, it's very static. There's one plot element and it's not to develop or consummate a series of events, but to expose him and the audience to different kinds of arguments and information.

Can you talk about what you do with the gaze in this last film? You seem to have taken care of the problem of the male gaze in a twist on Buñuel's dual actresses in That Obscure Object of Desire.

In the Buñuel, the female objects are interchangeable for the male protagonist. In *The Man Who Envied Women,* the male objects are interchangeable for the audience because there's no internal female character visualized. This seemed to me taking quite literally the problematic of the image of the woman as the object of the controlling gaze. Here, I removed her physical presence totally and doubled the man as an object by having two men play the same role. But it then becomes unclear how the gaze operates. The strategy removes it from narrative convention and there's something going on here that disproves a lot of this gaze stuff. The overheard heroine, because she is unseen, cannot be said to be the object of a controlling gaze internal to the film, but then neither is Jack Deller, though both of them are objects of identification for the audience. This is a case where the traditional axes of gaze, power, identification have been skewed somewhat, allowing the female spectator a less ambivalent access to the image through the voice of the heroine. The male protagonist is not, however, objectified through a simple reversal of codes. His "imaging" is constantly tempered by his powerful "discourses" and by his monitoring and mastering behavior, in the metaphor of the headphones, for instance. He becomes an emblem and agent of patriarchal abuse. His case, from a narrative standpoint, remains unsolved, unresolved. He is never brought "under control" as his cinematic "wild-woman" counterpart has traditionally been. That would be too utopian for my tastes.

Your approach to narrative has changed since you made Lives of Performers.

At that time I was doing a kind of parody of narrative. The performers read self-consciously from a script. It was a very distanciated kind of narrative. Then I would set up these tableaux of minimal situations all in that barren space that could be dressed with a chair or a suitcase to refer to a history of melodramatic objects and usage. So it was very stagey and artificial. When I talk about narrative now, I'm talking about the way it's done.

One of the most difficult sequences to read in The Man Who Envied Women *is the lecture sequence. In part because of the sheer length of it and partly because the significance of the space in which the lecture takes place is unclear.*

I made some strategic errors—or one, anyway. The subtext of the space of the lecture as being this loft up for sale can only be recognized as such at the end when you see the new kitchen and bathroom. I should have either started in the kitchen, or put in more clues like a realtor's sign or something. I could have handled it differently by putting in some additional clues to make you focus in on that space and its particular New York significance. It's especially opaque to a European audience.

It does elicit the most antagonistic responses from people.

Well, the trouble people have is they have so much trouble with that lecture that at that point they dismiss him [Jack Deller]. Later they dismiss him when he's talking to his shrink about women, doing that self-pitying, imperial rap. After that they want to hit him around a little bit. So they don't know how to take it when he starts speaking this Foucault stuff. Is this just some more bullshit? Is it being used for bullshit purposes, or what? I can justify that in terms of the complexity of the character. He's not totally bad, not a total schmuck, and he has some intellectual progressive things that are quite clear. Like, I have voices respond to those images on the wall. He talks about the cigar and cheap labor in Central America.

I must admit I didn't realize you had any sympathy for him at all.

Yeah, I do. There are women who find him vulnerable and appealing. Men are much harder on him, and men really object to him for that reason or to my creating that kind of character. They see him as utterly reprehensible and ludicrous, and they can't take anything he says seriously. But he says a lot of right-on things, including the Foucault stuff. Of course, the irony in the corridor scene is in what they're both doing. You see, I wanted to make a very complicated situation. I didn't want to make a very simple agit-prop sort of film. We see this all the time in the progressive and leftist documentary. In a way he's right when he says, "I'm a mass of contradictions, and what else can you expect under capitalism?" We get it right in some areas and in other areas we have these emotional needs and desires for autonomy and power that take various forms that may be injurious to those around us.

Still, for people who see him as all schmuck, he is simply an agit-prop character.

I think it is obvious that he is a pastiche and a construction. His speech is recitation from a collage of different things including real life. I think I make a calculating kind of film in which you can only go so far in identifying coherent positions either on my part or the characters' before you pull back and say, "Hey, who is this person? How is he made? He's full of conflicting information—what does that mean?" And then you have to deal with the information and not just with him. Like, can you dismiss everything he says because he's a schmuck? I don't think you can read this kind of film in this way. The fact that so many people do, makes me realize how these habits of reading films die very hard, and it continues to be challenging to make films where these viewing habits are constantly interfered with and questioned.

I showed this film to several men, most of whom denied any identification with this character, particularly those for whom such identification should have been appropriate.

I've been surprised at people I had in mind who did not recognize themselves. You can lead a horse to water. . . . I don't know if this person exists, but as I said, the characters are drawn from many different people, texts, and experiences. It may seem unlikely in this day and age that a progressive leftist would talk like Raymond Chandler. All those remarks about women made to the shrink are taken from Chandler's letters. That stuff is definitely dated, like when he says, "I never loved cheap women." You don't hear that expression anymore, but beyond the anachronisms of usage, there is this obsession and anxiety about knowing and controlling women. He cannot know women well enough. He constantly obsesses over this knowledge by which he assuages his anxiety. This, I think, is something that has taken a new form. The feminist man. Feminism as it is used by certain kinds of womanizing men. So it's plausible and perhaps is meant as some kind of object lesson . . . a warning [laughs]. Women recognize him instantly. Especially those from the academic community. They hoot and holler in recognition.

Do you have any of the same ambivalence towards the Jackie Raynal character?

No, because Jackie is even more obviously a construction. She appears in only one scene and speaks, or recites, from a single source, "The Pirate's Fiancée," an essay by the Australian journalist, theorist, feminist, Foucaultian, Meaghan Morris. Jackie too is using language for seduction, cast in the guise of the *femme fatale*. Now the hitherto repressed female image returns with a masterful voice. That whole scene is so full of irony and excess and tension that it works: the constriction of the space; the way they can only move a couple of steps at a time; the problematizing of the feminist space for feminist intellectuals; the railing against Lacan which goes on; the dream in the middle of it with its eruption of mistaken identities and roles—son/husband exchange by the collapsed mother/daughter—the Oedipal circus turned on its head.

So what about your next project. Anything you can talk about?

Very preliminary work. This is very different and suggests a story, which of course has problems. I'll have to think about that as the story materializes.

But in the past you've gone about the task of starting a project in a similar way?

Always in bits and pieces of things: a title, *The Man Who Envied Women,* came very early to me, as did the housing thing, which I was involved in. The character of Jack was one of the last things. I knew I wanted him to be talking to a shrink and giving a lecture. And of course I always like to layer different realities wherever possible, even if it doesn't make sense at the moment. So I had him lecture in a condo which is on the market, which, as I said, I did not make clear enough. Of course this refers directly to the way universities buy up poor neighborhoods. That could have been made clearer also. What he would say to the shrink, I tried to write, and it was maudlin and *Psychology Today*-ish. Then I came upon these letters of Raymond Chandler and that clinched it. I looked up women in the index and all this stuff fell out.

But when you apply for money to the various sources, how do you relate that kind of disjointed treatment?

When I started applying for money, I wrote a pretty coherent treatment which could have been a "real" film. That's what you have to do these days to make it sound plausible.

So the actual film resembled the treatment only vaguely?

Somewhat. The lecture I thought would be on economics. I thought the film would deal more with menopause than it does. It just sounds, of course, more coherent. It had a thesis that had to do with the contradictions of the main character. Those things were mapped out. Whether or not the film elucidates all of them I don't know. But I certainly had a treatment that sounded convincing. The toughest thing was the male character and how to develop or not develop him. I had some preconceptions about who he was and how to get that across. Someone who knows fictional technique and dialogue and all that would have had an easier time, but I had to wait until these things sort of materialized for me. I'm not really a fiction writer. That has its drawbacks when you have a plan. I'm going to run into the same thing again, but I'll deal with it in a different way this time even to the point of asking a writer to come in on the project.

How is the money situation for you as an avant-garde filmmaker in the age of Reagan?

For me it doesn't look good. If I want to make a film with locations and this length, I can't do it again. I can't raise enough money in this country and it's drying up in Europe too.

Do the returns on a film like The Man Who Envied Women *have any effect on possible grant money or backing from other sources for future projects?*

No, I don't think that's going to be an issue for me. I think it is an issue in the case of someone like Spike Lee, who now has access to other than public money. When I think about the films that are successful, I can't imagine moving towards that kind of filmmaking.

So, I guess for your next project you'll just have to cut back on the Star-Warsian special effects.

Special effects [laughs]? A freeze-frame of a door . . . for me that's a special effect!

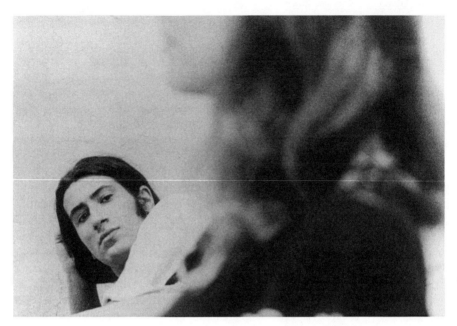

1.

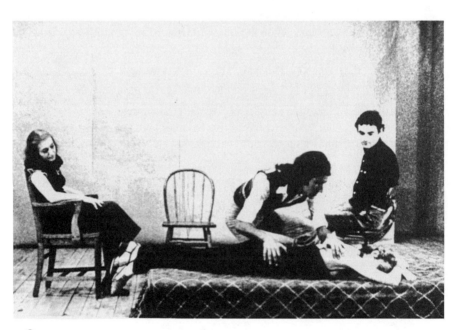

2.

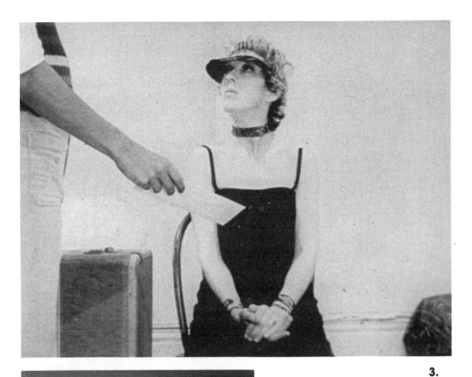

3.

4.

From *Lives of Performers*: 1. Fernando Torm and Shirley Soffer. 2. Shirley Soffer, Valda Setterfield, Fernando Torm, and John Erdman. 3. and 4. Valda Setterfield.

From *Film About a Woman Who...*: 5. Shirley Soffer and Yvonne Rainer. 6. Dempster Leech and Renfreu Neff. 7. Yvonne Rainer. 8. Frame enlargement.

5.

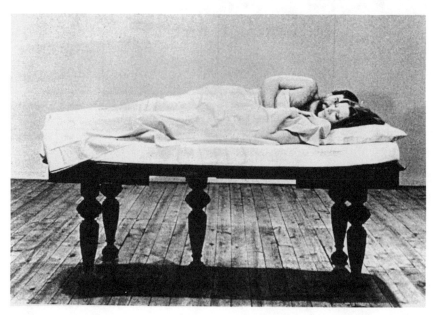

6.

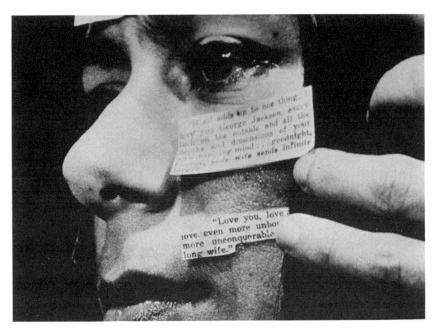

7.

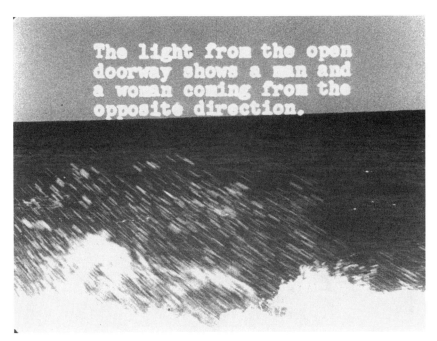

8.

9.

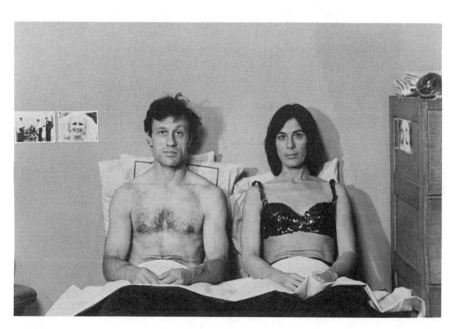

10.

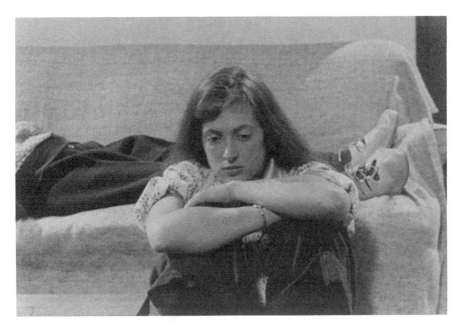

11.

From *Kristina Talking Pictures*: 9. Blondell Cummings. 10. Ivan Rainer and Yvonne Rainer. 11. Kate Parker.

12.

13.

14.

"The aim of all enemies of the State is the deliberate creation of an opposing power over and against this State, or the denial of *the State's monopoly of force.*"

H. Herold, head of the Federal Criminal Investigation Bureau (BKA), 1975

(Italics mine)

15.

From *Journeys from Berlin/1971*: 12. Annette Michelson and Gabor Vernon. 13. Cynthia Beatt. 14. Still. 15. Frame enlargement.

16.

17.

18.

From *The Man Who Envied Women*: 16. Thyrza Goodeve and Larry Loonin. 17. William Raymond and Trisha Brown. 18. William Raymond with a film clip from *In a Lonely Place*. 19. Yvonne Rainer and William Raymond. 20. Melody London, Jackie Raynal, and William Raymond.

19.

20.

Film Scripts

In the film scripts the dialogue and sound instructions are printed full width on the page. Descriptions of the image are in italic and indented and precede the dialogue they pertain to. The two elements are frequently interrupted and fragmented to indicate simultaneous actions. The following abbreviations are used:

b&w	black and white
CU	close-up
IT	inter-title
LS	long shot
MCU	medium close-up
MLS	medium long shot
MOS	"mit-out" (without; pseudo-German) sound
MS	medium shot
sync	sound synchronization
V-O	voice-over

Lives of Performers

Credits appear, black typewritten letters against a white background:

Lives of Performers
(A Melodrama)

CAST: Valda Setterfield, Shirley Soffer, John Erdman, Fernando Torm, Epp Kotkas, James Barth, Yvonne Rainer, Sarah Soffer

CINEMATOGRAPHER: Babette Mangolte

SOUND RECORDING: Gene De Fever, Gordon Mumma

Edited by Yvonne Rainer and Babette Mangolte
Written and Directed by Yvonne Rainer

The first shot following the credits is a title:

> Cliché is, in a sense, the purest art of intelligibil-
> ity; it tempts us with the possibility of enclosing
> life within beautifully inalterable formulas, of ob-
> scuring the arbitrary nature of imagination with an
> appearance of necessity.
>
> LEO BERSANI

Cut to a sequence of shots showing a dance rehearsal in progress. The seven participants move about a large shabby loft, executing simple walking steps, with frequent sharp changes in direction. One of them, a woman, appears to be the director, or choreographer. Although we see them speaking the sound track is silent. After about four minutes the sound surges up. The director is counting a repetitive "One, two, three, four, one two. . . ." A medley of voices discusses the steps, asks questions. None of this is in sync. The scene culminates in hearty laughter from the entire group. Cut to IT: At once our tension vanished.

The second sequence consists of six shots. The camera is stationary and frames a succession of six photographs against a background of assorted technical memos and notations concerning the film itself. The voices of the performers provide the commentary.

Yvonne: This is the first of eight photos from *Grand Union Dreams*. Shirley was a mortal, Fernando and Valda were heroes. I was one of the gods. It was done about a

Originally published in Yvonne Rainer, *Work 1961–73*. Reprinted with permission of Press of the Nova Scotia College of Art and Design.

year ago. In this first photo Epp and James are engaged in a duet. David and Yvonne have just finished dragging them on the fake grass in a small arc. When they stand they undulate their upper bodies in unison while passing the red ball back and forth. They are about to pick up the grass and involve it in their undulations. Valda waits. My question is: "What does it mean?" Are they celebrating something? Yes, that sounds good: Epp and James are doing a dance of pleasure at the advent of spring.

Shirley: It actually was spring when we began working on this piece and I first met you, Fernando. I think some people went over to your house after that first rehearsal.

Fernando: You asked if we had any booze. That was where I first had a hint of your humor—the look on your face when you asked.

Shirley: Yes, I remember the look you gave me. I thought "Oh, I'm discovered in my discomfort, but he's sympathetic."

Yvonne: Ah, there's the suitcase, and there's Trisha. Trisha has come down from Olympus and has laboriously poled her way toward the group of mortals who are putting the "squeeze" on the heroes, especially on Epp, who is squeezing the red ball. In this photo she has said "She is my very dear friend and I don't like seeing her caught in the middle." Trisha threads her way in and says to Epp, "You will soon see things of which you have never heard, and which you have never seen. Then you will understand things that I can never tell you. But you must stay awake. You may see them only once."

Shirley: And there's Fernando in the box . . .

Yvonne: . . . with suitcase. Why does Fernando have the suitcase? Is he going away or has he just arrived? Why is he in the box with the suitcase? Is he trying it out as a body-supporting device? And what is in the suitcase? Dirty sox?

Fernando: The complete works of Aristotle in Greek. (*Long pause.*) On the stairs. I was going up the stairs and I heard my name. I didn't even know who was calling me, but I felt it in my spine. Something about your voice, and I turned around and it was you.

Shirley: Uh-huh. I didn't know there was anything special about my voice at that time, but I distinctly remember seeing you on the stairs and realizing for the first time that you really were going to be taking this thing seriously and I felt a strong surge of liking for you, and that must have shown in my voice.

Valda: I was always aware of your presence. It was equivocal, sometimes sinister in that it didn't declare itself—especially on that ride we took into the Mennonite country with Shirley and Lena. I didn't know what you were about or who you were attracted to. . . .

Fernando: Actually, I hadn't intended to ask you to go, but somehow—meeting you by accident like that, passing through the doorway—I did it on the spur of the moment.

Valda: Yes, and I immediately asked if Shirley and Lena would come, because I didn't want to be alone with you.

Shirley: Then he kept coming to the house with those messages for you.

Valda: That really confused me—not that I thought much about it in a personal way—but rather, you know, in that way that one does when you are trying to figure out someone else's intentions, whether or not they are directed at you. So I didn't really think anything about him personally until you told me about those talks you had with him about me. I think then I began to look at you differently. Maybe with more curiosity. When we went to the theater that night I was very aware that you were sitting next to me. I don't know how aware I was that you had *manoeuvered* to sit next to me. Do you remember—when the whole audience stood up so enthusiastically—I turned and looked at you as if to say "O Christ, do we have to do this too?" and we stood up.

Fernando: Yes, I remember. Then later I sat next to you in the pancake house and at one point I took out a pencil and was writing something which you noticed in a certain way. I was embarrassed.

Valda: The night of our last performance you said after it was over that you'd be coming to New York and that you'd like to look me up. I told you my address and said that information had my phone number. Then later at that small party I was aware of you—for no particular reason. You were across the room talking to Donald. I made that gesture with the bottle of brandy—offering the last drop to anyone who wanted it before I wolfed it down—and finally you sprang laughing up and accepted the bottle. Then later you were lying down. As I started to leave, on impulse I went over and lay down on top of you, saying "Goodbye, Fernando" thinking it was the last time I was going to see you there. Almost instantaneously—as though you were expecting me to come to you—you grasped the back of my head and drew me down to your chest. You caressed my hair and sighed deeply. (*pause*) Then there was all that confusion about who would drive us to the airport. We didn't expect you.

Shirley: Yes, I didn't know what to think either, although I sort of knew. I guess I was just a little uncomfortable, because you had already showed me that piece he had written for you.

Valda: I regretted that later. It seemed too intimate to show anyone, even to Shirley, but I was still not ready to acknowledge your intentions toward me, so for the moment I had to pretend it was not as intimate or private as it later seemed to me. By the time you arrived to drive us to the airport I knew what was going on and I was getting excited.

Yvonne: What made you excited?

Valda: It was like the excitement of performance, experiencing my beauty and value when all those eyes are focused on me. I am at my best as a performer.

Yvonne: Why did you have to wait before getting excited? Don't you ever experience attraction to someone before you are sure whether or not they are attracted to you?

Valda: Yeh, sure. But I really wasn't in that frame of mind a year ago. You know what I had just come out of; I was very depressed, so I wasn't able to use my eyes too well. Besides, I really do enjoy performing.

Yvonne: OK.

Fernando: When we went back . . .

Valda: Wait. Yvonne, were you reading that?

Yvonne: What?

Valda: Those questions.

Yvonne: Yes. Why'd you want to know?

Valda: I just wondered. Sorry, Fernando.

Fernando: We went back to find your eyeshade, went upstairs, looked through the rooms. There was hardly any light.

Valda: I wondered why you didn't touch me, wondered why I didn't touch you.

Fernando: I stood on the landing beside the doorway as we were going back downstairs. I thought you'd have to squeeze through.

Valda: O God! You gave me so much room.

Yvonne: What else happened while we were rehearsing that piece?

Shirley: The hotel . . .

Fernando: The hotel . . . that's where I first got a sense of certain aspects of your mind that made you seem very different to me. I was lying on the bed and you were sitting on it . . . I can't remember now exactly what led to talking about Henry Miller.

Shirley: Somehow we got into who influenced him and I said Blaise Cendrars influenced him and we started to argue, only it wasn't an argument because I simply repeated my opinion while you repeated yours.

Fernando: Yes, I was trying to remember the name of someone else. I still think it was someone else—his name starts with a K.

Shirley: No, it was Blaise Cendrars.

Yvonne: So how the hell did that give you a sense of her mind? Did that seem like obscure information or something?

Fernando: It just had to do with that moment and yes, I guess her access to that particular information.

Yvonne: Here the mortals have become an inexorable wall, shuffling forward on Kleenex box-shod feet. On the right one of the gods—David—is walking about in great agitation in very squeaky shoes. Doug stands behind Valda, obscuring her face with a grey cardboard disc. Dong stands behind Doug with a microphone. Doug reads a speech from Jung about how if you don't pass through the inferno of your passions, you'll never overcome them. "Whenever we give up, leave behind, and forget too much, there is always the danger that the things we have neglected will return with added force." Somehow I transposed that into David's squeaky agitated walk. Understated passion. Fernando walks backwards before the greedy wall. (They are eating from a big pot, as you can see.) Fernando says:

Fernando: "See how cruel they look. Their lips are thin, their noses sharp, their faces furrowed and distorted by folds. Their eyes have a staring expression, they are always seeking something. What are they seeking? They always want something; they are always uneasy and restless. I do not know what they want. I do not understand them. I think that they are mad."

Yvonne: That's also from Jung. He quotes a Pueblo Indian about the white man. The mortals have become cruel white men.

Valda: I want to finish about the airport. I have to tell you this. When you kissed me goodbye, or rather, you were leaning against that rail with your feet crossed—the way you do—and I moved in to kiss you goodbye because people had begun to board the plane. You reached for the back of my neck with your left hand and drew me toward you. Your right arm was bent so your forearm was against your chest. As you pressed me against you and kissed me, my breast momentarily rested against your hand, which didn't move.

Fernando: Yes. Is that what made you think of those lines "all day he sits before you face to face, like a cardplayer. Your elbow brushes his elbow; if you should speak, he hears"?

Shirley: "The touched heart madly stirs."

Yvonne: Bullshit!

Valda: Oh for Christ sake, Yvonne. Get with it.

Yvonne: OK, OK, go on. I'm really enjoying all this.

Valda: Then I watched very carefully while you kissed Lena and I saw that it wasn't the same at all. You see, I was still not clear.

Shirley: It was so obvious.

Valda: As I said before, I wasn't in a state of mind to think of such things.

Fernando: When I got to New York I tossed a coin about whether to call you.

Valda: What would you have done if it had come out tails?

Fernando: I would have called anyway, but I would have felt it was all wrong.

Valda: You're funny.

Yvonne: Now the hero James is reaching the climax of his brief odyssey. Tannis in the wings—harpy or avenging angel—waits to mount his back at the most difficult stage of his journey. Fernando and Valda aid and impede him at the same time, supplying resistance and support to his forward lean. The gods wait expectantly on Mt. Olympus. This episode resolves itself as James—with Tannis riding piggy-back—clambers up the stairs. On reaching the top they crumple into the waiting arms of the gods, who then lower them to the floor on the other side of Olympus. As they are lowered, Yvonne reads from Jung: "At the beginning of the illness I had the feeling that there was something wrong with my attitude, and that I was to some extent responsible for the mishap. But when one affirms things as they are, without subjective protests, accepts the conditions of existence as one sees them, accepts one's own nature, as one happens to be, when one lives one's own life—then one must take mistakes into the bargain; life would not be complete without them. There is no guarantee—not for a single moment—that we will not fall into error or stumble into deadly peril. We may think there is a sure road. But that would be the road of death. Then nothing happens any longer—at any rate, not the right things. Anyone who takes the sure road is as good as dead."

Shirley: Such righteous sentiments. Now at this remove from that piece it seems terribly burdened with a kind of relentless truth-mongering.

Yvonne: What do you mean? In this last speech Jung seems anything but righteous. Righteousness implies a certainty that he is arguing *against*.

Shirley: It's the tone of self-congratulation or complacency of someone who has had a revelation and is laying it out. "Anyone who takes the sure road is as good as dead." Really! Maybe it's simply the fact of isolating such things from a longer text that bugs me. I just don't like the sound of it.

Yvonne: Well, you know, Shirley, that I have always had a weakness for the sweeping revelations of great men. That's why I'm going at this concert so differently. The line "O God, you gave me so much room" is really very much more moving to me than anything I used last year, even though on an aesthetic level I'm simply doing another form of story-telling—more intimate, less epic.

Shirley: What do you mean "O God, you gave me so much room"?

Yvonne: (*Explains*)

Valda: Were you saying that or reading it?

Yvonne: I was . . . remembering it from Hofstra. [Audience laughter.]

Shirley: I get it. Let's go on. I'm tired of all this.

> *The ensuing sequences take place in the same barren loft setting as the first*
> *rehearsal scene. The only accoutrements are three chairs, a single bed, or*
> *sofa, a suitcase, a package, and a letter. All dialogue is voice-over unless*

noted as "sync." Yvonne's and Shirley's speech is North American English, Valda speaks British English, and Fernando has a pronounced Latin American accent.

CU of script with Fernando's hand on it. Pan left over a patterned bedspread to wall. Pan right over Fernando's reclining body, past Shirley seated in a chair and speaking in Fernando's direction (MOS), to wall filled with posters. Pan left to Shirley, still talking.

Shirley: Shirley is saying how she put it off as long as she could and how finally she went up there to see the pictures of the rehearsal. Fernando is hardly listening.

Yvonne: Now she's thinking . . .

Shirley: I look like an old-time movie star! [Audience laughter.]

Shirley: She is complaining about how she doesn't want to do it anymore.

CU of Fernando's head. He looks toward Shirley. Pan over his body.

Yvonne: He says, "Then don't."

Shirley: She thinks about leaving the room.

Yvonne: She finds his inscrutability pretty hard to take . . .

CU of Shirley's throat. She leaves the frame, then returns. Camera tilts up to her face. She is looking straight at the camera.

Yvonne: . . . She wonders what he would do if she left the room. Would he feel remorseful, or would he follow her?

Shirley: She resents the fact that he always seems on top of the situation.

Shirley focuses up and to left of frame.

Shirley: She would like him to speak to her.

Yvonne: He's very tired of her . . . indecisiveness . . . He says, "What?"

Shirley: She says she doesn't know what to do with herself . . .

Again slow pan, right to left, over Fernando's body.

Yvonne: See, there's a lot of time . . . you don't have to talk all the time, just put in an occasional comment . . . I mean, you don't have to fill up that time with everything that may be going on . . .

Pan left-to-right, again to Shirley.

Yvonne: She wonders why he doesn't say anything. She really wants him to talk to her.

Shirley: She can't bear his indifference.

Fernando: He wants to know why she's afraid.

Out-of-focus CU, Shirley in profile in the foreground, Fernando in focus on the bed in the background. He gets up, moves out of the frame. Shirley comes into focus as Fernando's hand lands on her shoulder. Cut to Shirley's feet, low angle. She stands and faces him. Their feet come together. Tilt up to their hips.

Shirley: She says that she's always worked in a form that disappears as soon as it reveals itself. She does not want to be observed as fixed and final.

Yvonne: She embraces him because she realizes that he may feel as frustrated as she.

Shirley: She's surprised that she's told him about her ephemeral nature. [Audience laughter.]

Camera at hip level. Tilt from hips to Fernando's head, then down to Shirley's head on his chest, then down to their hips.

Yvonne: She wonders, what is it about him, she can't figure it out: his cunning or his docility. It always puts her on the defensive, makes her focus on herself.

Tilt from hips to feet. Shirley walks toward bed and sits down (profile). She stays in focus. Cut to tracking shot of Fernando walking away from camera toward bed.

Shirley: He asks her whether she's afraid of failing.

Yvonne: Here he's looking into her eyes.

Cut to different camera position. Shirley looks up at him, then leaves frame.

IT: She starts to leave, then changes her mind and rejoins him.

MS: Shirley and Fernando standing beside bed. Tilt down to their feet. Shirley sits down.

Shirley: She doesn't want to talk about it anymore. She feels he's not very sympathetic.

Fernando leaves frame and starts to walk around the room. Camera pans back and forth randomly, sometimes "catching" him.

Fernando: But Fernando's very confused. He doesn't know what she's talking about. She really confuses him. He loses the track of the issues all the time. He only asks, "Why don't you come with me?" But the only answer that he gets is, "Do you have any money?"

Yvonne: That comes a little later . . . There!

Shirley: She says, "Do you have any money?" [Audience laughter.]

Camera comes to rest on Fernando and Shirley sitting on bed. They look to their left (frame-right). Pan right to Valda standing in doorway. She is dressed very differently from the others, in a long dark formal gown. She crosses frame. Camera tracks backward to reveal wooden chair, in which Fernando then sits. Track continues, revealing Shirley on another chair and Valda on the bed. Cut to CU of Valda's face looking at camera. As she speaks (MOS), she continually shifts her position so that her head moves from the center of the frame. The camera re-centers her. She then shifts again, etc.

Valda: Valda is disconsolate. She is remembering a visit to John's house. It was in the country. She enjoyed the fresh air, the flowers and the birds, food, vegetables from the garden. She said it was so beautiful she thinks maybe she'd like to live there forever. She talks about a movie they saw together. They both cried. There was an old woman in the film whose performance affected her very deeply. As usual John had turned critical when they left the theater, and deemed his previous opinion sentimental. She's used to this kind of response in him.

Pan to MCU of Shirley looking toward Valda. Cut to

IT: I remember that movie. It's about all these small betrayals, isn't it?

Medium shot of Shirley, John, and Valda standing and facing the camera. They perform a dance that is comprised of a succession of turnings toward or away from each other, one person at a time.

Valda: You might describe it that way. It's also a story about a man who loves a woman and can't leave her when he falls in love with another woman. I mean, he can't seem to make up his mind. Or I could tell it from the point of view of the first woman: she loves him and endures his cruelties (yes, cruelties. You see, from her vantage point his weaknesses become—yes, become—cruelties) yes, endures his cruelties because he always returns to her, and although she won't acknowledge it, she really does think—no, feel—that she can't live without him. (How did she ever get into such a fix?) She also thinks that he loves her best and that that love will finally conquer all. After all, he always returns to her, doesn't he? Or I could tell it through the eyes of No. 2 woman: She loves him and wants him to leave No. 1. She even gets pregnant. Then her own husband demands a divorce; he's had enough. (How did she ever get herself into such a fix?) But I don't care to dwell on No. 2. (How can such things continue to happen?) As I said before, he can't make up his mind. Then No. 1 gets sick, so he stays with her but doesn't give up No. 2. Or rather, No. 2 doesn't leave him. I don't want to make it sound as though he holds the controls, even though the two women sometimes act as though he does.

CU of Shirley's face, looking directly at camera.

Shirley (*sync*): Which woman is the director most sympathetic to?

CU of Valda's face, looking frame-right.

Valda (*sync*): I think No. 1,

IT: Valda replies,

CU of Valda's face.

Valda (*sync*): maybe simply because she appears first.

MS: Valda in John's lap.

Yvonne: Now John is thinking of a particular event which happened about six months earlier. He had been outside their house and some muggers attacked him. And she had come out of the house and screamed. If he hadn't heard her scream, he would have plunged the knife that he had taken out of his pocket into his would-be attacker's throat. Later she had clung to him. She seemed excited and vulnerable, and he was very perplexed by this. He felt rather bitter. They made love, but his mind was half elsewhere.

Pan left to bed, which is against the wall. A suitcase is on the floor.

Pan back to chair. Shirley is now sitting in Fernando's lap.

Yvonne: I was reading a part that John would have read. I forgot to mention that I'm going to be . . . I don't know, did I mention, that I'm going to be taking some of John's parts.

Camera tracks forward until Shirley and Fernando are in CU. Shirley looks to right, gets up from Fernando's lap. Pan right to meet Valda, who is walking left. Pan left to meet Shirley, walking right. This is repeated until the women meet. (They actually are walking backwards so as to extend the time.)

Shirley: Valda says that they're waiting for Shirley, and it would be a good idea if Shirley were to go now. Shirley says that can wait because she has always wanted to speak to Valda to tell her how impressed she is with her. She was particularly impressed with something that Valda had said, which was that Asia is not clay in the hands of the West. [Audience laughter.]

Camera comes to rest on open doorway. Valda enters from left, pauses, looks over her shoulder, then exits. Fernando enters and looks after her.

Fernando: Here she says, "Wait a minute." Then she leaves, and he doesn't know where she goes.

MLS: Fernando on bed, Shirley on chair.

Yvonne: Here they're waiting for her to come back . . . and she doesn't come back.

CU of Shirley's legs. Cut to CU of Shirley's left shoulder. John enters, pausing behind her chair. During the ensuing action, camera dollies slowly back until scene is in extreme long shot with one of the standing lights exposed.

Fernando: Here comes John, to pick up Fernando. The train will be leaving soon, and he is worried about being late. He is going to Chile. [Laughter of performers.]

Fernando, holding suitcase, joins John. They both exit to right. Valda enters from right, sits on bed with her face in her hands. Shirley sits down beside her. The scene is now in extreme LS. Valda and Shirley alternately change their positions on the bed.

Shirley: Shirley tells Valda how fond she is of her . . . what a dear friend she is, and how she hates seeing her caught in the middle.

Valda: Valda replies that Shirley shouldn't worry about her. She thought she had made a decision, but now she's not so sure, and that's what's confusing her.

Shirley: Shirley's surprised, because she thought that Valda *was* sure.

Valda: Valda says it's not as easy as all that because other people become affected by the decisions one makes, and what will Nina and Theresa do?

Yvonne: Shirley tells Valda about a dream she had.

MCU of Sarah bouncing ball in slow-motion. A cat lies nearby.

Shirley: I had a dream about a wall. The wall is not concrete or metal; it is steel mesh like the fence in a schoolyard. There are no doors. Rather, it's the kind of a wall that I would like to climb rather than walk through a ready-made door. I do climb the wall, and it feels terrific. I'm stretching my body as I climb, feeling the pull on my legs and arms as I reach the top and climb over. I enjoy going down the other side. What I like about this wall is that I have no fear of being locked out or locked in. I can always get in or out by climbing by my own physical nimbleness and agility.

On the other side I find that I am in a schoolyard, which is, in fact, the schoolyard of the school across the street from the house where I was born. There are no children in the schoolyard on this day, although it is a beautiful spring day. I run around freely, the wind blowing in my hair. I am happy, bouncing a large volleyball. I bounce it up and down and against a brick side wall. It feels good just to run around and be free and have all that space to myself. I feel my body stretching and I am running around the yard very fast, but I am full of energy, not at all tired. I have an enormous sense of great physical well-being, of a stretching and toning up of all my limbs and the back of my neck. When I wake up I am really happy. I remember that I have caught a glimpse of something alive and free within me.

LS of Valda and Shirley on bed as before. Valda and Shirley embrace.

Valda: Valda thanks Shirley. She says she's made her feel much better.

Shirley walks to right and exits. Cut to medium shot: Shirley walks to right and exits. Cut to MCU of Shirley's legs walking to right.

Valda: Shirley says she'll leave now while she still has time to catch the train. She doesn't find it easy to go.

MLS: Valda sitting on bed, jiggling a foot. The cat lies beside her. After after 45 seconds, she leaves frame.

MS of plain wooden chair. It is in the center of the frame and faces the camera. Valda enters with a package and sits down. She starts to unwrap it, pauses, continues, takes out a printer's eyeshade, stands up.

Valda: When Valda received this package in the mail and saw where it was from, she was longing to open it, and could hardly wait until her friend left. But suddenly she felt less anxious. She wondered what she was getting into, receiving gifts from *him.*

She tries on the eyeshade, primping as though before a mirror. [Audience laughter is heard.] *She sits down, looking squarely at camera.*

Yvonne: The face of this character is a fixed mask. We shall have her wear an eyeshade to reveal her inner and outer appearance. The eyeshade hides the movement of the upper half of her face, but the lower half, where the

IT: One week later.

tongue works, stays visible. She must function with a face of stone and at the same time reveal her characteristic dissembling.

Fernando, seen from the waist down, walks in from left, holding the suitcase in one hand and a letter in the other. Valda takes the letter.

Fernando: Here he is coming back from Santiago, holding that funny letter that he doesn't know where it comes from.

Valda: Valda asks if they had a good time and he says, "So-so."

Fernando: And she asks him if he had missed her, and of course, he missed her a lot.

Valda and Fernando embrace and kiss behind chair. (He has removed her eyeshade and she has left the letter on the chair.) Camera dollies back to ML.

Valda: She decides to look at the letter later. She asks if he had received *her* letter and where he was in the house when he read it.

IT (with simultaneous reading by Fernando): I was in the living room talking to Nina, when Theresa came in with the mail and handed me a letter. I looked at it, saw that it was from you and stuck it in my shirt pocket. I had to finish my business with Nina. Later I took it out of my pocket on the way upstairs; I paused half-way up the stairs to open the envelope, read the letter hurriedly, then continued on up to the bedroom to sit and pore over it.

IT: He asks her what she meant by "ebb tide." She tells him.

MS of Valda and Fernando entwined in each other's arms on the bed. The chair is in the foreground, out-of-focus. The letter is on the chair. Valda

*disengages herself from the sleeping Fernando. Camera pans as she moves
to right, picks up the letter and walks to a pillar, against which she leans as
she reads the letter to herself.*

Shirley: I'm sorry about the whole thing, mostly for myself, of course, but after that,
for you. I think if you can stand it you should take him back. I will probably change
my mind and want him back, but I never, I don't know how to phrase it, except that, I
suppose, he is split, and I thought I could put them back together, but I can't, and you
have the constant half, and I am simply not satisfied with the other transitory half that
he gives me, that is the atrocious novel that is his emotional life, representing the evil
feminine principle. I don't know how I got stuck in this category, but I'm stuck there
in a neat little box labeled emotional, childish, demanding, bitchy, undisciplined,
unintellectual, pleasure-oriented, etc., ad nauseam, while you apparently are in an
equally untrue box labeled unemotional, mature, fair, disciplined, etc. Passion
versus companionship, sex versus work, child/mother versus sister/friend, and
countless more sickening, cliché-ridden, and superficial characterizations which I
am sure are as unfair to you as they are to me. But maybe you are stronger and
cleverer than me and can live with the pattern or break it. I can do neither. I think he
needs you. Anyway, he needs somebody who won't let herself be destroyed by him,
and unfortunately or fortunately, I am not that person. For one thing, I have less to
fall back on everytime he is cruel. Less work, less friends, less emotional independence. Less experience with his cruelty than you've had. You've had all that time
with him to build on. I thought that wouldn't be so important, because I thought we
would live in the present, but he won't. He's either wallowing about in his past, or
cruelly tempting us both with impossible futures, putting off making a life with me
until we go away, get a house in the country, have children, etc. All of which he can't
do, and even if he could, it wouldn't help because it's external.

Anyway, dear lady, I used to be afraid of you, but I'm not anymore. It's he who's
hurting me, not you. And I'm free to like you, which I do. I gather that you're
unhappy right now, but maybe that will make it easier for you and him to get back
together. He is very unhappy too, but now I can't help you. He doesn't really seem to
want those things that he perhaps reproached you for not providing. I think he wants
an essentially homosexual relationship, only with a woman instead of a man. Maybe
you can make a good life with him. I hope so. I'm sick of all this unhappiness all the
time. He doesn't deserve to punish himself so much. He's only bad because he
demands to be so good. And I think he really does love you, much more than he will
ever love anybody else. Most of the time I've felt that I am just some kind of strut, or
support, in some incredibly complex and probably painful and beautiful structure,
which is his relationship to you. Which should flatter you immensely, but it sort of
makes me feel a little stupid. I really think I deserve to have my own structure
somehow, built by someone and me about us. Anyway, that's what I think, and I'm
not sure what I feel I should tell you, but I feel some kind of compulsion to explain
things to myself by telling other people. And also, I just wanted to tell you that I like
you, and that you should take him away from me now. Not that I have him, but you
know what I mean. And really, I think it would be the best thing for him and me, and

maybe you, although it would be presumptuous of me to pretend to know what you need. But if you need a very complex love, he has that for you.

Toward the end of the above reading, Valda walks to left, puts the letter back on the chair, and lies down next to Fernando. Fernando props himself up on an elbow.

Fernando (*sync*): Do you think that I should say that?

Valda (*sync*): What?

Fernando (*sync*): I mean about admitting that I feel superior?

Long slow fade-to-black.

MLS: Shirley, Valda, and John seated in chairs, S and J facing each other and V between them, facing the camera, but inclining her body toward John and her face toward Shirley as the latter two engage in conversation (MOS). The bed is in the foreground.

Yvonne: Shirley is asking John what he thinks of the performance, what he thought of the last performance. And he liked some of it, and some of it he disliked intensely. He was in such a bad mood at the end of it that he couldn't even applaud and he couldn't come backstage. He apologizes; he says, "You wouldn't want me to pretend I was enthusiastic when I wasn't, would you?" And she says, "No . . . but I'm sorry that you can't take pleasure in a friend's success" [audience laughter] and he says, "Well, I must admit that a couple of hours later I felt really threatened by it and I was wondering what *I* was going to do next." And she's amused by that, and she says, "Well, at least you're forthright." . . . Shirley asks Valda, "How did *you* feel?"

Valda: Oh, I didn't really know what I was doing. There was so little time for adequate preparation, and I didn't always know what was expected of me. I mean, if I come in a door and see you two here, what am I supposed to register? Fear, surprise . . . nothing?

Jump-cut; MLS same as before, except that Valda's chair is empty. Valda enters from behind pillar at right, sees John and Shirley, then exits whence she entered. During the following jump-cuts, John and Shirley simply observe the comings and goings of Fernando and Valda, occasionally looking in a puzzled way at the camera.

Valda enters, sees John and Shirley, pivots to face upstage.
Valda enters with Fernando. Both are laughing. Valda notices John and Shirley, then moves toward Shirley.
Valda enters, followed by Fernando. He grabs her wrist, swings her around, looks into her eyes.
Valda enters, sits in the chair between John and Shirley. Fernando enters, sits on the floor with his head in Valda's lap. She strokes his long black hair.

Valda enters, followed by Fernando, who stands behind her with his arm around her waist. She loses her composure, starts to laugh. They both "break up," look at the camera.
Same as preceding. They don't "break up."
Valda enters, followed by Fernando. He kisses her head-to-toe.
Valda enters, lies on couch. Fernando enters, tries to rouse her. When she doesn't respond, he runs out. He then does a series of "double-takes"—starts to re-enter, looks at camera, exits, re-enters, goes to Valda, backs up, sits in chair. He then begins to converse with John and Shirley in a casual way.
MLS: same scene. Valda enters, walks to left. Fernando enters, leans against pillar. Pan follows Valda to far left wall, against which she leans. Cut to Fernando against pillar. Pan follows him as he walks toward Valda.

IT: I need to talk to you, to see you before me.

CU: Valda and Fernando embracing. Fernando fidgets.

IT: You're never still, are you?

CU: midsections of Shirley and John embracing.

IT: I woke up this morning feeling anticipation and excitement at the prospect of seeing you.

CU: midsections. John holds Shirley's hands at her side.

IT: I have behaved as though I am exempt from the conditions that I constantly impose on others.

CU: hip level. Valda and John embrace.

IT: I have such strong feeling for you.

I know.

CU: Valda's and Fernando's feet.

Fernando: I don't know what

IT: Fernando stands sobbing against the wall. Valda lays consoling hands on his shoulders.

Fernando (*continues without interruption*): to do next. I feel like a shell. I am so afraid.

CU: Valda's crossed legs, Shirley from the waist down.

IT: What he did to my children I shall never forgive him for.

CU: midsections. Shirley in chair, Valda standing.

IT: I am living a loneliness I never expected. I feel so vulnerable, so inferior, so unsure of myself.

CU: Fernando in chair reading, Valda bending over him. Fernando is framed from nose to book.

IT: The dream urged upon me the necessity of clarifying this situation.

CU: John's head, facing camera. He is seated. Fernando stands beside him, his fingers caressing each other mid-frame.

IT: The only feeling I am sure about these days is a complete loathing for myself.

CU: Fernando's face. Valda's profile is bisected at the left. Her hand touches his face.

IT: Look at me, just for one second.

Fernando looks at her.

IT: I'm not afraid to die, but I don't want to.

MS: Fernando and John sitting on bed. F is leaning against wall, looking at J, who looks somewhat dispiritedly at the floor.

IT: Have you ever considered the possibility that if a man likes you he doesn't necessarily want to fuck you?

MS as before. John and Fernando have exchanged positions.

IT: I dreamed of my mother last night, and of my wife. My mother was crying for me.

MS as before. Shirley leans against the wall, looking at Valda.

IT: All of this being the case, how can I continue to be his friend?

MLS: Shirley, Valda, and John seated in three chairs, conversing (MOS).

IT: We're going to be married.

MLS as before.

IT: Now that we understood each other, it was a relief to continue our talk on lighter terms.

MS: Fernando stands, leaning against wall and smoking.

Yvonne: Fernando's watching them.

Pan right past Shirley, Valda, and John in chairs. Only their heads are seen. Pan left to frame Valda. She looks to left, gets up, and stands beside chair, facing left toward Fernando (off-screen). Only her midsection is framed.

Fernando: She says to him that they were discussing the performance. And he asks if they want something from the delicatessen, because he was going to get some cigarettes. But she tells him to wait, that she wants to show him something, and also the delicatessen is closed. [Audience laughter.]

Pan left as Valda walks toward Fernando. When she reaches him, cut to

IT: Valda shows Fernando her solo.

A totally different space, possibly a museum space, although the walls are bare. It is much more polished, less dilapidated than the loft we have seen so far. Valda, dressed in the same long gown, performs a long solo dance with a ball. Her movements are executed in silence, vaguely resembling those of a temptress in a silent movie, and lit by an encircling follow-spot. The solo ends with her torso arched in an extreme backward curve as the ball, tucked under her chin, rolls down the front of her body, along the floor, and out of the frame.

Cut to MCU: Fernando and Valda beside the wall in the studio.

Fernando: Here they are back in the studio, and Fernando is saying to her why did she show him that, that he has seen it a hundred times. Then she says that she does it differently now, that she understands it better. But he says that it looks the same to him.

As camera begins tracking right, Valda turns to face camera, making an angry grimace. Track continues all the way right to frame Yvonne in MCU leaning against a pillar, and watching.

Yvonne: He asks if they're waiting for the others, meaning Epp and Jim and Yvonne. And Yvonne has come in, meanwhile.

Cut to rehearsal seen at beginning of film. Snatches of direction and conversation can be heard.

Yvonne: . . . The arms are always in this slot, Fernando . . . You see, the "string" between the hands is always parallel to the wall . . . This is the beginning, the end . . . They just about meet ahead of the thighs . . . parallel to the wall and perpendicular to the floor . . . and chase the right hand . . . use as few steps as possible . . . no no, not the cup, not the cup, the angle . . .

Valda: . . . should I be here? . . .

Yvonne: . . . Did you get enough, Babette?

Babette: . . . I stay a long time on Fernando, I pan again . . .

Valda: . . . The box was really very precarious . . .

Yvonne: I was in that box and I didn't think . . .

Various people enter the shallow box standing upended against the wall and assume static poses within its confines. It is not high enough to allow them to stand upright, thus making for rather uncomfortable-looking positions, frieze-like in their two-dimensionality.

Yvonne: . . . keep your body here . . . the paper, now keep your body to the wall . . . now the feet go to the window, the body faces the wall, not the paper, the wall. Paper, wall, window, closet . . . scissors, rock [laughter] Uh . . . where are we? . . . OK, I'm going to do a special thing here: we're going to start, some of us in the box, others of us . . . You will get out in character . . . OK, you're doing that, Fernando's in the box, Valda . . .

Shirley and Fernando lean against the wall beside the box and appear to argue. (MOS)
Cut to

IT: Emotional relationships are relationships of desire, tainted by coercion and constraint; something is expected from the other person, and that makes him and ourselves unfree.

Cut to the rehearsal space again. The box is now filled with people, a compact mass of writhing arms and struggling torsos. Valda stands serenely beside the box, looking on. Cut to

IT: I began to think of him in a particular way.

Rehearsal space: Everyone leaves the frame. Only the empty box remains.

IT: Final Performance:
                                         LULU
                                     in 35 shots
A series of 35 tableaux vivants *ensues, modeled after the production stills in the published scenario of G. W. Pabst's "Pandora's Box." Each shot begins with the performers holding poses in a given tableau, which then breaks up after 20 seconds as they prepare for their next positioning. Each shot contains a minimum of movement: flickers of eyelids, quivering of nostrils, and the final, very brief, disassembling that is itself aborted by the following shot. The chiaroscuro lighting and small changes of costume (a tie, a jacket, etc.) indicate an entirely different register of drama from that of the previous flatly lit scenes. The "melodrama" of the film's subtitle is finally being enacted. Even the intertitle announcing the final event appears in more aggressive typeface. The entire sequence lasts about twelve minutes.*

[There is no sound until the last three minutes, when "No Expectations" by the Rolling Stones is heard.]

The final shot ends with an abrupt fade-to-black as John Erdman, in cap and tweed jacket, walks toward camera.

Film About a Woman Who . . .

All of the credits are black type on white background.

Film About a Woman Who . . .

with Dempster Leech, Shirley Soffer, John Erdman, Renfreu Neff

and James Barth, Epp Kotkas, Sarah Soffer, Yvonne Rainer, Tannis Hugill, Valda Setterfield

TECHNICAL ASSISTANTS: Scott Billingsley, Epp Kotkas, Barry Ralbag, Karl Schurman

SOUND: Deborah S. Freedman, Kurt Munkacsi (The Basement), Lawrence Loewinger

TITLES: Neil Murphy

Excerpts from "La Sonnambula," Vincenzo Bellini, Orchestra and Chorus of the Maggio Musicale Fiorentino; "Maria Elena," The Baja Marimba Band; Three piano sonatas by Edvard Grieg, "Thanks," "arietta," "Native Land" played by Philip Corner.

[The sound of thunder and rain begins.]

Photos from the Mangolte and Soffer families.

Financed in part by fees derived from performances of "This is the story of a woman who . . . ," "Performance around an unfinished film," "Kristina (For a . . . Novella)"

and also by funding from The American Theater Laboratory, National Endowment for the Arts, Castelli-Sonnabend Tapes and Films, Change Inc.

Narrated by Yvonne Rainer and John Erdman

Cinematographer: Babette Mangolte

Edited by Yvonne Rainer and Babette Mangolte

Written and directed by Yvonne Rainer 1972–1974

D, S, J, & R on sofa watching slides. (MCU)

[Thunder and rain continue.]

Reprinted, with permission, from *October*, no. 2 (Summer 1976), pp. 39–67.

Y's voice: He feels a growing irritation. He had run into her on the way to the shooting. He hadn't seen her for a year. Some banter was exchanged. Now

>   *D scratches nose.*

he is reviewing the conversation in his mind. "She hasn't changed a bit," he muses to himself. His mind works in spirals as he watches the slides.

Earlier this week she saw them on the other side of the street and was surprised at her

>   *R crosses legs.*

response—mild distaste rather than the rage she had anticipated. The whole thing now seemed rather sordid. It was receding. She had ducked into a shop to avoid them.

He thinks about making love, then about being in love, then about performing. Then he thinks about her: his very gaze seemed to transform her into a performer, a realized fantasy of herself. Sometimes it was almost as if she were saying

>   *S looks at J.*

"Look at me, look at me—a small price to pay for my love in return." He finds himself agreeing.

>   *IT:* agreeing . . . *(w on b)*

>   *Projected slide (b on w):* But only momentarily. It is quite possible that by
>   this time he feels very bad. This stage of his life as a captive audience-for-
>   one seems based in artifice and as such must sooner or later come to a
>   close. He sighs to himself. "Such delicious artifice. Nowhere is captivity
>   less painful or more complete."

>   *IT: (full frame, b on w) same as above.*

>   *no image*

She tries to reconstruct the passage from the novel that had so impressed her. The best she can do is: "All is finally clarified. It is unspeakable, but clear. The reach of my jealousy, of my certainty of betrayal, engulfs me at every step. [Sound of rain fades out.] It is unthinkable that I live in this condition in intimacy with another person. And the possibility of living a life without intimate connections is equally intoler-able. Is it any wonder that the most plausible solution is to remove my existence? I see no way through my dilemma.

>   *Silhouetted backs of group on sofa watching slide of text beginning with
>   "dilemma" and ending with "what else?"*

I am not one to compromise; I wish I were; my life would be easier. The phone is ringing. . . . It's always been all or nothing for me. This statement is for ART, even though at this very moment I don't know where to turn." She can't remember, hard as she tries, the passage that had followed. It had suggested that such a dire solution might not be necessary. She is now wracking her brain to remember . . . What else, what else, what else?

Projected slide of S on beach.

The rain makes her think of when she was 18 years old, spending a summer in Chicago. She

Projected slide of S in field.

was sitting by an open window in a room with five other people. It had started to rain heavily. A

Projected slide of S with children.

woman on the other side of the room was talking about her baby sitter. She said, "I hope the stupid girl has sense enough to close the windows."

Projected slide of S and camel.

Without a second thought she reached over and shut the window. A stunned silence fell on the room.

Full frame photo of S and camel.

LS: J in the distance, facing the ocean.

S enters with square of glass, lies down, and frames J in the glass,

She thinks about the snow in Vermont and their last night in the cabin—the four of them lolling about the sleeping-loft warmed by a wood fire. Their talk had ranged over motion and phallic-vaginal body parts and illusion and comfort and back to sex-as-illusion. Again she repeats to herself the remembered phrase "Easy locomotion between comfort and discomfort." Now it all seemed like good social titillation. "Contempt again," she thinks. "But I can't help it. Social interactions seem to be mostly about seduction."

S in foreground high above J on beach positioning himself in spaces formed by her limbs.

MCU: J, S, and Sarah pose on beach as for a still camera.

Backs of group on sofa watching slides:
Wedding group
Three women and baby
Two women
Mother and son
Young man
Shirley and family
Shirley, Sarah, John
J and R with New York harbor in the background.

Full frame photo of J and R as above dissolves into

IT (w on b): Events of the past rose like waves and battering against her mind threw it into a wild commotion of shame, grief, and joy.

MCU: D sits watching TV. Sarah sits on floor leaning against his chair. She plays with a small clay bear. He occasionally looks at her. Camera moves in arc from right to left.

The man danced with the three-year-old child. It went on for a long time. He didn't take his eyes off of her. He manipulated her tiny soft limbs in time to the music. He bent down to her, lifted her up, turned her around under his hand, delicately balancing and manoeuvering her body, which at times his two huge hands all but concealed from view. She could not stop looking at the two of them. The sensuality of the dance fascinated her, and then as time passed it became bizarre. She began to be uneasy in the realization that he knew that *she* in particular was watching.

MCU: J & R pose for photo.

J's voice: First an emptiness like a great white bird soared through her. Then she began to think about particulars: the quality of his intelligence at the moment . . . , his insight into the nature of her struggle, his refusal to go along with her desperate . . . He had dragged it all out of her. Now she had to pay. Yet it was a relief that he was now carrying the ball. It was his turn to . . . and not dance the fandango in . . . And there was still so much she didn't know, which, if known, might have made her act differently. How much of the problem of their differences was real and how much was a smokescreen to conceal . . . ? Her mind clouded when she tried to answer. She had set him an impossible task. ". . . to allow me to . . . when I need to," she had told him. He had reminded her that *she* was not so . . . of *his* . . . She pleaded special circumstances. They argued. His voice was hard and curt. The die seemed cast. Yet in some way she trusted him. He would . . . They would meet again. If only he could say "But we really . . ."

LS: J in foreground, S very small on a bluff in the distance. He turns his head, scans sky.

Which was all very well for *her* to say, having jumped the gun in . . . Then that terrible accusation of his. She couldn't even repeat it, it . . . Yet it posed another question: "Is it possible that I have really . . . , that I will never make . . . Only in this way . . . survive." So be it. There are worse ways to live. Being so . . . may very well . . . She felt, however, little conviction. And finally, she grew calmer, almost resigned. They had both been . . .—her terror and the . . .—slowly eroding . . . and regard him . . . and pleasure.

LS: S in foreground reclining on her elbows. J and Sarah, very small way below her on the beach, walk away from each other.

MS from a high angle. S, D, and Sarah at table. S flips pages of book; D watches over bread in toaster.

[Silence for about 1½ minutes.]

Y's voice: She had dinner with him and his male lover and several of their friends. It was a noisy ebullient gathering. Some of her previous reservations about him were revived with renewed force. "He seems to be one way and then you meet his friends and you think 'How can he stand them?' And then you realize that he can stand them because he is *like* them in certain disagreeable respects." And yet she didn't want to dismiss him. "It isn't that I expect him to be only . . . want him to . . .

　　IT: Madame the healer. *(w on b)*

"Don't waste your time over these old-fashioned faggots," she admonishes herself, "with their pendulum swings from gentle passivity to nasty aggression. The ones who still refer to each other as 'she'."

　　MS of table from another high angle. D dunks toast in coffee and hands it to Sarah.

She likes him because he is so gifted and has done so much work on himself. He still thinks of art, however, as a form of self-immolation. "Why did you not write about *them?*" he had asked her. An indirect rebuke for her self-involvement. She had to admit that she really did believe that her own life was more interesting than that of anyone who might portray it in performance, or she couldn't deal with anyone else's life as interestingly as she could with her own. If this applied to her, it was equally true of him. But she didn't want to go into it at the dinner. And besides, it would have put her in a condescending position. He had never sought her advice. She didn't want to risk taking on needless responsibility with regard to him.

　　IT (w on b): When thinking this over, she became self-critical. Finally she gave it up and went out to the museum.

　　Fade-up on photo of Pantheon exterior. (color)

She had a kind of mind incapable of encompassing historical data. She could understand an event only through illustration—such as the plaster casts of people in death throes at Pompeii, the paintings at Versailles depicting the inflated gestures of Louis XIV. She visited the Pantheon at different times of day. She didn't

　　Photo of interior.

respond when he beckoned to her to come over to listen to the recorded lecture on the earphones. She knew that to know who was buried there would not make the visit any more meaningful to her. She stood in the great expanse of floor and enclosed light and felt her mind soar.

　　Color photos of:
　　Cluny tapestry
　　Etruscan fresco
　　Drawing of pillars

By the end of the day she was sick of madonnas holding up their male infants, saints holding their bloody foreheads, martyrs holding their heads, angels holding their fingers up, duchesses holding up their robes, dukes holding their

> *Greek relief*
> *painting of Coliseum*
> *painting of Roman scene*
> *Versailles*
> *Roman Forum*
> *Grand Canyon*
> *Las Vegas*
> *Borghese Garden*

falcons, soldiers holding their spears, lions holding up banners, and virgins holding up mirrors. "Everything is about seduction or death . . ." But then she thinks of her own recent situation and the word "resignation" springs to her mind. But she knows she can't resign herself to it and must sooner or later have a confrontation or simply end it. She would not add her name to his collection of dubious friendships.

> *Las Vegas on left, 1920s photo of woman and cat on right.*

After three days in that city she began to panic. How was she to face him when he arrived? What she had not allowed to intrude on her consciousness at home was now a reality: she couldn't go on with it. Even this brief interlude was enough to make her aware of a tremendous relief and renewed purpose. She had to tell him. She felt at once anxious and happy. How had she stood it for so long?

> *Woman with cat remains on right. Las Vegas on the left is replaced by title (w on b):* She lived there for a month without seeing anybody she knew. She talked only when buying food or dealing with tradespeople. She never heard or spoke her own language.
>
> *Moving image of ocean with (white) titles at top of frame:* In short, suddenly she found herself in a bad way.
>
> *No title. Camera pans to left.*
>
> *Title (over ocean):* The light from the open doorway shows a man and a woman coming from the opposite direction.
>
> *No title. Camera pans to r.*
>
> *Title (over ocean):* Somehow she suspects she has failed miserably again. She has failed to tell herself what she wanted. "Let him figure it out for both of us!"
>
> *No title.*

J's voice: She tries to go back to the earliest move that had launched this particular series of *faux pas*. Perhaps it was not too late to set things right.

> *(In the following section all titles are black type against a white ground.)*
>
> *IT:* An Emotional Accretion in 48 Steps

IT: 1 She confides to him a deep hatred she feels for someone.

IT: 2 Later she is offended when he talks at length about meeting with that person.

IT: 3

MLS: D and R in bed (on table).

J's voice: He is puzzled by her behavior.

IT: 4

MCU: D and R in bed. His eyes are open; hers are shut.

J's voice: She pretends to sleep.

IT: 5

MCU: D touches R's hand.

IT: 6 She imagines herself telling him to go away.

IT: 7

MCU (same as above)—D withdraws hand.

IT: 8 She decides to demand his affection.

IT: 9

CU: D and R.

R (*sync*): Would you hold me?

IT: 10

MCU: D takes R in his arms.

IT: 11 She tells him she's upset.

IT: 12

MCU: D speaking to R. (MOS)

J's voice: He apologizes.

IT: 13

J's voice: She whimpers.

IT: 14

CU: D and R kissing.

J's voice: He congratulates himself on clearing up the matter. He becomes aroused.

IT: 15 They make love.

IT: 16

CU: Kiss.

J's voice: She participates with pleasure, but something is still bugging her.

IT: 17

MCU: They both sleep.

IT: 18 The next morning she gets up early and works for an hour.

IT: 19

MCU: D sleeping alone in bed.

IT: 20

MCU: R removes her diaphragm.

IT: 21

MCU: D eats breakfast & reads newspaper.

IT: 22

MCU: R in shower, reaches for towel.

IT: 23

MCU: D at table, looking to right and talking.

J's voice: He analyzes the situation. She doesn't say much.

IT: 24 He continues to use the pronoun "we." He is pleased with his clarity.

IT: 25

J's voice: She feels uneasy.

IT: 26 He thinks the main fear "we" share is that getting gratification will result in a withdrawal of love by the other.

IT: 27

J's voice: She agrees that "getting what you want" is the only way to proceed, but she . . .

IT: doesn't express the annoyance she feels. Why is he talking about that now, and why is he saying "we"?

IT: 28

LS looking down steep staircase. Camera in hall. D comes out door and walks down stairs.

J's voice: He thinks the situation is resolved.

    IT: 29

J's voice: They see each other that night in a complicated social situation.

    LS: jumble of furniture and people.

[Duet & chorus from "La Sonambula" begins and continues through #48.]

    IT: 30 She is on edge, but

    IT: 31

    MCU: R with glass in hand talks and laughs. D looks at her, then whispers in her ear.

    IT: 32 "Let's go to my place."

    IT: 33 She agrees, but grudgingly.

    IT: 34 At his place she says she doesn't feel like making love.

    IT: 35

    MS: D & R in bed. He repeatedly "checks her out."

    IT: 36 He knows something is wrong.

    IT: 37

    CU: D and R in bed. Heads face camera. As they speak subtitles appear: (D) I feel good with you. (R) I'm glad.

    IT: 38 Something is bugging her.

    IT: 39

    MCU: D and R lying in bed.

    IT: 40

    MCU as above—R places her hand on D's groin (on top of quilt). He removes her hand and rolls away from her onto his side. She does likewise.

    IT: 41 In the morning she is hugely depressed.

    IT: 42

    MCU: D in bed. R, fully dressed and holding coat, bends over and kisses him, then leaves frame.

    IT: 43 She arrives home.

    IT: 44 She is very angry.

    IT: 45 She knows the crucial moment was when she said "Hold me."

IT: 46 Somehow she had betrayed herself. She hadn't wanted to be held.

IT: 47 (Do you think she could figure her way out of a paper bag?)

IT: 48 She had wanted to bash his fucking face in.

[Music ends in fiery blast.]

CU: R's face.

R (*sync*): I'd like to kick your ass in!

IT (w on b): "Oh Christ," she thinks. "Now he'll never screw me again." She is determined, however, not to back off. She will take the bull by the horns, so to speak, and try again. . . . His performance was magnificent. Afterwards she wept. Then she slept. As a pool of warm water spreading in the sunlight.

[About 30 seconds after *IT* ("Oh Christ . . .") appears, another duet and chorus from "La Sonambula" begins.]

IT stays for another 30 or 45 seconds, then disappears.

no image (for 1 minute)

IT (w on b): Her thoughts drifted back to the first time she heard the music. Her brother had just begun to collect 78's and Strauss, Mahler, and Beethoven daily flooded the house.

LS from rear: D & R on couch, S profile in chair at right.

CU: S's profile.

[Music fades down.]

R's voice: Doesn't that make you think of the movie?

[long pause]

S (*lip sync*): What movie?

R's voice: "2001."

S (*sync*): Oh yes, of course. Only in the movies can you send your mind away.

Y's voice: For some reason she is embarrassed about her reverie.

[long pause]

D's voice: I don't think she really wanted to die. She just wanted to be asleep, to

LS reversal of previous LS. Camera slowly tracks in to CU of S's face during the speech.

D (*sync*): not be alive, to stop the pain of that Saturday night.

R (*sync*): Always it was someone's (*she is now out of frame*) passion that started me off.

D's voice: I'm just not going to get excited about it. I know you're distorting things for the sake of fiction; exaggerating and displacing and so forth.

R's voice: That's such a relief. I had thought you'd be angry at the way I referred to your work. I would have done it so differently.

D's voice: I'd make a few changes myself. I would have had that inter-title, "I dreamed of my

> *Track ends: CU of S*

mother last night and of my wife. My wife was crying for me"—I would have shown somehow that he was *really* thinking of something else.

> *CU lasts 10 seconds longer. Then*

> *IT (w on b):* "I dreamed of my mother last night, and of my husband. My husband was crying for me."

> *IT (w on b):* She is really thinking about the way crumbs of food collect at the corners of his mouth when he eats.

> *LS: woman in long dark gown jumping.*

R's voice: And I would have put some jumps in that solo, and maybe a longer fade at the end of that shot on the stairs.

> *MCU: group configuration with photo figures. Ends in fade-out.*

> *MCU: Profile R on couch looking down at lap and toying with cigarette foil. D is seated as before.*

> *CU: R's fingers playing with foil. Image is to right of frame.*

> *MCU: R on couch to left of frame. D (off-camera) gets up (the sofa cushion moves). R looks to left of frame.*

J's voice: Now when she thinks of the work all she can see are the flaws. That part is too long, that too short, that too quick, that too slow.

> *MS: R on sofa at lower-right corner (camera is elevated). J walks into frame from top, goes to back of couch.*

> *MCU: R at center of frame. J rests his hand on back of sofa, then leaves left side of frame.*

> *CU: R's lap to right of frame.*

> *MCU: R at center of frame. J enters from left, sits half out of frame, then moves in to look into her face, moves out again, leaving his hand on sofa cushion. She takes his hand and presses it to her lips.*

Slow fade-out.

LS of street from 3rd-story window. J carries box of envelopes, which he drops as he opens a door. He goes in, closes door, comes out again, starts to pick up envelopes.

Y's voice: Her mind overruns with the faces of people gone from her life. This one made unreasonable demands, that one unacceptable criticism, this one let her down once too often, that one grew tired of her elusive reserve. Maybe it was true that in spite of all her protestations to the contrary, she really preferred her own company. She preferred, as Rilke said, to love her solitude and bear with sweet-sounding lamentation the suffering it caused her.

LS: N.Y. harbor from War Memorial Plaza at Battery Park. Ship enters at left. When it has almost disappeared at right, V-O begins.

She knew that he would be back. He had to work things out his own way. And he was assured of his prior claim on her affections. His arrogance at first astounded her, then finally could be forgiven in her anticipation of the pleasure they

CU: J and S lying on their backs on the beach, their heads toward camera. J draws S over onto him.

both knew would again be shared—even if it had to be postponed a whole year.

CU: previous action in slow-motion. J and S roll out of frame to left.

CU: slow-motion, J lying on his side, S propped on elbows. S leaves frame to left, her legs cross to right, her shadow is seen moving toward ocean into upper right corner of frame.

Then she remembers what the scene had reminded her of. The sky with its leaden clouds, the wet spray of the sea, the thump of surf against the rocks. The two weeks had fled past them. She didn't remember a single argument, not even the kind of manoeuvering for brief privateness that people do when they are together constantly. At this remove it seemed impossibly idyllic. Looking at those two weeks against the backdrop of later events, she was at a loss to understand the nature of his feelings. She herself felt like a fool thinking about it—deceived and humiliated. But she also felt a deep sadness. There was no denying her own happiness and sense of completion at the time. Had he ever felt such things in her presence—for even a single moment? She wondered.

LS: same scene as above. S rolls over onto J at very bottom of frame. Sarah cavorts with two dogs near the sea.

Photo of Mont St. Michel.

On the way back to the city she was careful not to touch him as they sat in the back seat of the car. When he unconcernedly—or calculatingly (she couldn't tell which)—shifted his position so that his knee grazed her thigh, she carefully

A succession of 40 stills of murder-in-the-shower sequence from "Psycho" begins.

disengaged herself from contact. By the time they arrived in town he occupied most of the seat, and she had squished herself into a cramped tight ball. She was enraged.

She stumbles out of the theater. Her disgust with the film and actual nausea drive her body into the street. She recalls roughly the location of the hotel and starts walking in that direction. Her gut burns and she has to keep spitting out the bitter saliva that collects in her mouth. The streets are dimly lit and deserted, the houses shuttered and silent. She wonders if she will find the hotel in time. At a certain point, not having seen any familiar landmarks for awhile, she realizes that she is lost and experiences a powerful exultation. The discomfort of her body, the presence of the night, her solitude—all give her an acute sense of the moment. She finds a vacant grassy lot, gropes her way past the open door of a parked truck, and vomits. Relieved, she straightens up and sees the looming outline of a huge gas storage tank and remembers standing in the street across from the hotel that morning watching two men on a scaffold painting the

LS: S walking in street at dawn.

tank orange. She then knows that she is now only a block away. Almost regretfully she goes directly to the hotel, willing to take care of her body, reluctant to terminate being lost in the sleeping town.

Subtitle (w on b): She groans at the pros-

Street disappears, leaving only subtitle for 5 seconds.

IT (w on b): pect of a new struggle with her prejudices. "Fuck it," she thinks, "not now, not now. The rich and the powerful really are beneath contempt."

IT (w on b): In any case . . .

CU: R at table dealing with trout, framed from mouth to top of stack of plates. D (off camera to left) drops utensil on floor.

[Sound of utensil dropping followed by mix of utensils-on-plate sounds, some in sync with R's fork and knife.]

R looks, wipes mouth, picks up utensil and places it on table (off camera), begins to eat.

J's voice: Yes. He said, "Willy, say goodbye to America."

R looks to left and smiles. Camera pans to left and down over table, passing smoldering cigarette in ashtray, rests on cheese and crackers. Hands come into view, spread cheese on cracker, camera follows cracker to J's mouth.

[Sound of loud chewing, not in sync with image.]

He chews, pauses, looks to his left. Hand comes into view, wipes corner of J's mouth, camera follows it to ashtray, then the cigarette to D's mouth. He inhales, exhales, looks to right. Camera pans to right to original framing of R.

R (*sync*): This? Oh, this was given to me by a friend of my brother's when I was 15. He and Ernie had practically been raised together. Then I didn't see him for a long time until Ernie discovered that he was living with his mother only a few blocks from us. He started showing up at our house. I guess he always had been homosexual. I remember him as a very young boy running around in his mother's nightgown with pears stuck in the bosom. By the time I saw him again he was extraordinarily handsome. Then he went to Mexico. And brought this back with him. It must have been the very first necklace I ever owned. I had a huge crush on him. I would cast long, lingering looks his way. He was very gracious about it, although I remember that when he presented me with the necklace his hand trembled slightly as he withstood the ardour of my gaze. Ernie saw him very infrequently during the next four years, and only when he invited him to his house. By that time my brother was married and had a [no pause in soundtrack]

CU: J's hand fiddling with fork.

remember him as a very young boy running around in his mother's nightgown with pears stuck in the bosom. By the time I saw him again he was extraordinarily handsome. Then he went to Mexico. And brought this back with him. It must have been the very first necklace I ever owned. I had a huge crush on him. I would cast long, lingering looks his way. He was very gracious about it, although I remember that when he presented me with the necklace his hand trembled slightly as he withstood the ardour of my gaze. Ernie saw him very infrequently during the next four years, and only when he invited him to his house. By that time my brother was married and had a baby. Sometimes I would be invited to dinner and he would be there. I

Pan begins to right.

remember—it might have been the last time I ever saw him—we left Ernie's place together one evening. [pause] He told me that by the time I was thirty I would probably be a very beautiful woman.

5 seconds after "woman" R's hand resting on table comes into view. As camera arrives at original framing of R's mouth, she speaks.

R (*sync*): I think the primary distinction has been betw . . .

IT (w on b): "I think the primary distinction has been between the teeth and the tongue," she says. There is a silence. The discussion then resumes without taking her pronouncement into account.

CU of S, Y, and R. Pan back and forth across their faces. The title, "Who is the victim here?" *appears at the top of the frame during the first complete left-to-right pan. The women are engaged in conversation, which is not heard.*

Y's voice: She finds herself looking at the other woman with curiosity. She has a way of talking—delicate, precise, and lilting—that reminds her of women she has had disdain for in the past. Effeminate women. Yes. Yet this woman's assertion emerges in spite of the style, and not unpleasingly. She is intrigued and self-conscious. The three of them talk about sexual fantasies. She keeps thinking about privacy. No, it isn't hard to talk about these things. It is almost too easy, almost meaningless, almost absurd. "What will I say to her when we meet for the second time?" she thinks. Then she realizes that the subject of conversation has come up because there are three of them. "An intimate revelation to her alone might demand a comparable gesture," she reasons. "With an audience of two my revelations are reduced to gratuitous display. I become a performer."

MLS: S and D stand in back of sofa, R in front. S & D walk to front; all 3 start to sit.

MCU: All three standing in front of sofa, heads out of frame.

They sit. S and D carefully disrobe R, one article of clothing at a time, from gloves to blouse.

CU: midsection of R and D, standing. She is wearing black skirt. D starts to untie drawstring. She covers bow with right hand and presents him with her left hand, from which he proceeds to remove three bracelets which he slips into the pocket of his tuxedo. The skirt is then pulled down by 2 pairs of hands (S has entered frame), followed by the panties. R sinks below the bottom of frame to lie on the sofa. S and D meet at back of sofa where he gives S the bracelets. They hover behind sofa, facing camera and seen only from neck down. D slides hand down surface of sofa and slowly brings it back up, which action is matched by R's knee rising then sinking.

CU: R's nude body on couch framed from neck to hips. She lies on her back. D's hand slides over her belly, breast, and down her left arm.

CU: R's torso and head, same posture as above. She toys with medallion, sits up, moves out of frame by leaning forward, lies back down.

MS: R lying on sofa with black skirt pulled up above bosom, S leaning elbows on back of sofa. Both of them watch D, who is seated in chair on wheels. He slowly slides his hand from R's ankle up over her calf, along her thigh, coming to rest at her crotch on top of the velvet. Camera has slowly tracked in, keeping the hand in center of frame, ending in CU.

Starts in CU—R's hips center, D's face to right, his hands grasping the top of the black bloomers she is wearing. As the camera dollies back, he slowly pulls down the bloomers. Both sides of the sofa come into view. S sits on the right, Y on the left, her face disfigured by peculiar patches. When the bloomers are almost to the floor

No image for 30 seconds.

Track resumes. Bloomers are now on the floor. Camera begins to track forward as D pulls R's pants slowly up over her legs. (He looks straight forward at the camera the whole time; Y and S keep their eyes on the pants.) Camera veers to left toward Y's face as the pants arrive in place. The patches on her face begin to be recognizable as newsprint. One is on her forehead, another on right cheek, another on chin, and two on her left cheek.

Dissolve into extreme CU of first clipping: I'm still floating drunk full of you. Do you mind if I indulge myself for a few minutes and recall those things which make me laugh all over? I like your long, unruly hair and the way it was sticking up in the front, that childlike mischievous expression on your face when I pushed it down over your forehead.

Dissolve into CU of Y's face. Y moves chin into view.

Cut to extreme CU:
I'm totally intoxicated, overflowing with you and wanting you more than ever before.

Cut to CU of Y's face. Y lowers face to show forehead. (This one is read aloud by Y's V-O.)

Y's voice: An hour and a half since the last embrace . . . you're still here, I see you, we are one, and this indestructible togetherness they'll never be powerful enough to wrest away from us . . . That so much love could exist anywhere, in any two people, even between us, I never realized. It makes me feel all fluttery and kind of weak, not enough though in the sense of succumbing to weakness, for it makes me feel so much stronger . . . my life-long husband.

Y raises face to bring left cheek into view.

Dissolve into CU:
It all adds up to one thing: I love you George Jackson, every inch on the outside and all the depths and dimensions of your awe-inspiring mind . . . goodnight, George, your wife sends infinite love.
Love you, love you with love even more unbounded, even more unconquerable. Your life-long wife.

Slow fade-out.

Photo of elderly woman in field.

Y's voice: She catches herself snorting gleefully at the scene of the two women being totally bitchy to one another. She remembers a similar scene—was it Dorothy Lamour, or Betty Grable?—in a movie she saw when she was no more than 9 or 10. One woman had ripped another woman's dress off. She had stayed in the movie theater long after her friends had left until

Dissolve into slow-motion fight between S and R. MLS

that scene came around again. She had laughed louder than anyone around. And she must have felt guilty about it, because she never told anybody, not her mother, nor anybody.

Camera speed changes 4 times during fight—16 f/s to 24 to 48 to 24. Fight lasts 5 minutes.

[After 2 minutes of silence, phone rings four times, followed by sounds of footsteps drawing closer and receiver being picked up.]

Y's voice: Hello? Oh hi, hi . . . Yeh, I just got it in the mail. You want to hear it? Well, I'll try, but your handwriting is sort of hard to read . . . OK, here goes: "This is the poetically licensed story of a woman who finds it difficult to reconcile certain external facts with her image of her own perfection. It is also the same woman's story if we say she can't reconcile these facts with her image of her own deformity.

IT (at top of frame): They thought her shit was more important than she was.

She would like to engage in politics, but she can't decide whether to join the big women or the hunchtwats. The big women have a lot to offer, but she has discovered

IT (at top of frame): Her shit got more attention than she did.

essential weaknesses in their proposal to use wads of counterfeit money for . . . doorstops? What is this . . . boxtops? Oh . . .

IT (at top of frame): box-stops

boxstops. Neither is she attracted to the naive notion of the hunchtwats that every connection brings bed-chains. Not that it's a matter of victims and oppressors. She simply can't find alternatives to being inside with her fear or standing in the rain with her self-contempt.

IT (at top of frame): Sit tight.

How long can you go on this way, mmm? You still think it's all going to come out right, don't you? For instance, if you get up in the morning and feel your feelings well enough you will receive the right gifts from heaven without ever having to ask for them or even define them. It should be smooth sailing now, right? Just

IT (at top of frame): Is she for or against herself?

deciding which side you're on should insure that all the best things in life will beat a path to your door. Right? After all, you've paid your dues, haven't you? What do you want? Her pretense of innocence must end.

IT (at top of frame): She feels like a fool.

Nothing is new anymore, thank god. Now at last she can use her head and her eyes. If the mind is a muscle then the head is a huntress and the eye is an arrow.

(no more titles)

Thanking you for your immediate attention to this matter, I look forward to hearing from you at your earliest possible convenience. Respectfully . . . blah, blah, blah, blah. . . ." Yeh, I think it's pretty good. I think they'll get the message.

[Crash of thunder.]

> *Sequence of shots dealing with Sarah in bed and her real and imagined nightmares. The first image and subtitle appear simultaneously with crash of thunder.*
>
> *Subtitles:*
>
> How bad can it get? Listen:
> 1   I appear to be self-sufficient.
> 2   I can behave as though you don't exist.
> 3   My face conveys a congealed intelligence.
> 4   You think, therefore, I have silent wisdom.
> 5   If I were wiser life might be unbearable.
> 6   I am a stern and unrelenting judge and critic. I do not forgive.
> 7   I use my energies for the solemn enforcement of absolute sameness. I do not tolerate frustration of any kind.
> 8   I refuse to compromise with a world to which I have been a total stranger from the beginning.
> 9   And if I make occasional concessions, I will not grant this privilege to others.
> 10   It is time for me to be silent, methodical, resentful, gloomy.
> 11   You are a sap to feel close to such as me.
> 12   I despise you.
> 13   I shall remove myself from your offerings.
> 14   I shall appear self-sufficient.
> 15   I shall appear to need nothing, YOU LEAST OF ALL, SAP.
> 16   I shall become still, feign death. [*Frame goes black during #16.*]
> 17   One false move and the jig's up.
>
> *CU: D's face looking at camera.*

D (*sync*): . . . because she has younger-looking breasts than you . . . because she has younger-looking breasts than you.

MLS: R "rushes" into her clothes in slow motion.

[About 10 seconds after beginning of shot]

D's voice: *I'll* leave. I don't want you to go down there alone this time of night.

Y's voice: Propelled by an avalanche of rage, her limbs catapulted her body into her clothing. She hardly knew what she was doing, and when her voice came out, it surprised her.

CU: R's face.

R (*sync*): You're not moving fast enough.

no image

Y's voice: He lost no further time and bolted out of the door. Then she became aware of her heartbeat. When it had settled down she thought that she had never been that angry in her whole life. She thought she knew how someone could murder.

MS: J, S, R, D cavort on sofa. At bottom of frame is subtitle: DUMMY! My life is such a mess.

IT (w on b): She grieves for herself.

Backs of J, S, R, D on sofa looking at slide of Luxembourg Gardens.

Y's voice: The places for sitting in the Luxembourg Gardens are individual chairs rather than benches. So one can make small adjustments in placing oneself in relation to a companion or the total view. [pause] She sees him and tries

MS: 4 people clambering on sofa as before.

to turn away, but it is too

Luxembourg Gardens as before.

late. He has already caught sight of her.

IT (w on b): It was impossible to face him. Everytime she turned to face him he changed his position so that they were always side by side in a 45° angle.

People clambering on sofa.

He tells her about his eidetic

MLS: J and R seated at opposite ends on sofa. He talks and smokes. She remains totally still. (Shot continues for 10 or 15 seconds after V-O ends.)

images. She listens intently, watching his darting eyes, the mouth moving, pursing, curving, opening, the slender fingers curving around the cigarette. Her eyes devour him. Her mouth becomes hollow with expectation. She moves her knees cautiously so that they are further apart. He doesn't notice, or pretends not to. She holds back, continues to listen, and the sensations pass.

People clambering on sofa as before. Shot lasts 3 seconds.

LS: D in snowfall walking toward corner of building.

What was it like for him when he was with her? Images with oily outlines waver in her reverie. She sees them eating together, but not the place; she sees them talking, but not their expressions. One of them may have just smiled in response to the other. She can't quite make it jell.

no image

But she feels her jealousy acutely. The knowledge of their past urbanity and mutual congratulations releases slivers of jealousy

Camera in car moving backwards shooting past CU of J to LS of R walking on other side of street. She goes into a diner. He stops car, gets out, crosses and goes into diner.

through her mind in a slow drip.

["Maria Elena" begins.]

IT (b on w): In her fantasy she speaks to his penis. Contingent on what she says it enlarges and decreases in size. The man does not otherwise move in his reclining position. Neither does he speak.

MCU: J seated on floor, leaning against couch; S kneeling—back to camera—and hovering over him. Her recurrent action—concealing his face from view by moving her upper body—alternates with the back-and-forth tracking that intermittently again reveals his face.

[Last notes of "Maria Elena" correspond to end of above shot.]

D, S, and Y in subway train. Y hands S a piece of paper which makes her laugh uproariously.

["Thanks" begins.]

"no image" is intercut with R, J, and S running back and forth in the rain, then with a CU of a woman's and a man's feet running back and forth indoors.

The four protagonists are seen from the rear observing a dance performed by Epp Kotkas and James Barth.

["Arietta." Dance moves in and out of sync with music.]

LS of Barth running in circle at previously seen Battery Park location.

["Native Land"]

Intercuts of LS and fragmented CU's of Kotkas and Barth performing from 20 poses derived from photos and drawings of Isadora Duncan.

CU: R's face.

[Final bars of sonata]

Ocean and rocky shore with titles at top of frame:

Several years later she would ask him, "Where were you when I was giving birth to your child? After all, I did it for you." He hit her across the face.

ENOUGH!

He laughs out loud.

Now she is thinking of his penis again.

no title (ocean remains)

She sighs with relief. Now that she knew the truth about her feelings she was free to love him again.

no title

You could always have an ocean ending.

Ocean fades out.

[Music ends.]

Final title fades out.

Kristina Talking Pictures

KRISTINA TALKING PICTURES

(This and all of the titles in the film are hand-printed on yellow ruled paper.)

A Film by Yvonne Rainer

Narrator *(female voice begins 20 seconds after title appears)*: I hardly dared to breathe. Is it finally ending, this crab-like groping along the bottom? I almost don't believe it, but it must be so. I've dared not focus directly on

> *MCU (color): Blondell seen from waist up looking out of window. Camera moves slightly up and down because it is on chest of "breathing" camera-man. Blondell wears a yellow-and-brown print blouse.*

that possibility for the past few days. I keep telling myself that if I look directly into the light I'll be thrust back to the bottom. You heard me. I mean, those depths wherein the body turns to gelatin and the brain lies in colloidal helplessness, listening to its own muffled cries.

Now the single bright shaft angling towards me from above remains fixed and clear. So I know I'm rising, or have started to rise, to the foreseeable surface.

"You're like an old fashioned diver," she used to tell me. "You hit the bottom and bounce back." There was almost no bouncing this time. A scuttled diver doesn't bounce.

Yet a familiar excitement is rising with me, like the brightness of imminent discovery.

> *M (b&w): Kate sits, faintly insolent, looking at camera.*

Perfumed images jostle rhetorically against tenacious objections. [10 second pause.] My actors will not move with indolent ease through painted landscapes filled with their spoils—their

> *M (b&w): Valda sits at a desk with her back to us, swivels to face camera, smiling broadly.*

houses, their kitchens, their bodies, their trophies.

> *Slow track, CU (b&w), l to r past shelf of books. A hand removes a book from right end of shelf.*

Reprinted, with permission, from *Afterimage*, no. 7 (Summer, 1988), pp. 37–73. Extensive quotations in this script from *Supership*, by Noél Mostert, © 1974, are used with the kind permission of the author.

Their faces are not swollen with a masklike beauty; their actions will not lead them, unquestioning as mindless automatons,

> *M (b&w): over David's shoulder. He bites into hero sandwich, spills catsup on book.*

into senselessly violent entertainment. If they become pawns or bullies, or cowards, or avengers, or victims, if they are corruptible or bored, it will be only for a moment. Faults as well as strengths will be acknowledged, while self-delusions will be corrected along with indiscretions, derelictions, transgressions and

> *M (b&w): Janet at table with picture puzzle. She looks up with a slightly startled expression.*

sins of omission. If their affluence produces an excess of self-scrutiny, it must also be said that this

> *M (b&w): Lil propped up against pillows on couch, talking towards camera.*

same self-scrutiny will result in scrupulous reassessment more often than evasion, protest and action rather than

> *MCU (color): Blondell at window as before. Camera pans left over out-of-focus wall, across another window frame. Facade of building across street comes into view through open window. Pan continues across 3 or 4 windows, coming to rest on open window in which can be seen woman in white blouse moving about in an office.*

paralysis of will. At the crunch, they may not walk away from the camera wearing a halo of rectitude or resignation, but they will at least be toughened by the reification of their high-mindedness, singleness of purpose, and moral strength. For after all . . . they are . . . in a sense . . . if nothing else . . . nothing less than heroes. [15 second pause.] All right,

> *CU (b&w): photo of real Kristina's face (a lion tamer in a German traveling circus).*

call me Kristina. That's not my real name, but let it stand. It's on my passport. I was born in a little town near Budapest before the last few wars.

> *(b&w): footage of tiger act in circus (Gunther Gebel-Williams).*

David's voice: Budapest?

Narrator: That's my uncle. He's quite young here. Jews were still allowed to work then. I remember . . . outside Prague . . . arguing . . . sitting by the window . . . trailer . . . early spring sunlight on my pudding . . . Daddy hit the table . . . my pudding jiggled. All of a sudden he slapped the spoon out of my hand. . . . "Playing with your food." Mama was crying. The President of Czechoslovakia was ushered into Hitler's new study. "At last," Hitler reported later, "I had so belabored the old man that his nerves gave way completely, and he was on the point of signing; then he had a heart attack. In the adjoining room Dr. Morell gave him an injection, but in this case it was too effective. He regained too much of his strength, revived, and was no longer prepared to sign, until I finally wore him down again." Uncle took me at night to a house. Two long tables . . . lights hurt my eyes . . . lady smiled . . . lips moved, no sound . . . Kiss . . . uncle . . . hand . . . terror. I never saw him again.

I was pretty happy doing the lion act for a while. But I'm afraid Emma Goldman and Virginia Woolf ruined me for the circus. Dominating brute beasts . . . How can that compare to what they did? . . . Now that I'm thinking about it, Martha Graham and Jean-Luc Godard were as responsible for my leaving the circus as anybody.

[After ten seconds, ticking of clock begins,

> *M (color): Kate asleep in bed, clock at bedside. She rolls over, opens her eyes, discovers time, jumps out of bed. Camera "meanders" over bed, green sequined bikini lying on radiator, brightly colored mat on floor on which is lying a yellow ruled sheet of paper,*

fades out as soon as above shot is established. Sound effects begin: shower curtain being pulled, running of shower, shower stops, shower curtain is pulled, toilet is flushed,

> *intercut CU of letter on floor (color):* Dear Kristina . . . By the time you receive this letter I will be . . . Don't ask me where, I have one urgent request: . . .

> *Camera continues scanning as before over floor, legs of chair full of clothing. Kate's legs walk into view. She pulls off pajama bottoms, pulls on trousers.*

tooth brushing, spitting. Silence.]

> *Camera moves again to letter, CU of letter:* that you forgive me. It was a dumb insensitive thing to do. Please forgive me if you can. I have very warm feelings for you. My only fault

[Sound of shoes walking briskly back and forth; increasing and decreasing in volume. Bureau drawer opens, shuts, opens. More walking, sometimes corresponding to Kate's walking in image.]

was to believe . . .

> *Kate sits on bed, pulls on boots, begins walking back and forth, in and out of frame, stuffs articles of clothing into black canvas bag on floor, hastily pulls covers over bed. Camera comes to rest on crocheted dress draped over chair. Kate's hand removes it and stuffs it into bag.*

[Silence.]

[Sync sound: zipping of bag.]

She zips bag shut, then leaves frame. Camera moves over letter, mat, open bottom drawer of bureau, base of bed, green costume on radiator, letter.

[Sound of elevator door opening, shutting, descending; murmur of people talking, another elevator door opens and shuts, street door opens, sounds of traffic.]

CU of letter: that we had arrived at a point sufficiently remote from our recent hurt as to resume . . .

Kate's voice: Taxi! [Car squeals to a stop.]

Cabby's voice: Where to, lady? [Door slams.]

Kate's voice: La Guardia. [Car takes off.] No, stop. [Sound of car squealing to a stop.]

Camera continues as before, mat, letter, chair, pipes, etc.

CU of letter: a friendship. I am deeply sorry. Yours, Raoul.

Kate's voice: Wait a minute.

Camera comes to rest on green costume on radiator. Kate runs in, picks it up, turns to face camera. She is seen only from the waist down.

[Sound of car door slamming.]

MS overhead: Kate lying on bed, the green costume, spread neatly across her hips and bosom, on top of her clothes.

Kate: To hell with it.

[Silence for 20 seconds.]

She remains still for the rest of the shot.

David's voice: The huge beasts lumbered onto the stage. The woman, a Teutonic Amazon in gold brassiere, corselet and sandals, was everywhere at once. Her bodily and facial set changed abruptly from moment to moment. Out of a stance with one arm raised in triumph, her face basking in applause, she struts past the brutes, feints

Succession of four stills
1. (color): Kristina and tigers

at one with a stick. Now she is hurling herself around the ring as she rearranges stools and paraphernalia for the next event. She is completely alone in there. She moves constantly. She pats them, shouts at them, darts up close only to pull back as the animal jabs.

2. (b&w): mother and baby elephants.

the air with its paw, then unconcernedly turns her back and persuades another—with a prod of its trunk—to sway slowly into position. Again she turns, and with an

3. (color): Kristina and sitting tiger.

imperious glance and small gesture orders a recalcitrant beast back onto its perch. Now and again the playful ease with which she sits in a lap, lies under a foot, or allows

4. (b&w): Ivan and Yvonne sitting up in bed.

herself affectionate contact with an animal

(b&w): Kate emerges from elevator, stops short as if startled to see camera.

is betrayed by a momentary expression of

(b&w): Group of people with hands in the air walking from right into deep space of alley that stretches away from camera.

constraint, or a faltering under real weight.

M (b&w): David sits up in bed, reading text aloud in sync.

At the finale her movements are sharp, seemingly purposeless, as the ponderous wrinkled hulks—

MCU (b&w): Kate stands with arms folded (reverse angle of previous shot) looking at David.

hesitating, refusing, cajoled—by mysterious, perhaps unspeakable, promptings—to finally rise to a

M: David as before.

ziggurat tower. One can only wonder what makes them cooperate in

Ed's voice: such unnatural acts. We

CU (this and the following series are in color): Ed's eyes. Camera tracks back to reveal lip sync.

watch in fascination, for the very movements which produce a purely human design give us an inkling of the beasts' movements when they mate.

Track continues, slowly revealing a large room in which Ed and Kate are seated on either end of a couch, Blondell in a leather chair opposite them. Other furnishings are a square wooden coffee table, a large square pillow on the floor. In the distance a wall full of photos can be seen. Two slender pillars vertically divide the space.

[Complete silence. The visible conversation of the three people is not heard.]

Narrator: Last night I made a great effort: bathed, put on makeup, wore my best outfit, went up to the Fields' for dinner. Managed not to eat or drink too much and had a reasonably good time. In fact, for most of the evening had a very good time. The host and hostess were, as usual, most gracious. Their efforts toward making their guests comfortable were successful.

CU: Kate, wearing same crocheted dress as in last shot, on couch. She stands up, head goes out of frame.

Kate: I don't like the acting.

CU: Ed looks up at her.

It's the tone of voice.

CU: Kate in slow motion brushes crumbs off of her knitted skirt, sits down. (Plate with toast is on sofa.)

Every sentence ends with a rise in pitch as though the characters can only ask questions.

CU: Ed as before. Blondell walks r to l between him and camera before he finishes.

Ed: Maybe that's an idiosyncracy of the language, you know—like Chinese.

LS: Ed leans against pillar. Blondell in leather chair. She starts to rise.

Kate's voice: Or like English as

LS: different angle: Ed still against pillar. Kate now sits in leather chair, balancing cup and saucer on knee, talks away from camera over her shoulder. Both wear different clothes.

Kate: spoken by the British?

LS from the kitchen: Kate in red blouse and same chair as in last shot, now looking toward camera. Blondell walks away from camera toward sofa and sits down.

I doubt it. British English seems a little ironic to our ears, even arbitrary.

Almost reverse angle: Kate walks diagonally toward camera, holding cup, wearing red blouse.

MLS: Kate (in white cotton blouse) sits down on trunk in front of wall of photos. Ed's crossed legs are visible at right of frame.

I don't find this the case when I listen to German or French spoken outside of the

LS: kitchen. Kate (in crocheted dress) walks from refrigerator to stove. Valda (in glittering gold and scarlet gown) squats before open refrigerator. Blondell in foreground on pillow, thumbing through magazine. Kate out-of-focus on couch.

movies. But that quasi-improvisational tone in his movies sounds very false, and it's not the kind of falseness that happens when people . . .

Same angle, wider shot: Kate on r side of couch, David on left looking at slides, Blondell leaves frame at beginning of shot.

"put on an act." It's just plain old

Different angle: David on couch. Camera immediately tracks laterally left to right.

unconvincing acting.

[Sound of paper crinkling begins, continues until end of shot.]

Blondell comes into frame, sitting on pillow, then Kate in leather chair. Finally Valda comes into view. She stands at an oak table, wrapping a large box in brown paper.

Blondell: How about people who speak English as a second language? How do they sound to you?

Camera stops tracking and tilts slowly up Valda's body.

Kate's voice: You mean . . . foreigners?

MLS: Kate sits on left side of sofa, laughing. She looks behind herself as David walks l to r, disappearing behind wall, without interrupting her speech.

Blondell's voice: Yes.

Kate: mmm . . . If they don't speak fluently they don't sound very spontaneous.

LS: Blondell at kitchen sink getting glass of water.

Blondell: Would you say they sound like bad actors?

[Sound of running water into glass continues into next shot.]

Kate: Exactly!

CU: Kate (in white cotton blouse and pants) gets up and starts swinging her arms back and forth so one open palm hits the other fist in front of her with a resounding smack. We see only her midsection.

CU: Ed's midsection profile. He duplicates Kate's movement. Blondell in background, leaning with her back to sink. She brings a coffee cup to her lips.

[Kate's hand-smacking is now joined by Ed's.]

Ed: Where behavior

Same angle, wider shot: Valda's forearm can be seen on right as she sorts pieces of puzzle. Blondell brings coffee cup down.

and theatre meet.

[Hand-smacking continues.]

CU: Blondell's face. She delivers a "knowing look" at camera.

[Hand-smacking now goes slightly out of phase.]

Slightly different angle, wider shot: Valda is completely in frame. Kate stands opposite Ed. They continue swinging arms until after Kate's punch-line.

Kate: Reminds me of the last time I tried to tell a joke. There's this little old Jewish lady trying to cross the street. A truck comes along and knocks her down. The truckdriver stops. Now, she's not hurt, see. The truckdriver says, "Look out!" And so she says, "Vy, you coming beck?" *(They all laugh. Ed sits on table.)*

My friend questioned the need for a Yiddish accent. So I repeated the punchline in my own intonation: "Why, are you coming back?" See,

MCU: Kate stands by open door to bathroom, again in crocheted dress.

the theatre has gone out of it. I don't care

MCU: Kate on toilet.

if that is his intention. I stop listening. [Pause, then sound of urinating, which continues into beginning of next shot.]

CU: Blondell's face top of frame as she bends over (dipping carrot stick). She straightens up, moves forward with r hand on hip (wears brown velvet pants).

Blondell: I agree. His early movies are full of . . . [bite, chew, chew, chew]

LS: Blondell in front of wall of photos, holding carrot stick, looking to her right. Kate comes out of bathroom and sits on sofa. Blondell turns to face her and sits down on trunk.

lightweights. They're either too young or too pretty or too middle-class or too famous.

CU: Blondell (now wearing dress) sits down on couch, looking frame right.

And as characters they're either disgustingly frivolous or

ML: David in black jacket at kitchen counter making a sandwich. Camera pans as he walks to r, bends over Valda sitting at the table with puzzle.

Blondell's voice: weirdly pious. And in those later movies it looks like they came straight from Fort Lauderdale to play at revolution.

Extreme LS: dining and kitchen area. At the beginning of the shot David sits down where Valda has been. Kate and Valda are at either end of the table. Blondell leans against counter, then walks toward

Kate: I'd like to see Doris Day or Elvis Presley talk about their experiences in Dachau. Would we take Yves Montand more seriously? And what is the difference

plant in foreground and waters it. Then she

between Yves Montand facing the camera and telling us and NIGHT AND FOG? . . . Or

picks up newspaper, opens it, and walks almost

a photo of emaciated corpses tacked on the wall?

David (*with mouth full of food*): There is as thin a line between poetry and banality as there is between horror and fascination.

out right side of frame,

Blondell's voice: What's so . . .

swerves sharply, crosses

poetic

right to left in front of camera.

sync): about . . . Yves Montand?

ML: Blondell on sofa. Camera pans left after her line.

Jump-cut to MCU: David sitting on other side of sofa. He is laughing (silently) in Blondell's direction. He becomes serious, looks away from her.

David: Had I been in Dachau would I have had the will to survive while so many perished? Periodically the question prods me like an accusing finger applying the final test of my right to exist . . .

He leans forward.

When I was a kid it took another form: "If the Nazis told me they'd kill my father unless I dived off the high diving board, would I do it?"

Valda's voice (*begins immediately*): I was sitting at an outdoor cafe. A

MCU: Valda, sitting behind table, talks (sync) straight at camera. (She wears the same gold and scarlet spangled outfit throughout the film. It is her particular insignia connecting her to the Kristina character.)

(*continues in sync*) little boy came over to me and said "You're in luck, you can travel. I shall never get away from this place."

Narrator's voice (*begins immediately*): She felt transparent, later thought about her face, and knew her face had given her away. Too intense, it must even be looking angry these days

CU: camera tracks right past photo-wall to reveal Blondell standing on r edge of frame, then returns to centre. (Blondell wears same print blouse as in opening shot.)

Blondell enters frame gesturing and talking toward someone off to the left. We don't yet hear her.

without her knowing it. She always checked it out in the mirror before leaving the house, but her face, like Nixon's, was catching up with her. What will it say today while my tongue wags? Like people in the subway whose faces sag into habitual molds of depression and fatigue in the absence of stimulus, will my face refuse today to respond, the eyes gleam, mouth smile, chin push forward and up? Today I will remember how to enjoy myself among people, express interest, concern, etcetera, look into the face of my conversant just often enough to convey sincerity . . . Keep panic and bitterness at bay.

Blondell (*sync*): . . . the Kid . . . the Fuentes household [She is improvising an account of Julio Cortazar's short story *The Bestiary*.] . . . The Kid is a violent man . . .

lip sync stops. We continue to see Blondell telling her story.

Blondell's voice: One day I said to myself: I am forty. By the time I recovered from the shock of that discovery I had reached fifty. [Sound of apple being bitten into.] The stupor that seized me then

CU: Slow l-to-r track over photos: faces of Gustav Diessl, John Erdman, Nixon, Kristina, stills from "Potemkin" and "The Man Who Knew Too Much," postcards of landscapes, dirt roads, a highway, photo of extermination camp corpses.

has not left me yet. I often stop, flabbergasted, at the sight of this incredible thing that serves me as a face. I had the impression once of caring very little what sort of figure I cut. While I was able to look at my face without displeasure I gave it no thought, it could look after itself. The wheel eventually stops. I loathe my appearance now: the eyebrows slipping down toward the eyes, the bags underneath, the excessive fullness of the cheeks, and that air of sadness around the mouth that wrinkles always bring . . .

Blondell (*sync*): "Says that the tiger is in the Kid's study."

Same shot: Camera passes over larger-than-life still of grinning Cagney and reproduction of Rembrandt's Anatomy Lesson.
Wider shot of Blondell and photos as before.

Kate's voice: What book does that come from?

Blondell: What?

Kate's voice: What book is that from?

Blondell: *The Destruction of the Dutch Jews.*

> *MCU: Ed from rear and above sitting in wicker chair by pillar. He looks to r as he talks.*

Ed: Even stars die.

Blondell's voice: What?

Ed: (*disconcerted*) Oh . . . uh . . . no. I was just thinking about ageing. I mean, stars . . . you know . . . planets.

[pause]

> *He looks down. We do not see his lips.*

Ed's voice: The sound of my own voice is intoxicating. Sometimes the only way I can

> *MCU: Ed in wicker chair from front. In the background on the left, three dark female figures mill about. His lips do not move.*

believe my own thoughts is to talk. Saying the words gives them credibility.

Ed (*sync*): Yes, that kind of liberalism would be suspect, but I don't think that kind of person even exists.

Blondell's voice: What kind?

> *He looks thoughtful, strokes his beard, then begins.*

Ed: The sensitive intellectual or artist agonizing over the nature of his existence in the face of world poverty, over-population, pollution and depletion of natural resources. He keeps up with the most objective accounts of international corporate struggles for power and wealth, with their attendant manipulations of supply and demand thinly masked behind outrageous lies. Our artist suffers a thousand pangs of conscience and crises of will over the temptation to be a passive onlooker. He contemplates alternative modes of action and protest, like voting, writing letters, meetings, committees, petitions, sometimes even violence . . . In other words, he is the epitome of the concerned liberal . . .

> *He smiles mischievously.*

But when it comes to women all he can think about is tits and ass.

> *MS: Almost reverse angle, Kate at stove preparing coffee. She stares at him, reaches for a box of coffee filters.*

Kate: I don't think he's any more improbable than someone who feeds stray cats and voted for Nixon.

> *She places filter, then ground coffee, then starts to pour in boiling water.*

Blondell's voice: Did you burn your draft card and tell the derelict to get out of the hall?

Ed's voice: Ha! Do you contribute to Amnesty International and ignore the scream in the street?

Narrator: On the day you took your papers and bottles to the recycling centre, were you told that you have cancer?

> *CU: from above, water going into coffee, steam rising.*

Do you believe in Chairman Mao and refuse to curb your dog?

> *Camera zooms away slightly from coffee.*

[Music starts (Offenbach's *Duet for Two Cellos*).]

> *LS: Lil sitting on front stoop with shopping bag. Kate comes out of building, looks briefly at her, walks briskly off to right.*
>
> *LS: sidewalk and building. Kate walks in from left toward camera, holding a bouquet of roses. She stops, tosses the roses one by one up—presumably toward an unseen window.*

[Music continues.]

> *LS: Lil on stoop as before. Kate walks in from right, stands talking to Lil, finally reaches down to help her up.*
>
> *Series of close-ups:*
> *Kate's hand under Lil's arm.*
> *Lil's hand grasping handles of shopping bag.*
> *Kate unlocking front door. Both enter building.*
>
> *MCU: Lil and Kate stand, backs to camera. Elevator door opens. They enter. Elevator door closes.*

[Music is suddenly muffled.]

> *CU: Lil and Kate, from waist up, inside elevator. Lil takes things from her shopping bag to show Kate. The last is an 8 x 10 photo of a star-filled night sky. Kate raises it above her head.*

[Music begins to grow louder.]

> *Ceiling of elevator, covered with "starpaper." Kate's hands smooth it around the edges of a rectangular opening. As the elevator rises, a brilliant light comes into view in the opening.*

[Sound of elevator door opening.]

[Music very loud and clear.]

CU: backs of Kate's and Lil's heads as elevator door opens. They leave elevator and disappear to left. Valda walks into view from right and yells in their direction.

Valda: I said "All that matter disappears into the black holes."

David, in raincoat, enters from left, comes into elevator. Valda observes him. Door closes.

[Music becomes muffled again.]

Door opens.

[Music very loud again.]

Valda is still there. David leaves elevator and frame, returns immediately holding a book, leans against door frame and talks to Valda. When they hear Lil's voice, both change their positions—David moving to right side of elevator opening. Valda stepping slightly forward—and look to left of frame. David starts to take off his raincoat. Elevator door closes.

Lil's voice: The sky is up above the roof, so blue, so calm.

[Music continues throughout voice-overs.]

Blondell's voice: Sure, Pirandello was naive. But Elsa Triolet . . . I dunno . . . You'd think having been loved by Mayakovsky . . . she . . . oh, I dunno.

Same shot, inside of elevator door.

Ed's voice: You're funny . . .

Lil's voice: A stone falls to the ground because of its love for it.

Narrator: After you sent your check to the American Civil Liberties Union did you discover your husband had a male lover? Are you appalled by torture of political prisoners and jealous of your wife's success?

MLS (b&w): Ivan sawing bookcase with electric saw.

[Music continues, along with faint whine of electric saw.]

Did you march on Washington and let a friend bully you to tears?

[Music and saw end here.]

Did you stop paying taxes to protest the war and do a song-and-dance when your daughter asked you?

MLS (color): Jeep. Valda and Sarah are inside. Valda looks out of window.

Sarah: "If I weren't your daughter, would you still like me?"

Succession of b&w shots of Valda's "song and dance," poses from Isadora Duncan with Sarah looking on. Three are outside in front of a large modern apartment building, three are in front of and within a freight elevator. The last is taken from Rembrandt's Anatomy Lesson, *with Sarah reclining like the corpse and looking dolefully out at camera.*

New shot: The "Rembrandt" tableau in color. Valda looks up from her book.

Valda: Oh let's forget about it and go to the movies.

IT: THE RETURN OF RAOUL

[Immediately there is a flourish of staccato orchestral music, fading to silence as soon as next shot is established.]

(Unless otherwise indicated, all shots in this sequence in color.)

MCU: Raoul and Kristina sitting up in bed. She is on the right, wearing the green sequined trunks and bra. He is bare-chested on the left. To his left is a photo of the original Kristina's face, tacked to the wall. He is recounting something to her. They laugh. She recounts something to him. They laugh.

[Complete silence throughout their unheard speech.]

They turn to face camera, smooth sheets. She adjusts hair, clothing.

[Sound of sheets fades up with a roar.]

They are ready for the "performance." He turns to her.

CU: His finger pointing to something on her chest above her right breast.

Raoul: What's that?

Kristina: It's a silver bullet-hole.

MCU: The two of them as before.

Raoul: That's no place for a silver bullet.

He brings her finger to his mouth and bites it. She smiles, starts gesture.

CU: Her finger on his nose.

Kristina: What's that?

Camera pans as he puts his nose on her chest. He removes his nose.

Raoul: A . . . dagger.

Kristina's voice: No, it's a . . .

MCU as before: he looks at her. She starts to turn toward him.

Raoul: What?

Kristina: It's a . . . nose

CU: Her profile turned toward him. His hand touches her lips.

Raoul's voice: And those?

She kisses his hand, looks at him.

Kristina: Lips . . .

She starts to make gesture with her hands.

And this?

CU (b&w): one fist moves slowly across the other with the dark blanket as background.

Raoul: Eclipse . . .

MCU as before: He covers his eyes with his hands.

And this?

[Long pause.]

CU: His hands covering his eyes.

He removes hands and turns towards her.

Kristina's voice: Lapse.

Raoul: What?

Kristina's voice (*after a pause*): Lapse of time.

No image.

(*After another pause*): What was it like?

[10 second pause.]

Raoul's voice: I was an engineer on the VLCC for

IT: VERY LARGE CRUDE CARRIER (hand-printed on yellow ruled paper.)

No image.

almost a year. It was a quarter of a mile long and as wide as a football field. In all that time I set foot on land maybe three times: twice in Rotterdam, once near Bordeaux, once in Cape Town when we broke down and had to be towed into port. That was nasty. We usually anchored 10 miles or so offshore, and only long enough to load or unload the tanks, so going ashore was

MS: dark brown blanket.

Camera pans left (positioned above and at side of bed) to reveal Raoul talking (in sync).

usually out of the question. When you walked out at night on that black expanse, away from the bridge and the decks, you didn't even feel the presence of the sea. The steel catwalk traversing the ship's length ran on as far as the eye could see and beyond. You felt an arid metal acreage spreading invisibly all around, and its impact was one of menace: a mechanical desert of indefinable purpose imposed upon the sea's own emptiness. It was filled with wind signs, not those of masts and rigging, but of abandoned structures on a plain. The sea itself lay somewhere a long way below the remote and unseen edge of the deck on either side, and what saltiness reached one's lips had the taste of steel . . . I once calculated it would take a car travelling sixty miles an hour 12 seconds to travel the length of the ship.

She talks briefly (MOS). He looks at her, then away.

. . . 250,000 tonner.

Again she speaks (MOS).

The Japanese are now planning a million tonner. Economy is the main determinant in the design of these leviathans. Instead of two or three propellers there is only one; instead of two boilers there is only one. If that one boiler starts to fail, the ship is in a desperate state. Without steam, the engines go, and all electrical power with them. As steam dwindles and the propeller stops turning, the lights fail, and so do radar, echo sounders, and all other modern navigating paraphernalia—the fire-fighting equipment, cargo handling and control, deck machinery, and all those marvellous new computers which are supposed to decide course, prevent collision, check wages and diagnose illness. It all goes. All

CU: Her face (camera at left corner of bed). Camera moves down her body, blanket,

blink, flicker and die. All that is left is a useless drifting shell. With power gone, it lies helplessly adrift, waiting for a tow from another ship, or, if near some coast, the hulk is set by wind and current toward shore, where it is likely to go aground, break, and pollute the coast. They aren't

back to her folded hands, his hand now over hers.
His hand leaves frame. Camera keeps moving.
She reaches to end of bed. Camera pans to CU of his face.

built to last. The old passenger liners lasted as long as 40 years. Five is middle age for a tanker, and 10 is approaching senility. Keeping a tanker running after that is a nightmare of constant struggle with breakdown and an almost non-existent margin of safety . . .

He turns to her.

Do you know what the Coriolis force is?

His lips continue to move, unheard. CU: Her profile (camera front of bed as before).

. . . affects a ship with the mass of a tanker are not completely known, but they do have to navigate differently than they did before, and in critical situations often by pure intuition.

Kristina: Hm.

> *She talks (MOS). Camera tracks back to MCU. There is now an additional photo to the left of him: an old man with a bloody forehead sits on a bench, surrounded by three younger men in uniforms.*

(*sync*): . . . go away? What was so terrible about that?

Raoul: There were other incidents. We happened to leave a party at the same time. She said that she was afraid of being on the street that late and asked me to wait with her until a cab came. I refused and walked away. I was thinking of you.

> *MCU: He is on the left edge of frame. A photo of an old-fashioned circus act is on wall above her head. In it two dogs balance on a see-saw. A woman balances on a large sphere in the middle. Two other women, or girls, look on.*

We were on an island in the Caribbean. We had stopped to investigate an abandoned half-demolished factory. I looked up and saw bats sleeping among the beams. I have a horror of animals that may be rabid. I ran out of the building. She didn't at first notice my absence and lingered inside. Finally she came out to look for me. When I explained, she looked at me reproachfully.

> *She looks at him. MCU: half of her, all of him.*

Kristina: She was pregnant and had found an abortionist. She asked me if I would lend her the necessary funds. I told her I would. Meanwhile I was going through some difficult memories with my shrink, about my being an adopted child, and my early fantasies about my real mother, about not being wanted by her and all that. Under the circumstances I felt I couldn't in good faith lend anyone money for an abortion, not even a good friend. I asked her if she could get the money elsewhere. She had only a few days left before her appointment. She said that if that was the way I felt she would have to. She told me I was illogical and disloyal. We drifted apart.

> *CU: upper half of her face and circus photo above on the wall.*

They had lined us all up—all 15 of us—to administer the spanking to my brother, who was lying over Mrs. Lytton's lap with his pajama bottoms pulled down. He was to receive the usual ritual punishment. When it came my turn I didn't refuse. I hit his bottom like all the rest.

When I was 18 I lived for awhile on the third floor of a rooming house on Clay Street. I had a kitchen, (*slightly out of sync*)

> *MCU (b&w): from front. She is leaning against him. He scratches his nose as she begins. The photo of Kristina has been replaced by one of a row of men with their hands in the air.*

MCU (color): same as preceding shot. He brings hand down from his nose.

(*sync*) but shared the bath with a Swedish girl across the hall and a couple in their 50s who had two rooms adjacent to my kitchen. All that separated me from them was a thin tongue-and-groove wood partition. When the husband came home in the evenings I could hear their conversation.

MCU (b&w): He scratches his nose. (This switch from color to b&w and back again happens two more times in the course of this scene. With one exception the color takes are in sync, while the b&w shots are not.)

One night I went out to go to the bathroom. It was locked. On returning to my room I glanced through the open doorway of the Swedish girl's room and saw her boyfriend sitting up in bed. Barely a minute later the wife from the end of the hall leaves her place to go to the bathroom. It is still locked, and apparently she gets the same glimpse of the boyfriend that I had just gotten. She barrels back to her husband lickety-split, shrieking about what she has just witnessed. They both rush out past my closed door. The husband goes down to get the manager while the wife loudly upbraids the young woman for her immoral conduct. She counters as valiantly as she can in her own defense. "It's none of your business" and "We aren't bothering anyone," etc. By now the husband has returned with the manager, a kindly 60-year-old woman whom I was very fond of. She is no match for the vituperative couple, who continue to demand that justice be done.

I am now hardly hearing anything; so frozen am I with anger and fear and indecision, it is like a nightmare of confused, unpleasant noises outside my door. Even when the harpy's voice filtered through and I heard "She wouldn't do such a thing," even then I couldn't bring myself to tear open the door, as if on cue, and scream "That's not true; I have men up here all the time!" But I couldn't move. The horrid pair stayed there until the boyfriend had left. I remained still, stunned by what I had heard, appalled at my loss of nerve.

He caresses her hair.

Raoul: You were only 18 years old. No one can say that was the best time in your life.

She nuzzles against him.

CU (b&w): A sinkful of dishes with a man's hands washing them. He has powerful forearms.

Raoul's voice (*replacing sound of dishes and water*): A black rain fell. Leaks, spills, dumping, foundering, running aground, exploding, fire on the sea, fire storm, hurricane winds, oily mist, black rain. Plankton generate one-third of the world's oxygen. Oil on the water, oil on the skin of the sea, oil on the plankton, oil on your nipples, oil in your vagina, oil on my penis, oil on the penguins. When the plankton go, so will our pleasure.

CU (color): A piece of yellow ruled paper attached to the side of a face. Black hair and an ear are visible, also movement of the jaw muscles. Words on the paper are hand printed: Why is the prospect of catastrophe so readily softened by poetry?

David's voice: [He speaks in Chinese, about travelling, for about 15 seconds.]

Camera pans to right as David turns his head to reveal full face and his speaking lips.

David *(sync)*: I shouldn't forget to mention that protein is now being derived from oil.

Camera continues pan to right until a yellow ruled piece of paper on the wall comes into view with the words: They recited their stories as though the power of their words might reveal paths of action or absolution. That they had long been implicated beyond all possibility of extricating themselves—this did not occur to them. They still regarded the world of external events as a source of raw material for their own efforts and develop-

Camera pans right, framing another identical piece of paper:

ment, and not as a factor conditioning them. They imagined themselves to be totally independent agents, able to withdraw or transcend at a moment's notice. They possessed a finely tuned capacity for commiseration and passionate protest. Yet, they continued to feel that, despite their professed horror, at their center they remained uncommitted and untouched.

MCU (color): Raoul on extreme right of frame, 3 photos to left of him (women walking in a cobble-stoned street has been added).

Raoul: . . . comfortable, even luxurious quarters. Swimming pool, cinema. They changed the feature twice a week. Long black leather sofas and armchairs in the wardroom. A bartender at one's beck and call to serve 8-year-old Glenfiddich whisky. A well-stocked library: Fitzgerald, Dostoyevsky, James, Sartre, Graham Greene, Conrad, Dos Passos, Jacqueline Susann. Dartboard, short-wave radio, tape recorder, record player, TV, video tape deck. Good food and lots of it. Sometimes, in the evenings, there was a feeling of emptiness in that room, when the men became listless or bored with each other, and as an awareness of the remoteness of the ship settled in.

Film slowly becomes under-exposed.

It was the feeling of being inside a walled-in community upon one end of a desolate island whose opposite shore few ever bothered to visit and some scarcely knew. You couldn't help wondering about it from time to time . . . The worst part was going down to clean the empty tanks and check for corrosion.

Very dark here. Begins to return to normal.

Kristina's voice: Their lifespan is about 18 years, quite a bit longer than that of the males. The conditions of life for the males are harsher. Once they're past their prime they are driven out of the pride, usually by competitive younger males. Alone, the lion must fend for himself, without the advantages of co-operative hunting. The lioness is in heat for a few days at a time and at variable intervals of between 3 weeks and 3 months. During this time she mates about every 15 minutes with the same male, usually the first male she has encountered. By his presence he keeps other males away. Sometimes, if several females are in heat at the same time, he will mate with more than one.

Camera starts slow track forward.

Strangely enough, most mating periods do not result in the birth of cubs. It isn't known whether this has to do with ovulation, fertilization, or abortion in the female. The gestation period is 14 or 15 weeks. The cubs—about 2 or 3 in a litter—are tiny at birth. They are usually born when the cubs of the preceding litter are 20 to 30 months old. The births by different females in the same pride are simultaneous. Another peculiarity is that after new males have taken over a pride, there are very few births

Track ends in CU of photo of women in street.

Camera pans right past photos, Raoul's face, Kristina speaking (sync), photo of eyes on file cabinet, sign on window, pausing on out-of-focus building across the street.

for a period of 6 months. Are the lionesses too nervous to conceive? Or perhaps the presence of the new lions causes abortion among the females that were pregnant when they arrived. The cubs are dependent on the adults to provide them with food until they are 2 years old. Only 20% of the cubs attain that age, however. The high mortality rate is attributable to a number of causes. At times when food is in short supply some starve, sometimes older cubs steal meat from the younger and weaker. And very often they are killed by hyenas or by new adult males that have taken over the pride.

Camera pans left, pauses on sign:
PHOTO OF E-
RECTION OR
PENIS ENTER-
ING VAGINA

When they are three, they leave the pride in which they were born, in small groups. After two years of a nomadic life, they are likely to find a pride they can take over.

Pan continues left, past new sign on cabinet:

Oh God, I'd give up everything for this

past Kristina's face, framing Raoul's face as he speaks.

Each pride has a territory roughly 3 miles in diameter.

Raoul: Danger of asphyxiation and explosion 90 feet down into the bowels of the ship. I was always reminded of the anomalous comparison with the great sailing ships. The sailing man went aloft into the sky with exhilaration in fine weather and a fierce sense of elemental combat in bad. Descending into the tanks, on the other hand, removed us from all that visibly mattered. It was like being swallowed up in a black hole.

> *Pan continues left past Raoul and above a new row of photos: war ruins, desert, WW I army convoy, newspaper photo of 3 of the first POWs to return from Vietnam. Camera comes to rest on the latter one.*

Raoul's voice: I came home from the war.

[Intervals of silence between sentences in this series last from 5 to 15 seconds.]

I sit in the big armchair.

They come over for dinner.

They talked about the Marx Brothers.

> *b&w: Doorframe. Camera tilts down, pans right, tracks back to reveal Kristina at a table, then Raoul, at first immobile, then eating.*

We ate meatloaf.

I stare at her rings.

> *b&w photo: first of a series of 4 of Kristina's face, eyes closed, mouth slightly open.*

> *Table scene continues. 3 others are seated at the table. John pares an apple, talks (MOS), Janet assembles a jig-saw puzzle. Shirley sits with her back to the camera.*

Kristina's voice: He is wondering why I find it hard to look at him.

Raoul's voice: Paul wonders aloud why Kissinger's promise to reveal the real reasons behind the Red Alert was never kept.

Raoul's voice: Earlier we laughed about the mice. "If you put the leftovers in the mouse hole, the mice won't come out."

> *Same b&w photo of Kristina's face (No. 1).*

Kristina's voice: He thinks about the field mice in the Sahara.

Raoul's voice: We went out to a neighborhood bar. Kristina stayed home.

> *Photo No. 2 of Kristina's face, slightly blurred.*

Kristina's voice: He fantasizes about holding me in his arms.

> *Photo No. 1.*

Raoul's voice: A fight erupts. The huge hulking bartender roughs up an intoxicated customer.

Photo No. 3, even more blurred.

Kristina's voice: He remembered the tracks in the snow, for some reason.

Photo No. 2.

Raoul's voice: I find myself reminiscing with Paul about a certain evening several years earlier.

Photo No. 3.

Kristina's voice: It had been an excruciating evening. He would rather not talk about it, but Paul has resuscitated it like a long-lost love. Perhaps it will seem funny now, or droll.

Raoul's voice: Paul says, "Raoul, you're being fatuous."

Photo No. 4. The 4th version of the photo is so distorted that the eyes and nostrils are black holes. The face expresses at once ecstasy, pain and horror.

MS: The group at the table seen from a different angle. All are now silent and still, with the exception of Janet, who continues to assemble puzzle. Camera slowly tracks in to frame her hands shuffling pieces.

Kristina's voice: He hears the hammering of the SS.

They shout up to my window.

When they come up they are unusually subdued.

We make desultory conversation.

Raoul's voice: I had phoned her from the bar.

Kristina's voice: He notices that I sound tired.

Raoul's voice: We say goodbye and agree to meet the next day.

Kristina's voice: We have dinner together.

He looks at me as if

Raoul's voice: We had dinner together. I did not at once tell her the news of her daughter's accident.

[10 second pause.]

Photo No. 4.

Kristina's voice: He is waiting for the right moment

Color: Kristina and Raoul sitting up in bed as before. He is shaking his head. Photo of POWs is on the wall.

to tell me he loves me.

Raoul (*sync*): . . . as we sat . . . The night before such a descent,

Another take occurs in silence. We can read his lips because he is saying exactly what we have just heard him say.

as we sat in the luxurious wardroom

Second take in silence.

brooding over our amply filled glasses,

Second take in silence.

it sometimes struck me with an acute sense of dislocation

Second take in silence.

of dislocation how the seaman's life had changed.

Second take in silence.

In this atmosphere

Second take in sync.

atmosphere of material attainment and privilege

Different take (sync).

and privilege, we were denied

Different take (sync).

denied the comfort of even a lingering instinct

Second take in silence.

to rail against an albatross.

MCU: Raoul and Kristina from right corner of bed.

From here to the end of this paragraph Raoul's speech is from one take, but the image is cut so that their movements advance in short, overlapping, repetitive stages (with the result that there is no lip-sync).

From the Persian Gulf to Europe via the Cape of Good Hope you go through four seasonal changes—from northern summer to tropical to winter at the Cape, back to tropical, and then into summer. The South Atlantic has a character all its own. It is not a sinister

He leans back.

sea, but one where nothing is what it seems; and whose perversity begins with the deceptive serenity of its surface, where dead calm is placed upon the backs of the

She brings her knees up.

massive swells, which roll smooth and crestless under it. They are known as Cape Rollers, and they gain their

Lip-sync is re-established.

they gain their size and momentum from their long journey up from the seas of Antarctica. The South Atlantic is a cold sea under a hot sun, and so adding to its perversity and richness: enabling many cold sea creatures to exist in the tropics. The whale, the albatross, seal, walrus, penguin.

The next sentence, spoken in sync, is fractured as the image alternates between two different shots: Raoul and Kristina from the front and from a higher angle at the left corner of the bed.

It is the sea of which Melville said . . . It is the sea of wh . . . sd . . . sea of . . . rolled by . . . Melville said "All the waves rolled by like scrolls of silver."

Kristina turns her head toward him.

Kristina: "That's so . . ."

Five different takes of this motion follow in silence.

She is looking at him.

". . . beautiful."

[Silence.]

They converse for about 45 seconds (MOS). She points to his side of the bed. He reaches for a pitcher and glass, pours liquid from the one into the other. She drinks, starts to take glass from her lips.

[Sounds of pitcher hitting glass, pouring, traffic, her swallowing.]

Medium CU from overhead and side of the bed (b&w). She hands him the glass, he puts it down (outside the frame). He talks without being heard. She is looking at him.

[Sound of glass being put down.]

[Silence for about 20 seconds.]

Raoul (*not in sync*): The chill wind into which we had been pushing on our way down the South Atlantic set itself behind us after we turned the corner at the Cape and warmed at once, and then grew steadily balmier as we

Camera tilts up, pans slowly left over wall. Windows, radiators, pipes, black floor on the other side come into view.

moved north. It was still a strong blow, however, even though we didn't feel it. We lay behind the sound of it, and scudded along the crests, the whole ship softly enclosed by that mysterious stillness and peace of the following wind. The waves were so high that they broke level with the deck, their crests rustling as softly as the tearing of silk.

A group of people with their hands in the air, walking very close together, pass from the lower left to the upper right. Camera continues its leftward movement, comes to rest on the black floor now empty of people.

[About 15 seconds of silence.]

Narrator: After my daughter had died I had no desire to see Raoul again. It really was finished. Strangely enough my decision seemed to release a flood of dreams. My sleep began to stir with a profusion of characters and landscapes, disproving my previous certainty that the loss of a dream

MS (color): Sarah sitting on a high kitchen shelf holding a microphone.

life was to be my punishment.

Sarah: I was living with a large group of people in a forest commune by the sea. People resembling Raquel Welch, Hollis Frampton, Leon Golub, and other people I knew or was familiar with in some way, were there. I wandered happily back and forth from shore to cliff to various rooms, visiting and chatting during the course of the day. I gradually began to be aware that everyone was becoming increasingly excited as the day passed.

Sarah pauses as she pushes back her hair.

They were expecting the leopard. Someone told me "You know, the Indians never came to this place because of the leopard." I didn't know whether I was frightened or excited. The animal finally came. He appeared almost docile unless someone moved fast. Then he became nervous and growled. I kept wondering if he had had dinner. I was on the verge of allowing him to pass very close to me when I lost my nerve and fled to a room already crowded with the timid. The rest of the group followed him about, secure in the knowledge of their numbers.

CU: blurred still of Sarah's face from above shot.

Narrator: Unlike many dreams, this one stayed with me. I couldn't get it out of my mind. Unfortunately, it augured the end of the pleasure I had derived from this particular period of dream activity. Finally I went to see . . . and told her about it.

MS (color): Valda in driver's seat of jeep talking through open window. Projection of tiger act is seen on rear side window.

Valda: Do you think there is a network of identification among women who have been ripped off by men?

CU (color): Kate in cotton blouse sitting on floor in front of sofa. Lil's space-shoed feet can be seen behind her on sofa.

Kate's voice: She's talking about me and . . . I won't acknowledge that.

Kate (*sync*): I wouldn't exactly describe it as being ripped off.

She bites into a slice of toast.

Kate's voice: I did acknowledge it. Damn!

Closer shot: Kate's hands meet over her head, her mouth is open in an angry grimace.

Cunt!

MS (color): Valda in car as before.

Valda: She always talked as though her problems were unique and she'd come and unload on you and then leave and you were left with this enormous burden and of course she never wanted to know anything about your difficulties.

CU: Kate's eyes looking up to right. She brings her mouth into view.

Kate's voice: She's gained weight.

Kate (*sync*): Did you see her at the end?

MS: Valda in jeep as before.

Valda: No, I was away. In fact, I can't now remember when I last saw her, which bothers me. But it was because I wasn't acknowledging that it really was the end and that we'd never see each other again.

Kate's voice: Did you write?

Valda: A few postcards.

Kate's voice: What's . . . Raoul up to?

Valda: Oh, he's going with . . . He's so young he can really bounce back from these things. Of course, I don't know the details, but I think he's doing all right.

Kate as before. She chews toast.

Kate's voice: Wow! That was easy.

Publicity still (b&w) of James Cagney.

"Cagney's" voice: Yes, I thought it was odd that she didn't mind being ignored. She always said "I don't like being 2nd or 3rd or 4th . . . I like being first if I'm noticed at all."

Kate's voice: You know everyone thought she was strong.

Kate as before, looking up to right.

Kate (*sync*): But she wasn't strong at all.

"Cagney's" voice: Well, she went on working.

Kate: And that's always respected.

Cagney still: DOORWAY TO HELL

"Cagney's" voice: Yeh, I hadn't realized how they had elevated the word "cunt."

Kate as before.

Kate: I wouldn't exactly call it elevation.

Cagney still: KISS TOMORROW GOODBYE

"Cagney's" voice: OK, maybe "isolate" is the word. They isolated it as something women should be exclusively involved with and expressing.

Kate chewing toast and smiling smugly toward upper right.

Cagney still: THE ROARING TWENTIES

[Kate says nothing. Shortly Lil's voice is heard.]

Lil's voice: It takes four years for a bottle to drift around the world.

[Silence for 10 seconds.]

"Cagney's" voice: I guess there's a need for that kind of thing. It keeps the mind busy.

Color: camera begins tracking left past Kate sitting on floor. Lil's legs and feet are visible behind her. The rest of Lil's body comes into view. An apron is folded over her arms. She seems to be sleeping.

(Lil is never seen to speak when we hear the old woman's voice. It is by simple deduction that we identify the voice as hers.)

Lil's voice: And the strange thing is

CU (b&w): Two furry legs and genitals of an animal.

that even before I

Tracking shot continues: legs of group walk from right into deep space.

started to have intercourse with a man

b&w: Group walking with their hands in the air.

where you can get pregnant, I always was already

Tracking shot continues. Valda walks into frame from right. Both she and camera stop travelling simultaneously as she reaches the window.

afraid that even by kissing I could get pregnant.

[Lil's voice fades down.]

Image is suddenly darker as Valda raises window and looks out.

Valda: He's not here.

Camera tracks right. Valda and window pass out of left edge of frame.

Lil's voice: First of all 3 days or 4 days before you menstruate you get in a mood of headache, you don't feel so well. Then you start to bleed, then first little, then more, then it gets stronger, stronger, stronger. And then in the

b&w: Left to right track with loping tiger.

end it dribbles and it gets pink, and then you (*her voice begins to trail off*) 8 days are gone of the month.

Previous indoor tracking resumes. Orange wicker chair comes into frame, then sofa, with Lil reclining, then

Kate's voice: What?

Lil's voice (*very low*): Then you have maybe 8 days where you feel normal, and then you start already again to . . .

Kate sitting on floor. Looking up at David in raincoat sitting on arm of sofa. Kate looks away from him at the recumbent Lil, releases his hand and gets up.

David's voice: Can she hear us?

Lil's voice (*very low*): I was a . . . You never become really a normal being, because the moment you start to have sexual intercourse . . .

Sofa from a slightly different angle. Kate sits down on sofa. Lil is still reclining, but her head is outside left frame line. It is apparent that Kate is speaking to Lil.

Kate: So they're gathered for their midday meal . . . The Kid is reading a newspaper . . . Rima's very quiet . . . Nino prattles about the snails. After they're through with coffee Luis asks his usual question, "Where is the tiger now?" Isabelle jumps up from the table and says "I'll go and ask Don Roberto." A few minutes later she comes back and says, "The tiger's in the Kid's library."

Kate stops talking and looks at Lil.

Lil's voice: Do I get it, don't I get it? My god, if something has happened, what a mess! What am I going to do? And so I was always in fear and the fear only ended when . . . (*her voice fades out.*)

purses her lips, nods in a conciliatory way, resumes story.

Kate: And the Kid is very annoyed, of course . . . Rima goes away for some sugar. Isabelle follows her. On the way back they almost bump into the Kid who's on his way to the drawing room to read his paper.

> *Cut to black. At left side of frame sofa comes into view as camera tracks right to left past Lil. Ends in black. Same shot is repeated. Both are in b&w.*

because his library has the tiger in it. She fails to hear the Kid's scream . . . But everyone else hears it . . . The dogs bark . . . and over and over Luis keeps saying, "But she said it was in the Kid's room, she said it was in the Kid's room" . . . and Isabelle clings to Rima . . .

> *Three-and-a-half-minute sequence of b&w shots comprising a "choreography" of victimization, beginning with tracking left to right past 4 people bouncing slowly up and down on sofa. Each shot is between 2 and 10 seconds in length. The camera is always moving past or toward: a row of people with their hands in the air, a group of people retreating from the camera with expressions of horror, photographs from the wall collage, a group of "corpses" on the floor, a group of tigers walking in an arc, a pride of lions, an oil tanker seen from above, etc. One exception to the moving camera format is several shots of an intersection of two narrow city streets where several performers enter and leave the frame while walking in the gutters. The last shot in this series is tracking in CU past a jumble of bodies on the floor.*

> *Cut to black.*

Narrator: For the next 3 weeks we worked especially hard. Her fervor was contagious. She would arrive an hour early to practice the steps, repeat a fragment of the choreography over and over again until she was satisfied that her execution of its nuances meshed exactly with her conception. I neither criticized nor commented. How could I interfere with this passionate involvement which daily—before my very eyes—molded and transformed my original puerile notions. The others at first sat about disinterested, waiting for direction. Then as they began to pay closer attention to her motions, to the tiny adjustments of timing, gesture, tilt of the head, etc., as though infused with the fires radiating from this intense presence in their midst, they called upon resources of imagination and energy they—and I—would not have dreamed they possessed. Rising to meet the challenge of their revealed intelligence, I focused with ever more precision on configurations that soon were entering an arena of shared interests and purpose. The work progressed at lightning speed. At rare intervals I observed from a distance and marvelled at this paradigm of communal activity. No matter that I alone had instigated it. We now found ourselves engaged in patterns of social interaction that could be viewed as both primitive—in the ideal sense of a community of shared belief—and utopian.

Raoul was the first to crack. So intent were the rest of us on the daily tasks and so happily absorbed that I did not at first take much notice of what now seems like blatant evidence of his discontent. If anything, I attributed his erratic behavior to fatigue, or coming 'flu—as indeed he himself did at the beginning of his aberration. He sat at the sidelines more frequently, with a somewhat dour expression. At times he would disappear altogether while we worked on a section that did not require his actual presence. This would not have seemed unusual had not the precedent already been established for those not directly involved to provide enthusiastic suggestions and comments.

Then he began to be late. Finally he missed a rehearsal . . . and didn't call. By then I knew something was amiss. I naturally attempted to reach him by phone, and was at length successful. He was quite uncommunicative, downright evasive when questioned directly. I could find no apparent reason for his sudden despondence. He would only concede that he couldn't continue the work. This was hardly the Raoul I had known. I was nonplussed. No amount of cajoling or questioning on my part could dissuade him. He remained obdurate. When I became angry and resorted to words like commitment and responsibility, it was to no avail.

We were all concerned about him, but after the first day, as though by unspoken agreement, no one referred to Raoul's absence. Even when someone reported that he had left the country, there was hardly a comment. A subtle lag in concentration

b&w: intersection of alley and street seen earlier.

began to be felt . . . The work went on.

Man appears at right, walking in the gutter and following the curb around the corner until he is out of sight.

b&w: narrow street corner from overhead. Feet of group of people appear at top of frame; they walk in with their hands over their heads. The next five shots show the same group successively nearer to the camera and getting closer to the corner until in the final shot the camera is at street level and they are rounding the corner.

Color: Narrow street stretching away from camera. Kate walks from behind right of camera into deep space. There ensues a series of 14 or 15 shots, each one beginning at a point further down the street. Kate remains the same size in the frame but the joining of the shots is such that the rhythm of her walk is not interrupted. The camera is stationary in each shot.

Narrator: I'm fucking around in more ways than one. Take better care of yourself. More discipline. Being alone—no one dependent on me—burdens one constantly with the possibility of letting go in Daddy's sense of "following the line of least resistance."

Man enters frame from behind right of camera. He gradually catches up to Kate,

I won't succumb to be Beauvoir's grim prognosis for the unhappy childhood: "You have to have luck." You have to have stamina and will in spite of their intermittent loss. I must keep my stamina up and will shall follow.

snatches her handbag, and runs past her toward the other end of the street. She stands, facing the camera, as he rounds the corner.

LS (b&w): Kate demolishes chairs in slow motion. Many short cuts, most of them showing her in the act of raising a chair above her head, so that the emphasis of most of the movements is up rather than down. In the middle of the sequence is a series in which the chairs themselves, or parts of them, fly upward, discretely and repeatedly, and then downward in the same manner.

Narrator: Max, I heard you died. In the park, a cruiser's death. What quirk of fortune brought you to that trashy end? After all, you were my first access to the finer things: a reproduction of the Sistine Jehovah and Adam, André Gide, tall Nuremberg bureaus, Tom and Jerries at Christmas never equalled since, Chinese rugs, fresh herring, *Parsifal,* soignée young men who spoke of axiology, cast-off wives of virile poets who wept on your shoulder and graced your parlor. The parties in your long flat inundated my impressionable vision like a gilded freight train in endless and singular passage. One night you described in meticulous detail Cocteau's *Orpheus.* I waited patiently, knowing my time would come. At last you paused and asked "Have you seen it?" "Four times" I said. At which you roared your Teutonic lion laugh. Later you were to say of me "All she needs is a kick in the ass." Your old-world nostrum for new-world adolescent psychic ills. But you did teach me the finer things. And came to a trashy end nonetheless.

[Pause of 15 seconds or so.]

Lil's voice: I dreamt I had sex with Marlon Brando.

LS (color): Kate finishes jigsaw puzzle at table. Blondell, behind her at the kitchen counter, prepares carrots for juicing.

He said "Why don't you brush your teeth? You have the breath of a lion, and besides, it's all over, the days and the people that pass in the street."

Blondell turns on juicer.

Narrator: Mama, I heard you died last night. In your sleep, I was told by your son, as though one could still distinguish your sleeping from your waking. I know what he meant. He meant it was peaceful. As though your long-deteriorated brain had not already found its fair share of peace, a lion's share, to tell the truth. Now you have slept your last, as though you had not already died a thousand painless deaths. Poor woman, you never could ask me to stop counting. In not entirely good grace I wish you your final peace and rest. [Juicer goes off.] But why can't I stop this bloody counting?

Blondell turns around with glass of juice, leans against counter.

Narrator: This

Blondell: Do you want some?

> *Kate turns in chair to face her.*
>
> *The first image in a series like the previously seen "choreography," all b&w: Tracking toward people bouncing up and down on sofa, toward someone trying to put a spoon in the mouth of blank-faced girl (Kate) sitting on floor against sofa,*

Narrator: is a boat . . . a barracks . . . a barricade . . .

> *past people milling or sitting disconsolately—some handling a large box, another a photograph . . .*

a bloody shame . . .

> *past bodies slumped across sofa, over man's*

Procrustes' Bed . . . Rosetta Stone . . .

> *body spread askew over sofa . . . past Valda sitting on floor against sofa while others*

a bridge of sighs, a vale of tears . . .

a bulwark . . .

blockade

> *bounce on it; one steps over her legs . . . toward group huddled as if with cold; toward another group from which Kate*

tip of the iceberg

> *separates herself—camera follows her gaze down to inert figure of man on floor; quick, fixed shot of photo of man running past soldiers*

chain of events

> *. . . past corpses on floor, 3 people huddled and talking, again corpses on floor . . .*

a battered reef, bar-room brawl, barrel of laughs . . .

> *toward chain of people standing on sofa, slanting up toward Valda, who is cantilevered from the arm of the sofa, like a ship's figurehead. At the end of the shot camera is underneath her, aimed up at her looming figure.*

beholden to everyone . . . behooves us to stop . . .

beginning of the end

[No sound.]

Color: circular track around group sitting on floor, laughing their heads off. In front of them Blondell stands on a chair holding a wooden pointer, "lecturing" (no sound) and pointing to words of a text (from The End *by Samuel Beckett) printed on the blackboard next to her. The words can be absorbed if one reads fast:*

The memory came faint and cold of the story I might have told, a story in the likeness of my life, I mean without the courage to end or the strength to go on.

At the end of the track the camera moves in to CU of Janet's face. She is the only one in the group who has remained solemn.

Narrator: For me it was photos of Bergen-Belsen and Dachau that I came across by chance in a bookstore in Santa Monica in July, 1945.

MCU (color): The back of Valda as she dials telephone. A 7-digit number is legibly inked on her left forearm, which she refers to as she dials. When through she puts receiver to her ear.

Valda: Dearest Kristina: Perhaps I should use the typewriter, try to keep a more objective attitude, but I would rather not, at least not for the moment, not for this letter, not for my memory, which is still incapable of comprehending what I experienced, not for the coming days and weeks. I would rather persist in walking about in this flat land of mindless present and feel my body shivering when I think of you and beams of pure light leaving my eyes while I have visions of endless numbers of black pages turned over in my memory after I saw you.

Color: Extreme wide-angle shot from corner of kitchen. Valda stands in the far corner bounded by windows. The shape of one window is etched at an angle by sunlight on the dark floor.

It is as if one had seen the origin of one's own mind and how it might have worked if it had not been distorted and petrified with anger and fear. I feel I can fly over the fields of ruins in my memory and all of it is alive and continuous and makes sense. All this since I met you.

Pause as she places one foot on the box in front of her.

It may seem like a childish expression of helplessness for me to insist on writing you love letters just because I think there would not be any other way to cope with the unnameable impetuosity that I have lived through and still do and desperately want to continue without any real perspective—of course I know that, don't be afraid—after having been with you. It took me a few days

She glances out of window. Camera begins to move forward (hand-held).

to sort it all out and give myself an explanation for my behavior so that—me too—I could "feel beginnings of a reintegration into a social fabric." How nicely you put your words that cut my throat which still wants to breathe with you. As I have reason to suppose that you knew . . . Anna?

Anna (*cues her from off camera*): the explanation.

She again glances out of window.

Valda: the explanation already by the time I was struggling with my distraught projections, I would rather spare you the detailed report of my insight even though it might offer some diverting variation on the standard case histories even for such a scholarly historian of psychic nature as you appear to be. (Right now I fantasize you laughing out loud and your laughing voice echoes in my body.) It is autumn here and sea gulls from the Dutch coast pass by the house to settle for the winter at the river.

She turns and opens window, speaks,

I'll be right down.

[Sound of traffic now intrudes.]

then faces camera again.

Last night I went to Antwerp to see L. and to breathe the sea. On the way I had a vision, which made me feel I was with you again. I was driving very slowly over a bridge. The girders, against the night sky, were black and white lines [the Herbert Clark music begins, very low in the background] switched on and off by the passing light beams of the car. And all of a sudden out of the clear night a white mist drifted over the road in the shape of a horse, a night-being to console me in my longing for you—with its dream-like form and careful motion.

[Music erupts at full volume with cornet solo.]

Valda stands silent for about 8 seconds longer.

b&w: from overhead. A tanker enters frame at upper left corner, leaves at lower right. (Actually, the helicopter was tracking from right to left.)

[Music continues, uninterrupted.]

CU (color): Camera moves over words on blackboard to first of credits, which are hand-printed on yellow-ruled paper that has been used through-out film. The separate pieces of paper are here pasted against the chalk-inscribed sentence from The End *seen earlier on the blackboard. Before and following each section of credits the camera scans portions of this sentence.*

CAST

Burt Barr	Kate Parker
Frances Barth	Lil Picard
James Barth	Ivan Rainer
Edward Cicciarelli	Yvonne Rainer
Blondell Cummings	Valda Setterfield
David Diao	Sarah Soffer
John Erdman	Shirley Soffer
Janet Froelich	Sasson Soffer
Epp Kotkas	Simian Soffer

NARRATOR: Janet Froelich
VOICE OF JAMES CAGNEY: Richard Tobias
ASSISTANT CAMERA: Byron Lovelace, Marite Kavaliauskas
SOUND ASSISTANT: Anna Delanzo
CONTINUITY: Epp Kotkas
GAFFER: James McCalmont (Grace Tankersley, assistant)
GRIP: Peter Miller, Hank Dorst
PRODUCTION COORDINATOR: Caila Abedon
CATERING: Mimi King

CAMERA
Roger Dean   Babette Mangolte

SOUND RECORDING
Lawrence Loewinger

Edited by Yvonne Rainer

I am indebted to the following people for their words and music:

Samuel Beckett (*The End*)
Simone de Beauvoir (*The Prime of Life, Force of Circumstance*)
John Cage
Herbert L. Clark (*From the Mighty Pacific*)
Julio Cortazar (*The Bestiary*)
Noel Mostert (*Supership*)
Lou Myers (*The Old-Age Home*)
Jacques Offenbach (*Duet for Two Cellos*)
Georgia O'Keeffe
Victor Shklovsky (*Mayakovsky and His Circle*)
Susan Sontag (*On Photography*)
Albert Speer (*Inside the Third Reich*)
Paul Verlaine

Financed in part by grants from New York State Council on the Arts and Creative Artists Public Service.

[Music abruptly fades out.]

© Yvonne Rainer

Camera tilts down past last credit to reveal last words of The End *printed on the blackboard:* to go on. *Movement continues past edge of blackboard, white wall, white screen.*

Journeys from Berlin/1971

Image black.

[Sounds of bath water, key being turned in lock, voices of man and woman, hereafter referred to as "she" and "he" and always off-screen.]

She: Mmm . . . It's good to see you. What've you got there?

He: Close your eyes and open your mouth. [Sound of bag rustling.]

Printed titles crawl upward from bottom of frame, white-on-black:

WORKING TITLE:

JOURNEYS FROM BERLIN/1971

A FILM BY YVONNE RAINER (1979)

She: Ooh, strawberries. Strawberries in winter. (*laughs*) Well, almost.

He (*like a carnival barker*): Fresh orange juice, Hawaiian pineapple, real strawberries . . . I'm tired.

She: *I'll* cook.

Titles crawl upward:

Let's begin somewhere:

In 1950 a draft for a political criminal law in the Federal Republic of Germany contained the following sentence: "The danger to the community comes from organized people."

April 27, 1951.

Voice of young girl reads: April 27th, 1951. Yesterday I went to an assembly in 306. A girl sang "Come come, I love you truly" from *The Chocolate Soldier*. As she sang I began to feel the most peculiar sensations. Cold shivers were wracking my entire body. Clammy currents ran all over me. I thought I was sick, but

Very distant aerial-tracking view of Stonehenge.

when she had finished, the shivers left me. Very often these sensations come to me when I hear or read of some outstanding human experience of bravery or perseverance, or a story of great emotional appeal. Sometimes these stories are absolutely corny or excessively melodramatic, like the one Louise Utis told in Oral English the other day about a G.I. who corresponds with a girl whom he intends to marry as soon as he returns from the war. His face is left badly scarred and he is also crippled after a battle. The day before his ship is to dock in the U.S. the girl is hit by a car. She suffers a serious brain injury which results in blindness. There was some dramatic closing which I can't remember. At any rate, during the last few sentences I had the chills. I really fight against them because basically I reject such stories for their contrived nature and unreality. Intense drama is always so removed from my own life that it leaves me with an empty feeling. I was also irked by the melodramatic manner of delivery . . . Then what in God's name do those damned shivers mean?

Titles crawl upward:

On July 7, 1956, the Federal Republic of Germany passed a conscription law requiring males between the ages of 18 and 45 to serve in the army for 18 months. Residents of West Berlin were exempt from this law. As a consequence, a great number of students from other parts of West Germany came to West Berlin to study.

[Sounds of kitchen activity.]

He: I really don't mind. Let me do it.

On August 17, 1956, the Communist Party (KPD) was banned by the Constitutional Court of West Germany. The federal government had applied for the ban as early as 1951.

Divertissement, or Dance of the Red Herrings: On August 13, 1961, at 12:35 A.M. in the Potsdamerplatz, the first concrete blocks were laid for the wall that would separate

Young man's voice: It's 300 feet wide and has 9 rows of

Cut to comfortable living room (color). An 18-year-old boy sits in a chair facing ¾ away from camera toward a fireplace. On the mantelpiece are objects and family memorabilia. He strokes a cat on his lap as he talks.

obstacles. The first is a wire mesh fence 5 ft. high, and the 2nd is a 5 ft. alarm fence. Then there's a path for German Shepherds that are trained to attack. [Off-screen barking. Cat reacts in fright.]

Titles again crawl upward:

East from West Berlin some five hours later. By some fluke you were spending the night in West Berlin.

On June 2, 1967, Benno Ohnesorg, a student at the Free University of Berlin, was shot in the back of the head during a demonstration against the visiting Shah of Iran. It may not be inappropriate to remark here that I presented my work at the Theater Festival in Shiraz in 1976. (Karl-Heinz Kurras, the police sergeant accused of the killing, was eventually acquitted.)

She: No luck, huh?

On Tuesday, April 2, 1968, Andreas Baader and Gudrun Ensslin, then 25 and 27 years of age, planted bombs in two Frankfurt department stores. In October they were brought to trial and sentenced to three years' imprisonment.

She: Where'd you look?

He: All over . . .

On April 11, 1968, an attempt was made on the life of Rudi Dutschke, head of the German Socialist Student Party, by Josef Erwin Bachmann, a 24-year-old house-painter. He said he had done it because he couldn't abide Communists. (He was sentenced to seven years' hard labor, and in 1970 he committed suicide.) This too occurred in West Berlin.

He: It's like 1969, when I was sleeping on sofas.

She: Don't worry. Something will turn up.

Several days later, in Berlin, Hamburg, Munich, Frankfurt, and other German cities, students demonstrated at the printing plants of Axel Springer, publisher of some fifteen right-wing newspapers and magazines. The attacks were a reprisal against the inflammatory anti-left opinions expressed in Springer's papers. In Munich a student and an Associated Press photographer died after being hit by stones. Among those arrested in Berlin was Ulrike Meinhof.

The stage was now set for the transformation of political opponents into political criminals: Interior Minister Ernst Benda called for the introduction of preventive detention. The only historic precedent in Germany was the Nazis' "protective custody."

Aerial footage of Berlin Wall.

Girl's voice: May 29th. I am so tired of this wrangling. Tonight it started with Daddy's anarchist friends' conscientiousness and ended with men's sexual potency. My mind's whirling. I don't know what's wrong. I feel so phlegmatic. I should have written this sooner, for only the vaguest shadow of an impression remains. Yesterday in World History Mr. Fast was pointing to various countries on the map while carrying on about world strategy. His standing there and talking about I don't know what suddenly appeared ludicrous to me. I felt laughter burbling up in my throat. It didn't come out, but then there was something else: What is there to separate the toiling masses all over the world? He was talking about strategy and diplomacy. Are these needed among us, the real people and owners of the earth? Or are they required only by the governments? I seem to have a child's outlook toward it all. I don't know anything about diplomatic relations, yet in my mind these commercial bonds between countries are reduced to futile and eternal fiascos.

Titles continue to crawl:

In June, 1968, the Bundestag passed emergency legislation extending the powers of the Federal Criminal Investigation Bureau (BKA) and secret services and giving the government extraordinary powers in case of national emergency.

She: Probably the beginning of a backlash . . .

In 1973 H. Herold, head of the Federal Criminal Investigation Bureau (BKA), wrote: "The situation requires a firm move away from the restrictions of the traditional functions of the police. They must transform themselves from a subordinate object with merely executive functions into initiators of social change. . . . a sort of institution of social hygiene."

[Muffled disco beat is heard.]

Dissolve to view of city street through third-floor apartment window.

He: You still on jury duty?

She: No. It's finally over.

He: What's that?

She: The neighbors. It's Friday.

[Sound of utensil hitting floor.]

He: Whoops.

She: I'll get it.

Cut to black. Titles crawl from bottom of frame:

Not long after 8 AM on Thursday, May 14, 1970, Ulrike Meinhof and four others helped Andreas Baader to escape

[Music becomes more strident,

from the German Institute for Social Questions in the Dahlem district of West Berlin, where he had been given permission to do research by the Tegel Prison authorities. Georg Linke, an elderly librarian, was severely wounded during the escape. After this Meinhof went underground for the first time.

fades out.]

Cut to view through window of train moving through industrial landscape. (color)

She: Everything about it is unsettling: The enormous waiting room holding 300 people, the roll calls, the endless waiting, the traveling down to the courtroom en masse—40 at a time—then more waiting outside the courtroom, the joking and laughing which stick in your throat when you see the relatives of the defendant, who—by the way—is almost always black, sometimes Puerto Rican, and always male. So the relatives come out of the courtroom and one of them—a woman—is sobbing uncontrollably. That was the first time I realized that someone's life might be in my hands. You know, I was quite prepared to fulfill my civic duty . . . not that I felt particularly qualified, not like the pious schoolteacher I met in the hall who said "Better us than others less qualified." Then you realize when the lawyers finally question you that this is hardly the point, and that you've got to psych out the lawyer's game and be prepared to lie if you want to get on a case. There was a rape case . . .

> *Cut to another view of city street through apartment window. (color)*

I was asked if I thought I could deliver an unbiased verdict. I said "I'm not sure." "Is there anything in this case that might prevent you from being impartial?" I said "Well, yes. The charge of rape is highly emotional, and I've never been in this situation before." Naturally I was dumped. The people who were accepted as jurors said yes or no and that was that. By the fourth time around I had wised up.

[Sound of music lesson is now clearly heard.]

> *Cut to room: two women are seated on the other side of half-closed double sliding doors. The space between the doors and the camera is empty and barely visible, while the other room is brilliantly lit. One person is teaching the other how to play a baroque recorder. The shot is in color.*

Patient's voice: First it was just a sense of the bed trembling and an image of a slightly swaying road experienced from the interior of a moving car, along with the words "What a silly notion, an earthquake in Germany." And I hardly paid any attention because I knew it must be a dream because I kept on falling asleep. Then there came a sound somewhere between the skittering of leaves on a sidewalk and rhythmic pitter-pattering of rain or mouse feet and it got louder and louder along with stronger shaking of the bed until it was right by my head and by that time I was brushing it away with my hand and throwing off the covers and shouting "Hey!" It rapidly receded as I turned on the light. I pursued my dominant thought that it was a mouse—even though nothing had touched me and I know that a mouse on a bed makes a different sound. I looked behind the floor-length curtains, closed the double doors, saying to myself—perhaps aloud—"So that's how they get in." Then I heard the people upstairs. It was 3 in the morning and they were up, in itself an unusual occurrence. Had my "Hey" awakened them, or had they had the same experience? Had "it" gone through the whole building? A thought intruded: that it was a visitation, in much milder form of the conflagration of 25 years previous. Periodically the old building shuddered in recollection.

> *Cut to a long barn-like interior, stretching away from the camera for roughly 150 feet. In the foreground, on the right side of the frame, sits a woman with her back to the camera. She is seated behind a desk upon which the arrangement of various objects changes from scene to scene: a*

porcelain dog, a gun, child's pail and shovel, telephone, vials of pills, etc. On the other side of the desk another woman, about 50 years of age, is seated facing her. She has not been seen before. Although she doesn't speak, one somehow associates the voice on the soundtrack with her presence. She is, indeed, the "patient," and the woman with her back to the camera is the "therapist." Way in the background can be seen shadowy figures, lit as though by light filtering in through the windows that look out onto a busy street. At the beginning of the shot four or five of these people are seen to be lowering a bed that had been standing upright—with a person strapped into it—and facing the camera. Others sit in chairs scattered about. Some read. There are about eight of these figures in the background.

The framing of this scene never changes horizontally, only vertically. Since the focal axis of the camera corresponds to the line of focus between patient and therapist—just to the left and neither above nor below—a slightly sloping, wedge-shaped platform is used to change the vertical framing. When the therapist is played by the man (taller than the patient) the desk and two chairs are placed on the platform so that his angle of vision (and that of the camera) slopes down toward her with the result that in the upper part of the frame is seen only floor with the feet of the background figures occasionally walking in. When the boy plays therapist the position of the platform is reversed to slope up away from the camera, thus revealing the ceiling of the space.

We are not mistaken in reading "superior" and "inferior" into these positionings.

[In the text of the "session," unless otherwise indicated, the patient's words are always in lip-sync. She is always played by the same performer. The words within square brackets [] have been elided from the soundtrack. She begins to speak as soon as her voice-over has ended—"shuddered in recollection."]

Patient: I'd like to keep going. Maybe something productive will come of don't be surprised at anything you hear. . . . So . . . living with contradiction. You know I've never threatened you with. . . . I've never held the threat of [   ] over your head an average of five or six blacks executed by hanging every Monday morning for political terrorism at Pretoria's central prison, according to reliable reports rejection and disappointment are two things I've always found impossible to take. . . . Look, it's very simple. We got married to get his first wife's demands for more child support off his back. Marriage didn't mean shit to me—neither commitment nor capitulation. My mother and father had already had two children before they got married. It was strictly a legal formality dictated by ignorance and linguistic [   ]. And you know something else? There appears to be no instance in 19th century Russia in which a man followed his wife into exile in Siberia. So what about feelings? Once they are revealed, the future is as closed as ever. Then I went to bed. Shortly afterward he came over and was ready to leave but I said, Oh come on in. Then I put in my diaphragm. We talked. He said, "I'm not a sex machine." We talked. Ok, ok. Rapport-achievement time was exactly 32 minutes and 10 seconds a chronically retreating promise, a promise that finally could no longer be invoked to justify habit. . . . An exemplary life lacks the eagerness of a mistreated dog. [Pause. She opens her mouth, moves forward in chair as if to speak, then leans back without having said anything. Dissolve.]

If I seem to have gained a hard-won dignity, it's thin ice over a bottomless lake of disbelief. When the first test of my weight shatters the ice, I can say "See, what did I tell you? You sell fata morgana." Being moved isn't going to get us anywhere, either, not anymore anyway. The funny thing is that if I behave as though I'm not so [   ] then it is more a matter of deploying the bourgeois artist even at the expense of artistic activity. Might not the interruption of my artistic career be an essential part of a new function? But what do *you* know from symbolic illumination? Bupkiss. . . . Forgive me, I have no right to blame *you* for my not being in a situation where I can say "We have begun a great thing. Two generations perhaps will succumb in the task, and yet it must be done." [pause] And don't give me that blindfold look, without expression, like a dead rabbit's. Well, yes, every now and then I would get a shooting pain somewhere deep inside, like in an organ, and then there would be nothing. But now it makes me think of *her,* and her last days, monitoring her diseased body as she must have done, and waiting for her chance—taxes paid, son's day off, it had to be done before Passover. Mayakovsky wrote "I don't recommend it for others." *He* would rather daydream about a golden future than focus on the frustrating present, whereas I would rather focus on the tolerable present than think about the

terrible future. (*"Terrible future" is spoken in unison by patient and therapist.*) You must think that's funny. (*From here to "if I can help it" she "baby-talks."*) Yes. Sometimes I lie on my back with my legs up when the sun is out. Not making babies. I've got a sun-dress and white knickers and new shoes. It's all on the wrong foot. I can't see you because you are black; when I am away from you I don't think about you. I'm not going to remember if I can help it. . . . Ah, what's this? (*She picks up pair of pliers from the desk.*) This is nice.

> *Cut to CU tracking along a mantlepiece filled with objects, photos, memo-rabilia, ending in hand holding a news clipping containing the same story that the patient reads in voice-over.*

Mender, teacher, cook, dustbin, other. And, what's this? "Tokyo (UP). A burglar has surrendered to the police after finding much more money than expected in a bag she stole a few days ago. The police in Yokohama said they had arrested the woman, identified as Shigeko An, 40, on charges of theft for allegedly stealing a bag containing $100,000 in cash from the house of a company president. 'She apparently wanted just a small amount of money to support her living,' the police said." . . . Prosecutor, banker, indus-

> *Cut to original scene. Therapist is still a woman.*

trialist. It's no good. Have you got a seashell anywhere? I want the sound. I am the wind. I am American. I have no desires. [The phone rings.] Look out.

Woman therapist answers phone.

Male voice: Breathing.

Therapist starts to hang up receiver. Cut to continuation of this action in a new scene by a male therapist. In the background is a rolled-up carpet, and at the very top of the frame can be seen the legs of five people seated in a row of chairs just behind the carpet.

I know, the essential element in being alive. You have a large mouth that can approximate a smile when one corner rises at the end of a sniff. But it doesn't fool anyone. It is really a sneer. You always seem to be talking out of

People in background bend over and push the carpet so that it begins to unroll. Cut to flipped image—left and right reversed. Carpet rolls out flat.

the other side of your mouth. You too are the person I invent. They said only the most guilty would be chosen as targets.

Image again reverses.

Body into words, words into action, maybe later. . . . No, I *didn't* hear of anyone voting for the metric system, if only to make new mistakes, invent moral facts, transcend Duchamp's beauty of indifference, [   ] children, understand the motives that prompted my act, think about The People, holy causes, the war of humanity against its enemies, maybe later. Think about the earmarks of leaping through hoops, consuming debts, things worth the trouble, tests of devotion, genetic codes for opening refrigerator doors, onward onward, simple precautions against [   ] but not before I have come to an understanding of motive and purpose, patience patience, in the case of Sofia Bardina, 1883, in exile in Geneva, physically deteriorated, without friends, in the case of Alexander Berkman, harassment, neglect, sick, despondent, 1936, in Nice, apropos of which I've been noticing that many people are a lot nicer when they are tired or sad. . . . I mean being. . . . no, going. . . . mm, or doing. . . . making. . . . [long pause; then she looks straight at therapist]. . . . living forever.

Therapist: A bad cold would cure me of that desire.

Patient: Actually, West Berlin has the highest suicide rate in the world.

Fade-to-black. Crawling titles rise from bottom of frame, white-on-black:

In January, 1972, the minister-presidents of the ten states that comprise the Federal Republic of Germany decided to exclude from public employment all those of leftist background or sympathies. Teachers, lawyers, civil servants—even busdrivers—were affected. Such blackballing was seen as a weapon against rapidly increasing successes by the Left in West German education. Chancellor Willy Brandt himself signed a "Berufsverbot."

In May, 1972, bombs exploded in the officers' mess of the Fifth U.S. Army Corps in Frankfurt; at police headquarters in Augsburg; in the car of the wife of Federal Judge Wolfgang Buddenberg, who had signed most of the warrants for the arrest of Baader-Meinhof members; in the lavatories of the Springer building in Hamburg; in front of the clubhouse of the U.S. Army Supreme Headquarters in Heidelberg. In all, 36 people were injured and four died. The Red Army Faction claimed responsibility. In the following month you were surrounded by police as your lover cut your hair by a country road near Cologne. Your activity—along with the sticks of rhubarb lying on the back seat of your car—marked you both as suspicious characters.

On Thursday, June 2, 1972, at 7:30 A.M., Andreas Baader, Holger Meins, and Jean-Carl Raspe were captured in Frankfurt.

[A cat's meow is heard.]

On Tuesday, June 7, 1972, at 1:30 P.M., Gudrun Ensslin was captured in Hamburg.

She (*V-O*): Hey, Louis, come get your dinner.

On Wednesday, June 15th, 1972, at 7 P.M., Ulrike Meinhof was captured in Hannover.

Tracking in close-up along a mantlepiece filled with objects, beginning with sticks of rhubarb, then a stack of books, a photo of Vera Figner, a hero sandwich, a brandy glass half full of "candy kisses," a photo of Meinhof, box of frozen fish, a paving stone, a tin can, gun, photo of elegant staircase, photo of Vera Zasulich, photo of concentration camp corpses. Bowl of strawberries comes into view.

She: Hey, give me one of those, will you?

The last object is a large granite architectural detail.

[Sound of pages being turned.]

Cut to new shot, the first in a black-and-white sequence in which a man and woman are seen walking in the vicinity of an ornate and unexplained piece of architecture. Throughout the film these two people are used to illustrate anecdotes and events described in voice-over by the narrators. They will be referred to as "Cynthia" and "Antonio," the names of the performers. They never speak.

[The following dialogue and texts are all in voice-over. The sound-track also contains much clattering and clanging as "he" prepares dinner, in some instances complementing the readings, as when his chopping accompanies her description of the savage response of the Tsar to the Nihilists.]

Cynthia and Antonio (b & w).

She (*reads*): I was invited to become an agent of the Executive Committee of the People's Will. I agreed. My past experience had convinced me that the only way to change the existing order was by force. If any group in our society had shown me a path other than violence, perhaps I would have followed it; at the very least, I would have tried it out. But, as you know, we didn't have a free press in our country, and so ideas could not be spread by the written word. I saw no signs of protest—neither in the rural governments nor in the courts, nor in any of the other organized groups of our society; nor was literature producing changes in our social life. And so I concluded that violence was the only solution. I could not follow the peaceful path. [Sound of cabinet doors opening and closing.] What're you looking for?

He: Flour.

She: There . . . no, lower.

He: Ah, got it . . . Who wrote that?

She: Vera Figner.

He: Y' know, there's really no basis for comparison . . .

> *View of London intersection through open window with railroad yard in background (color).*

She: mmm . . . It's interesting: one of the first violent things Meinhof did was to lead a bunch of people in tearing up that house in Hamburg where she had lived with her husband and two children. He had been unfaithful to her . . . It would be so easy to make a connection . . .

He: Gossip, pure gossip. And it's *not* that interesting. It has nothing to do with her politics.

She: What—his infidelities or her tearing up the house?

He: Both. She didn't turn to violence as a political option because of *him*. And even if she had . . .

She: But such things can't be entirely ignored . . .

He: If you ask *me,* they *should* be . . . Well, tell me, why not?

She: Because they happened, that's why. Because it shows a muddled vindictive streak in her nature that got in the way of her social thinking. A lot of their violent acts were carried out in a spirit of personal revenge rather than social justice.

He: Do . . . you . . . have [rattling of silverware]

She: What? [Sound of train approaching, builds to crescendo, then fades out. The sound corresponds to train passing in background.]

> *Tracking along mantlepiece (color).*

He: Never mind . . . paring knife . . . um . . . yes . . . social justice . . . You're still thinking of your beloved 19th century Russians, aren't you?

She: Listen (*reads*): Once when I saw some peasants on our estate kiss the border of my father's coat when he returned from a long journey, I cringed with shame. My first realization of inequality and injustice grew out of these experiences in my early childhood. I saw that there were those who commanded and those who obeyed, and probably because of my own rebellion against my mother, who ruled my life and who for me personified all despotism, I instinctively sided with the latter.

He: Well, there you *are!* She . . . what's her name?

She: Angelica Balabanoff.

He: Balabanoff. You're not putting *her* down because her politics grew out of her rebellion against her mother, but where Meinhof is concerned . . .

She: Well. . . . Ugh, what's the matter with me. Your argument is sneaky. It's not a question of what one grows out of, but what we do when we're grown . . . oh shit, . . Louis, stop that . . . You're probably right—one shouldn't make comparisons, and yet . . . and yet certain things come to mind almost spontaneously.

He: . . . such as . . .

She: Meinhof's generation didn't see serfs being flogged when they were growing up, but a lot of them probably saw Jews being taken away.

He: You saw the Japanese looking through wire fences on the West Coast.

She: Ye-es [hesitantly] . . . mmm . . . I guess there's nothing comparable in post-1968 Germany to "going to the people"—what the Russian intelligentsia did in the 1870's.

He: Sure. You had to be upper class to want to "go to the people." And there had to be a clearly oppressed class like the peasantry. Somehow foreign workers weren't visible enough in Germany ten years ago for radicals to take up their cause as an oppressed class. Maybe I'm wrong.

Aerial tracking over Stonehenge (b&w).

Girl's voice: Mon. May 12. Today I was downtown searching for a pair of shoes to fit my recalcitrant feet. I went into a Gallen Kamp's store and was waited on by a young woman. There was nothing extraordinary either in her appearance or her manner, but I couldn't help scrutinizing her and feeling vaguely disturbed as she bent over my feet fitting shoes onto them. I was ashamed of myself, forcing this woman to push shoes on—no, it wasn't as definite as that; yet tears came to my eyes as I left the store, having bought nothing. I don't know what is wrong now, but I am crying as I think of her. The dull, hardened look of resignation on her face and her deft motion in removing boxes from a tier of the endless shelves. And her mouth shaping "sure" as I said thanks. More and more frequently I feel this way when I buy things, especially clothing from weary sales girls. It isn't that I wish they would look happy (although this would certainly make me feel more comfortable), but I feel cheap, as if by purchasing an article from them and clinking coins into their palms, I am adding to the misery of their lot.

View of street through Berlin apartment window (color).

She: They were overshadowed by stuff like the Vietnam War and nuclear energy protests. . . . I wonder if middle-class German radicals went to work in factories the way you hear about educated leftists doing in other western countries, like France, and Italy—I mean with the intention of doing political work.

He: Even here in the U.S., and certainly in England . . . Good heavens, Amy, how long has this been hanging around?! Pfui!

She: Oh, stick it in the freezer. I've got to clean out that refrigerator some day. My point is that the Baader-Meinhof people preferred robbing banks and kidnapping to going to work in factories.

He: But even your Russians didn't last very long in the factories.

Aerial tracking over the Berlin wall (b&w).

Girl's voice: This morning I went to the Victor Equipment Co. for Junior Goals Day. I was the only girl among thirteen boys. I found that I was not interested so much in the machines as in their operators. I can't imagine myself living like that. All day long they stand there, turning something here, pushing something there, and on and on and on. The roar of the machinery is deafening. Then the women who work over the small and delicate pieces—they sit in a dingy room, all wearing hair nets and grimy aprons, pushing and inserting and cutting and placing. They could probably do it without looking. And the girls in the offices—I met one in the "Ladies' Room." She said, "They give me things to type, and I don't even know what they mean." Even if all the paper work could be dispensed with, someone must do the work with the machines. But all one's life, all day long? What a terrible existence. And that fat president, sitting back in his swivel chair and laboriously telling us what a democratic organization he has. According to him, all of the office workers share his pride in his company. Poor slaves, they are all properly servile to him. In their starched white collars and pressed pants and hairless, washed-out faces. Ugh. What do they think? Do many think of what actual good they are producing for man's existence?

He: And anyway, the RAF didn't rob banks just to get money. They believed in lawbreaking as something positive. Meinhof wrote that the progressive significance of department store arson lies in the *criminality* of the action . . . So that must have applied to robbing banks as well. In their way they were just as nihilistic as the 1870's Russians.

View from window of moving train of industrial landscape (color).

She: At first they were socialists, and not revolutionaries, distributing leaflets and putting up posters. The Tsar's response was savage. People were banished for life to Siberia, even hanged, for being in possession of a leaflet. They died by the hundreds in the prisons—typhoid . . . insanity. Their first acts of violence were in self-defense. So I don't know why they've been called Nihilists.

He (*laughing*): OK. They weren't Nihilists. They were Amazons.

She: Yes, I *am* thinking about those Russian women. *Their* revolutionary fervor came about in a different way from that of their male contemporaries. You know, women weren't allowed in the universities in Russia. If they wanted education past the secondary level, they had to go to Belgium or Switzerland. And legally they were under the absolute authority of their fathers and husbands. If you couldn't get permission from your father to go abroad then you'd have to make a phony marriage with some man who was leaving the country. It was out of their *personal* struggles against their oppression as *women* that their larger revolutionary consciousness grew. . . . *Personal struggle* is the key phrase for me here, just as important as revolution or liberation.

He: Hhm. . . . Are you suggesting that the prerequisite for being a good revolutionary is suffering?

She: Perhaps . . . No, not necessarily. Let me read something else by Vera Figner. [pages turning] She's talking about the time when she was almost through with medical school in Switzerland . . . in 1875. She had heard [Sound of train becomes audible.] about the arrest of many of her friends in Russia and decided to return.

    Cynthia and Antonio (b&w).

(*reads*): "The spiritual crisis I underwent in order to make this decision was my last. My personality had been formed and tempered during those years of struggle with myself. After the decision was made, my mind was finally at rest, and I vacillated no longer. I set to work without a backward glance. Social concerns had gained ascendance over personal ones for good. It was the victory of a principle that had been imprinted long ago on my thirteen-year-old mind, when I read in the Bible 'Leave thy father and thy mother and follow me . . .' I left the university without earning my diploma; I abandoned Switzerland, where I had found a new world of generous, all-embracing ideas, and, still feeling the effects of my recent emotional turmoil, set off for Russia. I was twenty-three years old."

He (*pause*): Interesting . . . uhmm . . . Two things come to my mind: One—the oppression of women in the west has become more and more subtle. And [Sound of train fades out.]—The element of time. These things all happened a hundred years ago, and the memoirs you've been reading were written 30 to 40 years later. Things like violence get a lot more palatable at that distance.

She: And the reasons for it get clearer. Vera Zasulich—she was one of the first to attempt a political assassination. In 1877 she shot Trepov, the chief of the St. Petersburg police, as retribution for his having ordered the flogging of a political prisoner. The prisoner had failed to remove his cap in Trepov's presence. This is the statement she made at her trial: "I waited for some response to the beating, but everyone remained silent. There was nothing to stop Trepov, or someone just as powerful as he, from repeating the same violence over and over. I resolved at that point, even if it cost my life, to prove that no one who abused a human being that way could be sure of getting away with it. I couldn't find another way of drawing attention to what had happened. I saw no other way. . . . It's terrible to have to have to lift a hand against another person, but I felt that it had to be done."

    Stonehenge (b&w).

He: Who was it who said, "Violence is only justifiable when it opposes violence?" The biggest mistake of the RAF was their timing. The sins of their fathers made them impatient.

Girl's voice: Sat. June 30. How selfish I am. At Shinn's today Bud Thorpe asked me to enter the race tomorrow. A certain number of riders must race so that the winners can go to the finals in Ohio. He mentioned May Jeuner's being able to go if he gets one more entry. Something like that. I was embarrassed. Immediately I thought how poor a rider I am and how silly I would look coming in way behind the others. I am ashamed of this blatant expression of my ego, but I find it impossible to get rid of it. The pride lives with me like a tumor, obstructing, blinding, and painfully annoying. A monstrous, pussy tumor. When I told S. about the matter, he said "Well, if that's the case, why don't you ride?" I must live it down, I must. Of course I don't tell anyone else these thoughts. That's funny, too: my pride prevents me from telling about my pride. It's a good thing I can tell myself. That's a big step toward "self-realization."

He: OK, I'll take a stab at it: It stands for flight, romantic agony, futility of effort, history as impenetrable, unknowable, mysterious; the poignancy of the past, freedom from historical imperatives, mournful railway journeys, Godforsaken Sunday afternoons in the proletarian

[Disco music begins, swells toward crescendo.]

quarters of great cities, looking through the rain-blurred window of a new apartment, cutting one's toenails while listening to Pablo Casals, standing on a lonely, spray-swept beach, walking across a windy airfield to a waiting plane, saying goodbye to a loved one . . .

    Berlin Wall (b&w).

She: Stop, stop! Uncle! Enough sighs and shivers. You should be cast in bronze clutching that spoon aloft like that. Did you know that Sartre went to Stuttgart to visit Baader in prison?

He: Was that when Daniel Cohn-Bendit went with him?

[Music fades out.]

She: mm . . . maybe. Anyway, a reporter asked him "Why did you visit Baader and not Meinhof?" and he replied, "Well, it's called the Baader-Meinhof Gang, isn't it, and not Meinhof-Baader!"

[They both laugh.]

He: Just like Sartre to outfox reporters like that.

She: Oh, I thought he was beginning to dodder in his old age.

He: No, not possible. He's still as sharp as a tack.

She: Oh for God's sake—I was laughing at his decline and you were laughing at his triumph. You're so much more generous than I, allowing the famous old man to hold on to his intelligence.

He: Allowing? I wasn't allowing *him* anything. *I* want to hold on to his intelligence. [They both laugh. Phone rings.]

She: Hello.

Male voice: You're not alone.

She: What?

Male voice: Even Trotsky did it.

She: Did what?

Male voice: He said Stalin couldn't engage in discussion. He said Stalin smoked his pipe in a corner. He said Stalin was always sulking. A pox on all of them.

She: Who *is* this? [She hangs up.]

He: Who the hell was that?

> *CU of Cynthia laughing, immediately followed by Berlin Wall, as before.*

She (*laughing*): A heavy breather. [They both laugh.]. . . . What I was trying to get at before was that you have to know what your personal struggle *is* and then get to the other side of it. Pouring unexamined personal rage—or whatever—into social action is going to foul things up somewhere along the line.

He: But if one waits to become perfect . . . Did you ever read Emma Goldman on political violence?

She: No. I have a collection of her essays, but all I've read is her autobiography.

He: Look up the one called "The Psychology of Political Violence" and read the last two paragraphs.

She: OK. [Sound of blender, chair scraping, footsteps, blender goes off, pages turning] "Compared with the wholesale violence of capital and

> *Mantlepiece tracking (color).*

government, political acts of violence are but a drop in the ocean. That so few resist is the strongest proof how terrible must be the conflict between their souls and unbearable social iniquities.

"High strung, like a violin string, they weep and moan for life, so relentless, so cruel, so terribly inhuman. In a desperate moment the string breaks. Untuned ears hear nothing but discord. But those who feel the agonized cry understand its harmony; they hear in it the fulfillment of the most compelling moment of human nature.". . . . That's

A rowboat comes into view.

nutty. The first part is all right—"the wholesale violence of capital and government"—but the stuff about the weeping and moaning violin string, boy, she sure could do it up purple.

He: Wholesale violence . . . wholesale violence. What would Emma have said about Jonestown?

Girl: There are no reservations being taken for steerage on flights aboard spaceships.

He: What was that?

She: It sounded like "There are no reservations being taken for steerage on flights aboard spaceships."

She: Do y' think you'll be wanting soup? I have some from yesterday.

He: Let's warm it up. It's so hot in here. Do you mind if I open a window?

She: No. [Sounds of window opening, N.Y. traffic.]

View through closed window of Bowery street scene, NYC (color).

He: We have no reason to presume that Meinhof didn't go through the kind of personal struggle you're talking about.

She (*pause*): It's true, there aren't enough in the way of available translations of her writing. The little I've read sounds like hysterical rhetoric . . . She must have suffered horribly in prison. She and Baader and their friends were in prison for three years before they even came to trial. They were kept in isolation, in empty, white, sound-proofed cells with the lights on day and night . . . No wonder Rosa Luxemburg could write of her "joyful intoxication" as she lay in her Berlin prison cell in 1917. She had access to a garden, she grew flowers, she watched birds, heard them sing . . . That's it, that may be it: the Left was squeezed out all over again . . . If there had been a vital Socialist opposition to all that economic expansion . . . to those smug industrialists. . . .

He: Ulrike Meinhof might have been the first woman Chancellor of Berlin! Hey, let's eat.

[Sounds of dishes rattling.]

Fade-out.

Again the enormous space that contains the "essential relationships": patient to therapist, daughter to parent, mother to child, person to person, spoken fantasy to filmic illusion, interior to light of day, individual to society. The therapist is still male.

Patient: Mariannenplatz. No dreams. All this Berlin nostalgia. Cheek frozen to a mirror for five days. The pit above my left eye grew terrifyingly large, a gaping hole through which I could see my brain lying there like a piece of stale bread beside the tracks of the old tramline that emerge from beneath the Wall and disappear into the asphalt hardly six feet away . . . (*She keels forward, immediately sits up.*) . . . Ugh. No dreams. Much spaghetti, pulpy mass. Must stay alert, the head is the first sense to go. Taking Cures. Walls of water-logged palindromes. Days filled with non-events: train stations, aching shoulders, three days of carbohydrate-and-sugar consumption. Some people don't seem to notice their own body changes. Changes of the spirit, the weather, sleeping cycles, dreams. But when they awaken their bodies are still gone. They eat without hunger and their food is digested in their absence. No gas, no swelling, no awareness of minute changes in the distribution of weight. One day they can't button their pants and they say "Oh I must have gained weight." Or one day they find one leg shorter than the other. . . . Drink wine, eat salt, quell untidy desire with candy kisses. I can predict exactly where new pressures of clothing will occur the next day—buttocks, thighs, belly, breasts—what new topography will appear on my face: creases and barrows as conspicuous as the scars slashed by two world wars into the soil of Europe. Then one day they electrocute themselves on a fan in a hotel room in Bangkok. Now it is women who die forlorn and solitary deaths in warm climates, isn't it? (*She stops talking, pauses, unwraps a stick of gum and begins to chew it.*)

Girl's voice: Friday, September 28. What did I put down that date for? The tears are here again. Brush them away. Something just happened. Mama just finished listening to one of those one-hour dramas, a real tragedy. She said, "I shouldn't listen to those stories, they really move me too much. But I don't know what else to do with my time." And the tears came. Sometimes I feel an overwhelming tenderness for her. I don't know if it's love. Right now I am being strangely moved by my feeling for her. Daddy is away. I am relieved when he goes away, yet I often pity him. I look at the picture of them on my dresser. I have always loved that photograph. He was 34 and she was 29. They were young once and joyous together. What happened?

Patient: What? What do *I* know about family life! Family life. . . . In families everyone talks very fast. Everyone changes the subject. Everyone talks louder than everyone else. Everyone asks for things. Everyone tells everyone else what to do and what's what. Everyone knows what love is. Some members of the family don't say anything.

She continues to talk. We don't hear her.

Girl's voice: Bitterness and anger have claimed my father and my mother has become petty with her physical grievances. I gaze at their youth and try to fathom something that is much too big for me. What are my troubles but inconspicuous nonentities when placed beside this titanic force that haunts and dwarfs me? What a funny phrase—inconspicuous nonentities. Nonentities are extremely inconspicuous.

Patient: Rueful smile. Once when we were making love the thought came to me—

what a waste that the flow of our pleasure should begin and end with ourselves. Just once. And once before that as I started to masturbate, my mind was invaded by the image of American soldiers forcing a hand grenade into the vagina of a Vietnamese woman. Only once such a thought. He had the biggest hard-on I had ever seen in my life. I admit I had been indiscreet, but you have to realize how young and innocent I was then. I did whatever anyone wanted me to do. My friend—this guy I had gone to the party with—we got very drunk and it just seemed like the most natural thing in the world to go into the back room and . . . and then it seemed perfectly natural to tell the guy I was living with about it the next day. After all, I told him everything, didn't I? Well, he got pretty mad, but that very night he also got such an enormous erection as I had never seen the likes of. It scared me half to death. What in God's name had turned him on like that? It couldn't have been *me*. Shall I now subsume history under memory, confuse memory with dreaming, call dreaming seeing? Or push for some cheap theatrical effects and simply reverse at a moment's notice? Listen: (*she reads*) "I walked twice around the room. Then I said to him, 'I greatly value our good relations, but I don't love you.' " (*She stops reading.*) We came back through the checkpoint at midnight. It was like rushing to avoid turning into a pumpkin. We went immediately to a bar. While there we went out twice and came back with pizza. There was a franticness and restlessness. Later when we talked about it he said he always felt cold when he came back. (*She again reads.*) "But now she was beginning to lie. She spoke with passion but she didn't believe what she was saying." (*She stops reading.*) Now it is women who have obscure crises of will in cold climates, isn't it?

Dissolve.

New shot. Therapist is now a woman, as before, and the space is now a derelict warehouse much larger than the previous space.

Mariannenplatz. I saw two women sitting by the Wall. One woman's right hand and forearm were covered with mud, lingering on their faces where their beauty lies like a fish in sand and the unique stupidity that comes with a certain kind of self-absorption or that excess of sensitivity that comes so early and stays so long. Freud lived in an unpretentious building of eclectic design. The facade of the lower part is Renaissance style while the upper part is decorated with classical revival detail. Marble fasciae, sunburst ebony inlays, carved white oak depositories. The famous director had lunch with the famous conductor and said, "There are no poor people here in Berlin, are there?" Embossed mirrors, ivory-inlaid cornices, mahogany paneling, marble hips. Georgian survival, gilded scagliola, granite piers, the results are in: you, being a properly constituted authority, can lead me to believe I am completely lacking in redeeming social value. Pure white Pentelic marble, 23-carat gold leaf, marble dust stucco flaking from a lifetime of ignoring male workers, avoiding their sexual stares. The Gästarbeiters in West Berlin—the immigrant Turks, Yugoslavs, Greeks—were no different in this respect from anywhere else. What I mean is that I have to be careful. I find the idea of an authoritarian regime expropriating individual moral responsibility—I find this much too attractive. Such expropriation is just one step removed from institutionalized proof of one's worth, or being rewarded for talent and effort is like being congratulated for living, and being congratulated for breathing is just one step away from institutionalized proof of my expendibility. All this is much too irresistible, don't ask me why just now. How do I get from here to. . . . How do I get from here to egalitarian relations? I'll just *pretend* I'm there: True equality means extreme uncertainty. Who knows, true equality might even lead to a struggle for. . . . you know, I can't even imagine what it might lead to. How do I get from here to loyalty, commitment, and relatedness to people? Well, you may be right when you say my capacity for these things is as fishy as the glue that holds together the cooling pipes in nuclear reactors. So what should I do, trade in my overriding contempt for a little despair?

> *Dissolve.*

> *New shot. Same warehouse. A man is standing on a chair in the background. Female therapist remains.*

I tried that already. And people *still* exist *for* me rather than *with* me.

She: Emma Goldman describes visiting a factory in Petrograd in 1920. She found it in a forlorn state, many of the machines deserted, the place filthy and neglected. A new decree had just been enacted "militarizing" labor. She saw armed soldiers, the same men who had fought side by side with the workers during the October days, now installed over the workers as watch-dogs. The number of officials and overseers had also increased. She writes, " 'Of the seven thousand employed here, only two thousand are actual producers,' an old worker near me remarked. It had been hard enough to work on empty stomachs when they were not being driven. Now with the presence of the soldiers and the inequality of the rations it was altogether impossible."

> *Dissolve to original space. Patient is looking back at man on chair wiping his glasses and group of people huddled in distance. She turns to face female analyst.*

Here we are, locked in this hermetic, sclerotic embrace, beholden to no one. So *what* if we are the world? You owe me everything; I owe you nothing. Nothing but money. Paying you money gets me off the hook. What else do you want? Ha. Funny thing for me to be asking *you*. But if equality between you and me is the issue, no one is measuring the virtues and achievements of one against those of the other . . . Except maybe me. Oh Christ, why won't an asteroid land on us now? Why won't someone please get me off the cusp of this plague, this ellipsis, suspension, anticipation, this retraction, denial, digression, irony, this ravenous for admiration, this contemptuous of those who provide it. . . . It's probably true that this contagion started spreading in the 17th century when they brought in silvered mirrors, self-portraits, chairs instead of benches, the self-contemplative self, and the personal as a . . . slave? . . . the personal as a slave of autonomy and perfectibility. By now it's quite clear that where proleptic capitalism is concerned, both self-discovery and speaking past each other are express stops on the way to carpeting the ceiling. I asked them how to say "bow-wow" in German. His friend said to him, "Why is she asking that?" The reply came back: "Oh you know these Americans: they're curious about everything." Do you know that everytime your pulse throbs, one more human being has come into the world?

> *Cut to new shot. Therapist is now a 9-year-old boy. Man is still standing on chair.*

Boy therapist (*barks*): Wau-wau!

Patient: I had room for one elective, so I signed up for a course with Bob Hope. His first line was so ridiculous that I walked out.

Therapist: What did he say?

Patient: The course was called "The American Presence in Berlin" and his first words were: quote, a slow and protracted copulation which gave equal pleasure to both parties, unquote. Let's put it this way: You can't feel motherly and horny at the same time. Intake, fertilization, gestation, exhaust. It must sound a little gross to use the internal combustion engine as a model for procreation; it makes the new-born sound like a piece of shit. Mm . . . it wasn't supposed to come off quite that way. I'm very sensitive to something you quoted from Virginia Woolf sometime back, something nice about motherhood . . . No, can't remember. Anyway, since motherhood has always been as alien to me as manhood. [She continues to talk. We don't hear her.]

> *Dissolve into new shot. Boy is replaced by woman therapist. Man continues to stand on chair in background.*

Patient (*examines a fold-up ruler for about 10 seconds*): Oh God, here it is again: equality. If you and I are equal, then I owe you nothing. Yes, I think I've finally got it: If you and I are on the same footing, I owe you nothing because, as a consequence, you then become like me—a shit, in my eyes. However, if I am more than you, then insofar as I am an ethical person I will be generous toward you. And if I am less than you I will be grateful and beholden, especially if I need you. But just you watch out when I feel like your equal: I'll walk out without a backward glance and why should you *mind?* After all, if I am as good as you then you are no better than me, which makes both of us into shits, [   ] aaaaaahhhhhh (*long wail with flailing of hands*). How much longer must passion and intellect be put off by such stink-cabbage?! [10-second pause]

> *Rowboat is brought in in the background. Group clambers into it.*

Patient: No, we're not nearly there. The worst of my malignancies is still to come. At the risk of bragging, let me put it this way: You know how I hate famous people, especially live ones. What I am about to confess is so embarrassing that I must resort to the use of the third person singular. I must also emphasize that this person—

whoever she is—is the embodiment of a specific social malaise for which neither she nor I can be held accountable. Much as I would have liked to believe I am unaffected by the corruptions of modern life—and we're talking about *me* now—me, your original independent woman earning her own living, thinking her own thoughts, carving her own coattails. Then one day whady ya know, there she is being courted by Samuel Beckett, pursued across the ocean by Samuel Beckett, fallen in love with by Samuel Beckett. And then guess what? The very next day—and this is after two days of sex and loving companionship with Samuel Beckett—*très délicieux*—There he is, buying her clothes, with her along of course, in . . . in . . .

Therapist: Bloomingdale's?

Patient: OK, Bloomingdale's. And all she ever really wanted was a hug and a cuddle. Not shoes, believe me, not shoes. Look, you can tell me till you're blue in the face that you're not God. I may agree momentarily, but I'm not going to believe you, not for love or money. And I can talk to you until *I'm* blue in the face all about modes of production and exchange, surplus value, commodity fetishism, and object-cathexis. But when the chips are down who do we find in Bloomingdale's spending the sperm?

Therapist: What do you mean?

Patient: You heard me. I said [   ] And then to top it off I said to him, "I don't want to harden myself against my distress as the only way of coping with it." He misunderstood and thought I wanted to pardon myself for my new dress.

Therapist: *Who* misunderstood?

Patient: Samuel Beckett, goddammit, Samuel Beckett! And furthermore, my cunt is *not* a castrated cock. If anything, it's a heartless *asshole!* (*She shouts.*)

> At "asshole" the contents of a bucket of water are thrown—from off-screen—in slow-motion, left to right, across the frame, without sound.

[The phone rings.]

Therapist: Hello.

Male voice: My daddy called me Cookie. I'm really a good girl. I'll go along with anything as long as you'll like me a little. I'll even promise not to bring up all that business about being such a low element, such primeval slime, such

> Woman therapist bangs down receiver.

[Phone rings immediately.]

> Boy therapist picks it up.

Boy therapist (*irritably*): Yes!

> There is now a rowboat on the desk, and patient is wearing "slinky glasses."

Male voice: . . . such an amoeba, such an edible *thing*. I'm not one for fussing. Not like those movie women: Katy Hepburn facing the dawn in her posh pad with stiff upper chin. Merle Oberon facing the Nazi night with hair billowing in the electric breeze. Roz Russell sockin' the words 'n' the whiskey to the best of them. Rita Hayworth getting shot in the mirror and getting her man. Jane Wyman smiling through tears. I never faced the music, much less the dawn; I stayed in bed. I never socked anything to anybody; why rock the boat? I never set out to get my man, even in the mirror; they all got me. I never smiled through my tears; I choked down my terror. I never had to face the Nazis, much less their night. Not for me that succumbing in the great task because it must be done; not for me the heart beating in incomprehensible joy; not for me the vicissitudes of class struggle; not for me the uncertainties of political thought . . .

Patient: It isn't as though I haven't been through pain. I've been in the hospital, awakened screaming from the surgeon's knife, shivered and rattled all night between the ice blankets. No matter how bad it gets in the hospital, you know that no one wants to make it worse. This may be thin consolation at the moment of pain, yet it is light years away from [She continues to talk; we don't hear her.]

She: This is by Angelica Balabanoff: "I knew that I was a very fortunate person. The suffering and struggle of these intervening years—unlike those of my childhood and youth—had meaning and dignity because they were linked to those of humanity."

[Patient stops talking.]

Boy therapist still has receiver pressed to his ear.

Male voice: . . . not for me a struggle for meaning and dignity. As for humanity, save it for the marines, not for me. I'm nothing but a

Boy *therapist slams down the receiver. As it lands he is replaced by* woman *therapist. The rowboat also disappears; the desk is now empty save for patient's purse.*

He: He thought it would be easy, because weak women had done it. Shortly before he died he spoke of plans to carpet the ceiling.

Patient reaches for comb in her purse, which is on the desk. Series of closeups follows, tracing the passage of comb from purse to hair to other hand to other side of head. The sequence ends with her hand brushing lint from her left shoulder.

[A violent fluttering of birds' wings is heard.]

Slow-motion dummy auto crash test.

Tracking past numerous "apotekes" on Berlin streets (color).

Girl's voice: Wednesday, August 15. It is long ago and far away. The night before I was halfheartedly picturing myself throwing myself out of the window and splashing all over the backyard. It went round and round in my head. The resultant pain and grief and weeping. And the thought of the longed-for nothingness. And the selfless body, twisted, broken. . . . And the lifeless face and the rush of air and the last consciousness. And the final gasp of regret. The next day I went cycling in Marin. On the way back from Tiburon I suddenly looked up to see a chartreuse convertible hurtling at me. Then I heard screaming tires, and a hot, forceful breath brushed my cheek. And I rode on. I had nearly been killed. I had been near death. When the hot breath left, I felt in a terrible instant the pulse of life within me—the pulse that I cherish and will never willingly allow to die.

Young man seated in living room, same as earlier shot (color).

Young man: This is a can that's actually a radio. And it's made for impoverished or poor countries in which people need some sort of information. And it's basically a very simple one-channel radio that will pick up any radio broadcast. And it's just wideband . . . and it's powered by actually just a candle, or paraffin, it's burning and producing electricity through a thing called a thermocouple. And when the paraffin or the candle runs out, they can use dung-chips or cow-chips or manure or anything else that'll burn, to power it. And it doesn't have to look like a can, it can be painted or anything like that. And it's very simple and it's very cheap. And it's very simple to use. You have an earplug . . that's in here. All you have to do is light the candle, and these wires here are antennae . . . and usually there'll be only one station broadcasting in an area, and you can pick it up with earphones . . . like this.

He continues to speak. We don't hear him.

She: This one's by Vera Figner: "Despite our absolute certainty of the masses' revolutionary mood and readiness to act, despite our belief in the proximity of a social revolution and in its ultimate victory over the entire existing order, we made a strange distinction between our own fates and the radiant prospects of the revolution. About ourselves, we were always pessimistic: we would all perish; they would

View from moving train window, now b&w, and much more grimly industrialized.

persecute us, lock us up, send us into exile and hard labor (we didn't even think about capital punishment then!). I don't know how the others felt, but for me that contrast between a radiant future for the people and our own sad fate was extremely influential when I was considering how to apply my socialist beliefs in practice. That contrast was always an emotional undercurrent in the stream of ideas that flowed freely in Zurich. . . . If not for the persecution, I'm not at all certain that I would have become a socialist at that time."

View from train window continues. "He" now reads a section from Alexander Berkman's Prison Memoirs of an Anarchist.

He: " 'Pitt-s-burgh! Pitt-s-burgh!' The harsh cry of the conductor startles me with the violence of a shock. Impatient as I am of the long journey, the realization that I have reached my destination comes unexpectedly, overwhelming me with the dread of unpreparedness. In a flurry I gather up my things, but, noticing that the other passengers keep their places, I precipitately resume my seat, fearful lest my agitation be noticed. To hide my confusion, I turn to the open window. thick clouds of smoke overcast the sky, shrouding the morning with sombre gray. The air is heavy with soot and cinders; the smell is nauseating. In the distance giant furnaces vomit pillars of fire, the lurid flashes accentuating a line of frame structures, dilapidated and miserable. They are the homes of the workers who have created the industrial glory of Pittsburgh, reared its millionaires, its Carnegies and Fricks.

"Henry Clay Frick, in absolute control of the Carnegie Company, incarnates the spirit of the furnace. The olive branch held out by the workers after their victory over the Pinkertons has been refused. The ultimatum issued by Frick is the last word of Caesar: the union of the steelworkers is to be crushed, even at the cost of shedding the blood of the last man in Homestead. Millmen disobeying the order to return to work under the new schedule of reduced wages are to be discharged forthwith, and evicted from the Company houses.

"The door of Frick's private office, to the left of the reception-room, swings open as the colored attendant emerges, and I catch a flitting glimpse of a black-bearded, well-knit figure at a table in the back of the room.

" 'Mistah Frick is engaged. He can't see you now, sah,' the negro says, handing back my card.

"I take the card, return it to my case, and walk slowly out of the reception-room. But quickly retracing my steps, I pass through the gate separating the clerks from the visitors, and, brushing the astounded attendant aside, I step

> *Cut to "Cynthia and Antonio" sequence, which lasts for the duration of the Berkman anecdote and most of the Zasulik story that follows.*

into the office on the left, and find myself facing Frick.

"For an instant the sunlight, streaming through the windows, dazzles me. I discern two men at the further end of the long table.

" 'Fr—,' I begin. The look of terror on his face strikes me speechless. It is the dread of the conscious presence of death. 'He understands,' it flashes through my mind. With a quick motion I draw the revolver. As I raise the weapon, I see Frick clutch with both hands the arm of the chair, and attempt to rise. I aim at his head. 'Perhaps he wears armor,' I reflect. With a look of horror he quickly averts his face, as I pull the trigger. There is a flash, and the high-ceilinged room reverberates as with the booming of cannon. I hear a sharp, piercing cry, and see Frick on his knees, his head against the arm of the chair. I feel calm and possessed, intent upon every movement of the man. He is lying head and shoulders under the large armchair, without sound or motion. 'Dead?' I wonder. I must make sure. About twenty-five feet separate us. I take a few steps toward him, when suddenly the other man, whose presence I had quite forgotten, leaps upon me. I struggle to loosen his hold. He looks slender and small. I would not hurt him: I have no business with him. Suddenly I hear the cry, 'Murder! Help!' My heart stands still as I realize that it is Frick shouting.

'Alive?' I wonder. I hurl the stranger aside and fire at the crawling figure of Frick. The man struck my hand,—I have missed! He grapples with me, and we wrestle across the room. I try to throw him, but spying an opening between his arm and body, I thrust the revolver against his side and aim at Frick, cowering behind the chair. I pull the trigger. There is a click—but no explosion! By the throat I catch the stranger, still clinging to me, when suddenly something heavy strikes me on the back of the head. Sharp pains shoot through my eyes. I sink to the floor, vaguely conscious of the weapon slipping from my hands.

" 'Where is the hammer? Hit him, carpenter!' Confused voices ring in my ears. Painfully I strive to rise. The weight of many bodies is pressing on me. Now—it's Frick's voice! Not dead? . . . I crawl in the direction of the sound, dragging the struggling men with me. I must get the dagger from my pocket—I have it! Repeatedly I strike with it at the legs of the man near the window. I hear Frick cry out in pain—there is much shouting and stamping—my arms are pulled and twisted, and I am lifted bodily from the floor.

"Police, clerks, workmen in overalls, surround me. An officer pulls my head back by the hair, and my eyes meet Frick's. He stands in front of me, supported by several men. His face is ashen gray; the black beard is streaked with red, and blood is oozing from his neck. For an instant a strange feeling, as of shame, comes over me; but the next moment I am filled with anger at the sentiment, so unworthy of a revolutionist. With defiant hatred I look him full in the face.

" 'Mr. Frick, do you identify this man as your assailant?'

"Frick nods weakly.

"The street is lined with a dense, excited crowd. A young man in civilian dress, who is accompanying the police, inquires, not unkindly:

" 'Are you hurt? You're bleeding.'

"I pass my hand over my face. I feel no pain, but there is a peculiar sensation about my eyes.

" 'I've lost my glasses,' I remark, involuntarily.

" 'You'll be damn lucky if you don't lose your head,' an officer retorts. (It was early afternoon, Saturday, July 23, 1892.)"

"She" now reads from the memoirs of Vera Zasulich:

She: "Then I lay down to sleep. It seemed to me that I was calm and totally unafraid of losing my free life; I had finished with that a long time ago. It was not even a life anymore, but some kind of limbo, which I wanted to end as soon as possible.

"I was oppressed by the thought of the following morning: that hour at the governor's, when he would suddenly approach in earnest . . . I was sure of success—everything would take place without the slightest hitch; it shouldn't be hard at all, and not at all frightening, but nevertheless I felt mortally unhappy.

"I had not expected this feeling. And at the same time, I was not excited, but tired—I even felt sleepy. But as soon as I fell asleep, I had a nightmare. It seemed to me that I was not sleeping, but lying on my back looking through the glass above the door, which was illuminated from the corridor. Suddenly, I felt as if I were losing my mind. Something was irresistibly forcing me to rise, to go out into the corridor and there, to scream. I knew that this was mad, I tried to hold myself back with all my strength, and yet nevertheless I went into the corridor and screamed and screamed. Masha, who was lying next to me, woke me up. I was indeed screaming, but on my cot, and not in the corridor. Again I fell asleep, and again I had the same dream: against my will I walked out and screamed, I knew it was crazy but nevertheless I screamed. So it went, several times.

"Then it was time to get up: we had no watches, but the sky had begun to turn gray, and someone knocked at our landlady's door. We had to hurry to Trepov's before nine o'clock, before he began to receive petitioners.

"We rose silently in the cold semidarkness. I put on a new dress; my coat and hat were old. After dressing I left the room: a new cloak and hat lay in the traveling bag, and I would change into them at the station. This was necessary because the landlady would certainly want to say good-bye; she would praise the cloak and advise me not to wear it on the road. And tomorrow this cloak would be in all the newspapers and might draw her attention. I had had time to think about everything, down to the most petty details.

"It was already growing light on the street, but the half-dark station was completely deserted. I changed, exchanged kisses with Masha, and left. The streets looked cold and gloomy.

"About ten petitioners had already gathered at the governor's. 'Is the governor receiving?' 'He's receiving; he'll be right out.'

"A woman, poorly dressed, with eyes red from weeping, sat down near me and asked me to take a look at her petition—'Is this how they are written here?' There was some sort of discrepancy in the petition. I advised her to show it to the officer, since I saw that he was already looking something over. She was afraid, and asked me to show it to him. I went up to the officer with the petitioner and directed his attention to her. My voice was ordinary—there was no sign of my agitation. I was satisfied. The nightmarish feeling that had weighed on me since the previous evening was gone without a trace. I had nothing on my mind but the concern that everything should go as planned.

"The adjutant led us into the next room, me first, and put us in a corner. At this very moment Trepov entered from another door, with a whole retinue of military men, and all of them headed toward me.

"For a moment this confused and upset me. In thinking through the details, I had found it inconvenient to shoot at the moment I presented the petition. Now Trepov and his entourage were looking at me, their hands occupied by papers and things, and I decided to do it earlier than I had planned—to do it when Trepov stopped opposite my neighbor, before reaching me.

"And suddenly there was no neighbor ahead of me—I was first . . . *It's all the same; I will shoot when he stops next to the petitioner after me,* I cried inwardly. The momentary alarm passed at once, as if it had never been.

" 'What do you want?'

" 'A certificate of conduct.'

"He jotted down something with a pencil and turned to my neighbor.

"The revolver was in my hand. I pressed the trigger . . . a misfire.

"My heart missed a beat. Again I pressed . . . a shot, cries . . .

"Now they'll start beating me. This was next in the sequence of events I had thought through so many times.

"But instead there was a pause. It probably lasted only a few seconds in all, but I felt it.

"I threw down the revolver—this also had been decided beforehand; otherwise, in the scuffle, it might go off by itself. I stood and waited.

" 'The criminal was stunned,' they wrote later in the papers.

"Suddenly everyone around me began moving, the petitioners scattered, police officers threw themselves at me, and I was seized from both sides.

" 'Where is the gun?' 'She threw it—it's on the floor.' 'The revolver! Give up the revolver!' They continued to scream, pulling me in different directions.

"A person appeared before me. His eyes were completely round, and his wide-open mouth issued a snarl, not a scream; his two huge hands, the fingers crooked, were headed directly for my eyes. I shut them as tightly as I could, and he only skinned my cheeks. Blows rained down—they rolled me around and continued to beat me.

"Everything went as I had expected; the only additional thing was the attack on my eyes, but now I lay with my face to the floor, and they were out of danger. I felt not the slightest pain, however, and this surprised me. I felt pain only that night, when they finally locked me in a cell.

" 'You're beating her?'

" 'Already killed, it seems.'

" 'You can't do that! Stop! We must have an investigation!'

"A battle began around me. Someone was pushed away. They helped me up and sat me in a chair. It seemed to me that this was the room in which I had presented my petition, but in front of me, somewhat to the left near the wall, there was a wide staircase without landings, which went to the very top of the opposite wall. People were hurrying down it, pushing one another, making noise and shouting. This riveted my attention immediately; how did the staircase get there?—it seemed as if it hadn't been there earlier, as if it were somehow unreal, and the people

> *Cut to three shots of young man seen earlier, walking down street with his dog and into a brown shingle house.*

unreal too. 'Perhaps it's only my imagination' passed through my mind immediately. But then they led me into another room and so the riddle of the staircase was never solved; for some reason, I recalled it all day long, whenever I was left in peace for a minute.

> *Cut to view of Bowery from window, with sounds of traffic.*

"The room into which I was led was large—much larger than the first; large desks stood near one of the walls, a wide bench ran along another. There were few people in the room at the moment, none at all from the governor's retinue.

"Meanwhile, the news evidently had already spread to higher circles. The room began to fill up; one after another, military and civilian bigwigs arrived, and with more or less threatening looks headed toward me. A loud, energetic officer was in command. He called two soldiers with bayonets on their rifles, stood them behind me, and ordered them to hold my hands. He went to the center of the room, looked around, and evidently not liking this position, moved to another. As he walked he warned the soldiers: 'Be careful, or else she might stick a knife into you!'

"My foresight, and consequently my precise plan of action, did not extend beyond the moment of attack. But every minute my joy increased—not because I was in full control of myself (there was the matter of the staircase), but rather because I found myself in an extraordinary state of the most complete invulnerability, such as I had never before experienced. Nothing at all could confuse me, annoy me, or tire me. Whatever was being thought up by those men, at that time conversing animatedly in another corner of the room, I would regard them calmly, from a distance they could not cross." (July 24, 1877)

Fade-out.

[Sounds of eating, silverware, plates, etc.]

Printed titles rise from bottom of frame:

In the first four months of 1976 there were no dissenting votes in the Bundestag as the penal code was amended to make propaganda for violent acts against the State as punishable as the acts themselves.

Early in the morning of Sunday, May 9, 1976, Ulrike Meinhof was found hanged in her Stammheim prison cell in Stuttgart. She was 41 years of age.

On April 28, 1977, Andreas Baader, Gudrun Ensslin, and Jean-Carl Raspe were sentenced to life-long imprisonment for murder in four cases and attempted murder in 34 cases.

He: It might have been the guards. . . . I doubt if the government conspired . . .

She: . . . something really fishy about those deaths . . . How did the guns . . . specially constructed penitentiary . . . The place was built expressly for *them* . . .

On the morning of Tuesday, October 18, 1977, Baader and Raspe were found shot and Ensslin hanged in their Stammheim prison cells. Baader was 34 years of age, Raspe 33, Ensslin 37.

He: It might have been easy to smuggle stuff in. Baader had 800 books in his cell, a tape recorder, record player, TV set . . . but the matter of Irmgard Möller . . . she survived after . . . nothing's been heard . . .

Openly expressed doubt of the official government view that the Stammheim prisoners committed suicide has resulted in prosecution for "defamation of the state."

She: If it's true, what a tour de force, huh? All four together . . . Communiques have been published supposedly written by them: "Our last and strongest weapon is our bodies, a weapon which we have used collectively and with which we have threatened . . ."

He: This one is attributed to Baader: "They can't prevent a prisoner dying—which means in any case—they will be responsible . . . in the eyes of the public (and it will happen in public) this murder will remain their responsibility."

She: . . . that hoodlum.

> *Titles almost disappear at top of frame. Dissolve into close-up of woman therapist's hands shuffling photos of Meinhof, Zasulich, Figner, Berkman, Hayworth, Goldman, Wyman. Camera dollies back to original position. In the background are 3 people looking out of the windows and a man on the left edge of the frame reading at a desk. The patient closes the book she has been reading and speaks.*

Patient: All right. Mariannenplatz, 1971. Come to a full stop. Turn your back on noisy self-effacement; declare your memories bankrupt; put your papers in order; pay all the bills; feed the cat; conduct a perfectly calm, productive meeting, even make a few jokes. What's the difference: the decision has been made, no need to fear that your mind will be changed. It was even possible to stand my own company—the first time in weeks—now that the decision had been made. It really doesn't matter what the circumstances were—love, work, money, exile—self-imposed or otherwise. It's always one or two of those, isn't it, or three . . . So why did I choose that option, that monstrous flight, that search for a final exit? . . . Like the search for the unicorn that may eventually be captured in Nepal, affection grows more difficult than it used to be. . . . and regard for life.

> *Circular tracking over Stonehenge. View is now much closer.*

Girl's voice: Everything I've written has been put down for the benefit of some potential reader. It is a titanic task to be frank with myself. I fear my own censure. Even my thoughts sometimes appear to my consciousness in a certain form for the benefit of an imaginary mind-reader. And strangely enough, *I* am that reader of these pages; *I* am that reader of this mind. I have very strong impressions of my childhood "acting." Up to a few years ago, whenever I was alone I would "perform." I don't think I did anything unusual or dramatic at these times, but the things I did do I did with the thought in mind that I was being watched. Now this reaction is becoming more and more unconscious, having been transmitted to my actions, speech, writing, and my thoughts. This last is the most unfortunate of all.

> *Therapy session (with woman therapist).*

Patient: I walked to the drugstore to get the last prescription filled, impervious to the brilliant fall sky.

"Apoteke" across a Berlin street (b&w).

She: . . . unlike the victim of torture in Iran who, in her choicelessness, was able to write, "I know that I shall never see another sunset. In a sense, I am glad. The burns on my feet are all infected and the pliers used on me have left nasty gashes . . ."

Patient (*V-O*): It never crossed my mind that I might never see another brilliant fall sky.

She: Later on she writes, "It is your strength against theirs. It is your faith in a high cause, namely the defeat of an inhuman enemy who has forgotten all feelings of kindness, understanding, and compassion."

Therapy session.

Patient: Why remark on the sky when it would have not the slightest effect on my decision?

Tracking over objects on mantlepiece: strawberries, pliers, photos of Zasulich, corpses (b&w).

She: What do you suppose people mean when they use the word "humanity"? It sounds so pretentious.

Here, for instance: ". . . for to torture without compunction requires the complete denial of one's own humanity."

He: What's pretentious about it? The word simply describes what one has in common with other people—being human, capable of joy and suffering.

Therapy session.

Patient: I suspect the worst: There never was any humanity there to deny.

Therapist: Your suspicions aren't evidence.

Patient: I disagree. In this case my suspicions are the very corpus delicti. I plead guilty to an absence of humanity.

Therapist: Yes, I do seem to remember your saying that even your asshole had no heart.

Group struggles to bring enormous staircase through the rear doors.

Patient: Don't worry; I'm well aware of more plausible excuses: such as my injurious past. A cruel father, a doting father, an indifferent mother, a dead mother; I was the only child, first child, youngest, middle; I grew up in poverty, wealth, the 19th century? My daddy called me Cookie? My grandfather fled a pogrom?

Tracking over objects.

She: Angelica Balabanoff was the youngest of nine children. Olga Liubatovich's mother died when she was an adolescent. Elizaveta Kovalskaia's mother was a serf. Emma Goldman's father beat her. Vera Figner had elegance, education, intelligence, and the ability to conduct herself properly in all social circles. Vera Zasulich's father never sat her on his knee or called her Cookie. A racial bigot who had been accused and acquitted of bombing a synagogue burst into tears one day and sobbed that his mother always hated him and somehow he was getting back at her.

Therapy session. Profile of staircase in middle distance.

Therapist: All right, all right. For the sake of argument I'll concede your point:

Woman walks up staircase.

You're inhuman and no better than the torturer . . . So! (*very grandly*) What is to be done?! (*pause, then laughing*) How about a stake through the heart?

Stonehenge.

Girl's voice: Sunday, November 18th. How hard I try to convince myself that man is intrinsically good. If this were not so, what would be the use of trying to be good oneself? I think that by a good person I mean one who does not feel compelled to satisfy the demands of his ego. Such a one will be at peace at least with himself and will be able to accept himself as he is. Only then will he be able to love others. It is only with the conviction that his love will arouse the Good that lies dormant behind every soul's facade of hypocrisy and selfishness that one should seriously try to eradicate the querulous cries of the ego. For hypocrisy is itself hypocrisy, murky water that obscures the face of the seeking self.

Therapy session.

Therapist: . . . . or an enema of gentian root, garlic, and bezoar stone every morning for 10 days?

Stonehenge.

Girl's voice: I saw my ego staring me in the face. I ceased to listen to what they were saying because I saw that what I had been saying did not come from myself. What is my self and what is my ego? Who is the I and the self and the ego? Show me this monster who claws my senses and I will rend him to pieces.

Therapy session. Therapist reads aloud from a book. Woman walks down stairs. Cut to closer shots as she progresses through swinging doors and out onto street. Pedestrians, traffic are seen.

Therapist (*reading*): "The analysis of melancholia now shows that the ego can kill itself only if, owing to the return of the object-cathexis, it can treat itself as an object and if it is able to direct against itself the hostility which relates to an object and which represents the ego's original reaction to objects in the external world. In the two opposed situations of being most intensely in love and of suicide the ego is over-whelmed by the object, though in totally different ways."

She: Energetic, cheerful, and serene, Isaev always enlivened the group. At the same time, he was sternly conscientious; according to him, serving the revolution inevitably meant restricting your personal life. "Personal renunciation," he would say, "doesn't

> *At "renouncing" image flips upside-down as woman walks back in, through the swinging doors, and backwards up the staircase.*

mean renouncing one's identity, but rather renouncing one's eogism." All of Isaev's life forces and human aspirations were directed to the revolutionary cause. "Our task, our supreme task, is to gain justice for our Russian people," he frequently repeated.

Patient (*V-O*): It was almost like having a sense of mission. If a stone can have conviction and purpose, then that describes the way I moved unswervingly toward my objective.

> *Therapy session, as before.*

Therapist: . . . . (*laughing*) or should we apply a plaster of pigeon dung to your feet? . . . Come on Annette. (*in exasperation*) Sit up straight, sit up.

Patient: How little I want to know what lies ahead. (*She leans forward.*) Listen to me, will you? I'm trying to get at something . . . the matter of conscious choice. For me the exercise of choice always meant disregard of feelings. It still does, only now for different reasons.

> *Berlin Wall.*

She: Political imperatives have always been meaningless to me unless I started from scratch.

He: How so?

She: I don't easily empathize with other people's lives. Each time, I had to struggle for that as though for the first time. It never became a habitual reflex.

> *Therapy session.*

Patient: You always gave me the benefit of the doubt, didn't you? You accorded me the dignity which you thought I might eventually allow myself and others. I waited for that day to arrive, but it never did. Neither your efforts nor the things I achieved on my own—here and outside—ever brought about the change I so longed for.

> *View through glass of swinging doors at rear of space (color). People and traffic of London's East End.*

He: What about something like abortion rights? You had no trouble at all knowing where you stood on legislation cutting off abortion funds for poor women. I mean, you were able to empathize with poor women without batting an eye. So what's all this starting-from-zero stuff?

> *Therapy session.*

Patient: Somehow I always thought that that great American invention, "being in touch with your feelings," would make a better person of me. What a shock to discover that feelings can erode not only one's best interests but one's conscience. How shocking to discover that decisions are often so much easier to make without "being in touch" with one's fear, anger, and envy.

View through glass as before (color).

She: But that's just the point: I *don't* empathize with poor women, even on *that* issue. Some things are easy to take a stand on because they're so obviously unjust, and one has moral obligations and habits. What I'd really like to have are moral, or ethical, *feelings,* maybe even instincts, if that were only possible.

He: What do you think of this: "Principles and the inner life are alibis the moment they cease to animate external and everyday life." That's Merleau-Ponty, 1947.

She: Read it again?

He: "Principles and the inner life are alibis the moment they cease to animate external and everyday life."

Therapy session.

Patient: . . . and yes, how shocked I was to discover that some feelings are just plain foreign to me; so foreign that I find it hard to say the words for them. (*pause*)

Therapist: Are you going to try?

View through train window (b&w).

She: Nnoo . . . It doesn't apply. I'm not looking for a way out. I don't spend time every morning worrying about who picked the coffee beans that went into the coffee I'm drinking; whether he's sick or well, whether he has a radio, a wife and 8 children, whether he works 12 or 14 hours a day, whether he's working or sleeping while I linger over my second cup of coffee.

Therapy session. Staircase gone. On the left in the background a woman now sits at desk. Patient doesn't speak, but looks blankly at the desk.

Patient: (*V-O*): Kindness, understanding . . . compassion.

Therapist (*reading*): "There is another principle which, having been bestowed on us to moderate, on certain occasions, the impetuosity of egoism, or, before its birth, the desire of self-preservation, tempers the ardour with which we pursue our own welfare, by an innate repugnance at seeing a fellow-creature suffer. I think I need not fear contradiction in holding humanity to be possessed of the only natural virtue, which could not be denied them by the most violent detractor of human virtue. I am speaking of compassion, which is a disposition suitable to creatures so weak and subject to so many evils as we certainly are: by so much the more universal and useful to humanity, as it comes before any kind of reflection; and at the same time so natural, that the very brutes themselves sometimes give evident proofs of it."

View from train window (b&w).

She: Well, all right, obviously I do occasionally think of those coffee beans. mmm . . . (*long pause*) This is going to sound sappy, but I'll say it anyway . . . I'd like permission to make mistakes . . .

He (*after pause*): Who's stopping you?

Girl's voice: I will learn to love myself; then I will love humanity.

Therapy session.

Patient: I had no compassion for the life I wanted to end. I had succeeded in suppressing everything—thought, feeling, doubt—everything. I had achieved complete autonomy and perfect detachment. I was a free agent. I was empty and impregnable at one and the same time.

View from train window.

She: I just now made up my mind: I'm going to stop trying to become a better person. There's no adding up correct social behavior like revolutions on a prayer wheel. It's hopeless. They'll never let me in, so I might just as well attend to what has to be done right now, whether or not I myself benefit.

He: What kind of benefit did you want?

View through windows of swinging doors.

She: Oh . . . right feeling, passion maybe—the kind of passionate conviction the Russian Amazons had. I know its pure fantasy.

He: And what about mistakes?

Therapy session.

Patient: Nothing has changed.

She: Well, if you accept your own fallibility, and don't have such a stake in your own . . .

Patient: It could happen again.

Windows.

She: . . . in your own development . . . one might conceivably take greater risks . . .

Therapy session.

Therapist: You're the one who used the word "invention."

She: . . . in argument . . .

Patient: Huh? Oh, you mean, if there were no compassion we would have to invent it!

Windows.

She: . . . risks in using one's power . . .

Therapy session.

Patient: . . . Suicide, then, can be seen as a failure of imagination . . .

Windows.

She: . . . for the benefit of others . . .

Therapy session.

Patient: . . . a failure to imagine what may lie outside one's own experience . . .

She: . . . working with people . . .

Patient: . . . a failure to imagine a world

Windows.

She: . . . inhabiting one's own history . . .

Patient (*V-O*): . . . where conscious choice

She: . . . resisting inequities close at hand . . .

Therapy session.

Patient: . . . and effort . . .

She: . . . risks in love . . .

Patient: . . . might produce mutual respect

She: . . . mistakes

Patient: . . . between you and me.

Fade-out.

View from Bowery window.

She: I'd like to read one last thing: a letter from Meinhof to Hannah Krabbe when they were in prison, Meinhof in Stammheim and Krabbe in Ossendorf.

He: Who's Hannah Krabbe?

She: She was a member of the Socialist Patients' Collective that originated in the Psychiatric-Neurological Clinic of Heidelberg University . . . Uh, she and some others blew up the German Embassy in Stockholm, uh, in 1975 when the German government refused to meet their demand for the release of imprisoned RAF people. The letter is dated March 23, 1976, less than two months before Meinhof died. (*reads*) "That's bullshit—'psychiatric' wing. Like everywhere else a policy of destruction is being followed at Ossendorf, and the psychiatrists are cooperating, just as they have designed the methods of the secret police.

"Psychiatry, like imperialist science in general, is a means, not an end. Psychiatrification, as a device"

He: What?

She: That's what it says: "Psychiatrification, as a device of psychological warfare, aims to persuade the destroyed fighter of the pointlessness of revolutionary politics, to destroy the fighter's credibility. At the same time it is a police tactic designed to insure that political prisoners sprung by—as Buback puts it—compulsory liberation—will be of no use as recruits." Uh—Siegfried Buback was the Federal Prosecutor who was assassinated in April '77 by the RAF.

> *Converted video footage: A woman—recognizable as one of the two from the music lesson—sits in medium close-up in a very dark room and addresses someone just to the left of the camera. From her tearful monologue (which begins "Dear Mama") we learn that she is living in Berlin and has just seen a film,* Morgen Beginnt das Leben, *directed by Werner Hochbaum in Berlin in 1933. She describes the gasps and murmurs she heard as young members of the audience identified the street signs of neighborhoods that were otherwise unrecognizable. The film is their link to pre-war Berlin, a city "that is no more."*

> *By itself the monologue is somewhat sentimental. The reading of the Meinhof letter, from this point on, is inserted—in segments—so that it replaces parts of the on-camera monologue. This footage is also intercut with the recorder lesson seen at the beginning of the film.*

Woman: "Dear Mama: I think you would understand this, but it doesn't matter. I have to talk as though you would understand what I'm saying. Tonight I saw a movie, and I'll try and tell you very fast. Tonight I saw a film that was shot in a city that existed before the war. I'm living in Berlin and I saw this movie in Berlin and it's about Berlin 1933 . . . Werner Hochbaum is the name of the director. And it's a very simple story and it uh . . ."

". . . A man gets out of prison . . . his wife . . . her alarm clock doesn't go off . . and she's not there to meet him. And it shows them both wandering through the city looking for each other. He goes to her house . . . his house . . . She isn't there . . . Lots of superimpositions . . . flashbacks . . . like his face . . . as it . . . uh . . . against . . . against . . . what he's . . . he's remembering . . . I was walking home later that night and I was thinking . . . I was thinking, mama, why can't . . ."

". . . and were acting in a city that I knew, and everyone in the theatre knew, was soon to be blown to bits . . . and so we are touched by the artistic effort and by . . . the city that is no more and by the people that are gone . . ."

". . . spending five years in prison . . ."

". . . He gets out of prison and, uh, she gets up in the morning and . . . It isn't just one clock that tells you that it's morning, and nine o'clock. Half a dozen different church spires and bells . . . and in fact the . . . the tower of the then modern church that is actually right across from my house had remained intact. A church built in the twenties . . . red brick with a soaring square tower and a clock . . . and I hear it every quarter hour . . . and its bell . . . I don't know why I'm telling you this, mama . . ."

She: "What Bücker is doing there is not psychiatrification, it is terror. He wants to wear you down. In using terms such as therapy, brainwashing attempts, your reasoning is off, you're understanding things in psychological jargon, you are merely interpreting, whereas the attack is a frontal one.

"The Ossendorf method—like the prison method in general, except that in this case it is made aseptic, total by the perfection of the building and the penitentiary concept embodied in it and represented by Bücker and Lodt—consists in choking the prisoner until he loses his dignity (actually the German was more like 'becomes shitty'), his idea of himself, his ability to perceive terror. It's about destruction. Psychiatrification is just one aspect, one of the vehicles among others. If you allow yourself to become mesmerized by them, like a rabbit by a snake, you'll no longer notice the other goings-on.

Cut to recorder lesson.

" 'No windows'—sure. But that complaint reveals your shock at the sadism with which isolation was thought out, the perfection of its execution, the totality of the destructive will of the authorities, disbelief at the intensity of the antagonism which we encountered as fighters, finally, disbelief at the fact that fascism is effectively ruling here. In fact this is not just an allegation of ours but the exact term to describe the repression that hits you if you get involved in revolutionary politics in this state.

Cut to video footage as before.

"They can't psychiatrize anyone who doesn't allow it. Your wailing about psychiatry mystifies isolation. One has to fight against its effectiveness, and of course you people have to wage war against the chicanery of Bücker.

"So you had better demand—no acoustical monitoring, only visual monitoring at lock-up time, just as in Stammheim. But here also we had to fight for it, until we got rid of the pig who was listening in and could squat on the floor, etc. Repression is all you're going to get unless you make an effort.

"You're an ass; you're trotting out from your sewing box the demand that we should all be put in one prison and the line 'war prisoners' as if these demands could actually be used as a threat against Müller. That's nonsense. 'We'll have to concentrate and go for the application of the Geneva Convention.' What the hell do you expect from Müller?

Cut to recorder lesson.

"We are fighting against them and the fight will never end. They will never ease up the conditions of the fight. If you're only reasoning on the level of bourgeois morality you'll soon run short of ammunition, it's foolish. So watch yourself, for no one can do that for you while you're in isolation—not even Bernd."

"Ulrike"

Cut to black. The final title rolls up from the bottom of the frame.

[Sound of recorder stops.]

"The aim of all enemies of the State is the deliberate creation of an opposing power over and against this State, or the denial of *the State's monopoly of force.*"

H. Herold, head of the Federal Criminal Investigation Bureau (BKA), 1975

(italics mine)

Title disappears at top of frame.

Credits rise from bottom of frame.

CAST

Patient	Annette Michelson
Female Therapist	Ilona Halberstadt
Male Therapist	Gabor Vernon
Boy Therapist	Chad Wollen
Two women playing recorders	Yvonne Rainer
	Ruth Rainero
Young man with dog	Leo Rainer
Man and woman walking in front	Cynthia Beatt
of Berlin church	Antonio Skarmeta
Voices: "She"	Amy Taubin
"He"	Vito Acconci
"Girl"	Lena Hyun

People in background in the Whitechapel Art Gallery:

Anna Ambrose, Elaine Burrows, Mary Colston, Elizabeth Cowie, Mitch Davies, John Ellis, Leslie Eyles, Marion Foran, Francis Fuchs, Renee Glynne, Dave Green, Li Guy, Paul Hallam, Tony Harpur, Linda Hartley, Peter Jewell, Carola Klein, Robert Letts, David Maclagan, Helen Mc-Clure, Orly Ofrat, Stephen Quay, William Raban, Ian Sellar, Charlie Ware, Bruce Wilson, Beth Worth, Liz Wren

CINEMATOGRAPHERS

London, Stonehenge, and New York	Carl Teitelbaum
Recorder lesson	Wolfgang Senn
Man and woman walking and Berlin streets	Michael Steinke
Young man with dog	Jon Else
Berlin Wall	Shinkichi Tajiri

SOUND RECORDING

London	Larry Sider
Berlin	Christian Moldt
Berkeley	Dan Gillham
Voices and Effects	Helene Kaplan

CAMERA ASSISTANT IN LONDON: Anne Cottringer
DESIGN COORDINATOR: Miranda Melville
CONTINUITY: Renee Glynne
GAFFER: Jonathan Collinson
ASSISTANT GAFFER: Glyn Fielding
PRODUCTION SUPERVISOR: Nita Amy
PRODUCTION ASSISTANT: Judy Leveque
PRE-PRODUCTION: Donna Grey
EDITOR: Yvonne Rainer
ASSISTANT EDITOR: Ryan

Special thanks to:

Whitechapel Art Gallery
Boston Film and Video Foundation
Jay Anania
Marcia Braunstein
Phoebe Cohen
Michael Grieg
Ilona Halberstadt

Jacqueline Lesschaeve
Laura Mulvey
Michael Oblowitz
Anna Ratti
Beth Rectanus
Schuldt
Peter Wollen

Sources of information and quoted material not previously acknowledged:

A. Alvarez
Jillian Becker
Walter Benjamin
Noel Carroll
Ronald Clark
Sebastian Cobler
Magda Denes
Leo Deuel
Barbara Alpern Engel
Hans Magnus Enzenberger
Sigmund Freud
German Information Center, New York

Jane Kramer
Peter Kropotkin
Jacques Lacan
Wilfred Owen
Cesare Pavese
Sophie Perovskaya
Clifford Rosenthal
Jean-Jacques Rousseau
D.W.Winnicott
Sheldon Wolin
Ely Zaretsky

This film has been made possible by:

The British Film Institute
Deutscher Akademischer Austauschdienst

New York State Council on the Arts
Center for Advanced Visual Studies, M.I.T.
Christophe de Menil
Beard's Fund, Inc.
The Rockefeller Foundation

© Yvonne Rainer, 1980

The Man Who Envied Women

CU of man's face. He is smoking and speaks toward left side of frame.

Jack Deller: Doctor, I'll tell you all you want to know about my sex life. I'll confess to hitting my wife and throwing the cat off the 3rd floor balcony. I'll even describe in minute detail the peculiarities of my shit . . . Just don't ask me how much money I have in the bank.

[Music]

> *Slow zoom out to reveal a screen just behind him and to his left. The title* Screen Tests *appears, followed by the opening shots of* Un Chien Andalou. *As the man in the projected film (Bunuel) goes out onto balcony,*

[Music fades out.]

Trisha (*V-O*): It was a hard week. I split up with my husband and moved into my studio. The hot water heater broke and flooded the textile merchant downstairs; I bloodied up my white linen pants; the Senate voted for nerve gas; and my gynecologist went down in Korean Airlines Flight 007. The worst of it was the gynecologist. He was a nice man. He used to put booties on the stirrups and his speculum was always warm.

> *On "speculum" we see the CU of woman's eye being slit.*

[Coffee shop ambience.]

> *Cut to backwards tracking shot past booths in coffee shop. First we see a man reading a newspaper, then two women having a conversation, and finally the camera comes to rest on Jack Deller #2 reading* The New York Times. *He is wearing large headphones and appears to be eavesdropping on the two women's conversation.*

Woman #1: What do you call 12 dead men at the bottom of the sea? . . . A new beginning. . . . What is the best way to a man's heart? . . . Through his chest.

Woman #2 (*laughing*): Dyke-bar jokes.

Woman #1: Until that moment he had treated me as a person rather than a woman.

#2: Like balancing on the tip of a man's penis.

First published in *Women & Performance: A Journal of Feminist Theory*, vol. 3, no. 2, issue #6. Reprinted with permission. Extensive quotations in this script from *Michel Foucault: Power, Truth, Strategy*, edited by Meaghan Morris and Paul Patton, © 1979, are used with the permission of Feral Publications.

#1: I'm not trying to pin him down or anything . . . just get him into bed.

#2: Nicaragua will have no choice but to resist. If Reagan invades, I'm joining the Sandinistas.

#1: She told me I'd never be a committed feminist until I give up men.

[Music fades in.]

> *Cut to lateral tracking shot past brilliantly lit arched windows of a library.*
> *As blackness replaces the last window . . .*

[Music fades out.]

> *Man peering from behind a wood and fiberglas screen.*

Trisha (*V-O*): Oh. Oh. Oh. The biting man, the man who looks, the man who offers the little girl candy in return for . . . They were all there in full regalia: top hats and tails, I the nude on the grass, I

> *Manet's "Dejeuner sur l'herbe."*

> *Upside-down pirouetting pointe shoe.*

with the cock in my mouth, I

> *CBS weatherman on TV.*

married to the CBS Weatherman, I

> *Lid of suitcase being closed.*

keeping the lid on the

> *CU of hands shuffling fund-raising appeals: CISPES, SANE, etc.*

suitcase that contained my father. Of all the weeks he might have picked to pop out,

> *Video image on monitor of street demonstration against anti-abortion*
> *legislation. Banner in background reads* No More Forced Labor.

he had to pick this week . . .

> *CU of sign on back of demonstrator:* No More Nice Girls

He chose this week to pop out of that suitcase and dust himself off.

> *A hearing room. A man at podium (Robert Storr) ends a speech.*

Robert Storr: How the hell're we going to do our work?

[Boos and applause.]

> *He walks away from podium. Camera pans to man in glasses seated in*
> *audience (Jon Hendricks).*

> *Wide shot of empty movie house. Audience begins to trickle in.*

Trisha (*V-O*): Rage at men. The noun: rage at men. Why now? Why can't it be put off indefinitely? I'm not up to it this week. I have nothing more to say about that subject. . . . Don't say anything about it. . . . Let it speak. . . . In a manner more suited to

> *Same hearing room as before. A lawyer (Norman Siegal) is speaking at podium.*

Norman Siegal: I believe that the city's actions on this point verge on deliberate indifference. There was not a single minority group, not even a single minority artists' group, in the pool . . .

> *ICAIC poster of smoking gun-camera.*

Thank you.

> *Hearing room. Siegal leaves podium.*

[Wild applause.]

Trisha (*V-O*): In a manner more suited to the closure of courtroom drama than to the nameless dread that pursues you from your first moment of awakening to . . .

[Babble of voices, laughter.]

> *Steering committee of "Artists' Call against U.S. Intervention in Central America." 15 or 20 people sitting in a large circle in Leon Golub's studio. Camera pans left to right.*

> *CU of Daniel Flores Ascencio.*

Daniel Flores Ascencio *speaks of strategies (his voice is not very clear):* . . . I explained to them . . . because the support is needed for Artists' Call . . . it would be very important if they change the petition to be delivered by the 21st in this country . . . Now the President of the Young Socialists tries to aid representatives, including Europe and Latin America . . . They're going to revise the resolution and make it part of the agenda . . .

> *CU of Jon Hendricks.*

Jon Hendricks: The problems are . . . we need to find ways of getting the posters up on the wall . . .

> *CU of Daniel Flores Ascencio.*

Woman's voice: . . . so many Spanish names are on the poster . . .

Hendricks' voice: . . . I had thought in the exhibition . . .

Daniel Flores: In the exhibition, yes, but I am talking about printing the names on the poster . . .

Woman's voice: . . . But it wouldn't be clear at all where they are from . . .

Flores: . . . But I think it would be nice if we could include some of them . . .

Jack Deller #1 in "therapy session," i.e., in front of screen as at end of opening shot. Clip from "Dark Victory" is seen on screen.

Trisha (*V-O*): The signs were there from the beginning. When we were deciding to live together, one of the first things he said to me was, "I'm not such a bastard as I used to be."

J.D. #1: This must have been about 15 years ago. I met her while I was still married to my first wife. You know what she said to me on our first date? She said, "I'm really a very good girl." Thirty-five years old and she was still calling herself a girl. [He continues talking without sound (*MOS*) as Bette Davis and George Brent speak in the projected "Dark Victory."]

Steele: Have you been a good girl?

Judith: No.

Steele: I thought not.

Judith: Why?

Steele: I knew you wouldn't be, I knew you couldn't be.

Judith: You mean—a good girl? Why, the idea. Well, I am!

Steele: Did you drive in for lunch and come right back?

Judith: Father, I cannot tell a lie.

Steele: What did you do?

Judith: (*Shows off new shoes.*) Bought these shoes.

Steele: Very pretty, very nice. What else?

Judith: (*indicates dress*) This, and some other new frocks I know you'll like.

Image on screen changes to Hollis Frampton's "Otherwise Unexplained Fires." Two men seem to be conducting a scientific experiment. Camera zooms slowly in so that interior film occupies the full frame, alternating shots of trees, fire, and a mechanical chrome man on a horse.

[An unidentifiable mechanical sound begins, followed by music.]

CU of legs working out on a "NordicTrack." The sound from the preceding shot can now be identified.

[News broadcast (woman's voice) of the downing of Korean Airlines Flight #007.]

Freeze frame of legs.

[Sound of NordicTrack stops.]

Titles appear:

The Man Who Envied Women

A film by Yvonne Rainer

with William Raymond, Trisha Brown, Larry Loonin, and Jackie Raynal

Legs on NordicTrack Resume Motion.

[Sound of NordicTrack resumes. (The broadcast is continuous.)]

Camera dollies back to reveal J.D. #1 on NordicTrack. A wall of books is behind him. The room appears to be his study.

Trisha (*V-O*): It *was* a hard week. Alicia went off to Antioch. I moved out of Jack's house and into my studio. I received an eviction notice. I passed my 50th birthday.

Jack!

A woman in a hat and raincoat enters the frame. We see her in the following sequence only from the rear. We assume that the voice we hear is hers. In actuality, her voice is always off-screen.

CU of hand turning knob on radio.

[Volume of news broadcast decreases.]

Medium, J.D. on NordicTrack.

Trisha (*V-O*): Jack, I'm going now. I . . . I'll pick up the rest of my stuff next week.

J.D.: I'd like to know when. I don't want to come in and find you've been here while I'm out.

[Phone rings.]

J.D. gets off N.T. and goes toward desk.

MCU: J.D. sits on side of table while answering phone.

J.D.: Hello.

Linda: Hello . . . Barry?

J.D.: Barry? There's no Barry here. You must have dialed the wrong . . .

J.D. is looking offscreen. Cut to CU of Trisha's hand removing video tapes from bookcase.

Linda: Who is this? You sound like Jack Deller. Sorry, I must have dialed your number by mistake. Freudian slippers (*laughs*).

MCU: J.D. as before.

J.D.: Oh hello, Linda. I can't talk right now.

Linda: That's OK. I'll be in touch. Bye.

> *Wider shot from across the room. Trisha stands in foreground, her back to camera. J.D. half sits on table, facing her.*

Trisha: Jack, I'm sorry, I can't say exactly when. I'll call you when I know my rehearsal schedule.

J.D.: It doesn't matter, you still have a key . . .

> *He walks around to other side of table. Camera tracks right, then forward toward a number of images on the wall. Neither Trisha nor J.D. is now in the frame. A battered bicycle leans against the wall below the images, next to it an ironing board is set up.*

Take your ironing board out of here . . .

> *CU of ironing board. Trisha enters and starts to fold it up. Camera tilts down and tracks left.*

and take your art off my wall.

Trisha (*V-O*): I'll do it later. I haven't time now.

[Door slams.]

> *MCU: J.D. on NordicTrack. He ducks his head in response to slam.*

J.D.: (*shouting in direction of slam*) Then turn the radio back up!

> *He gets off N.T. and leaves frame.*

[News broadcast ceases.]

> *During the following speech hand-held camera "explores" a corner of the study: the battered bicycle, a dustpan containing fragments of glass, the bookcase, two wooden ducks perched on a shelf.*

Trisha (*V-O*): When he was courting me he loved my reserve and independence, what he described as extreme shyness and supreme self-confidence. After four months of living together his reason for starting an affair was that I didn't love him. How that same reserve, shyness, and independence all became evidence of indifference is beyond *me*. The bigger question is, after that first infidelity of his, how did I manage to keep myself in ignorance of all the rest? Her answers were both simple and somehow veiled,

> *Camera has settled on J.D.'s striding legs on NordicTrack. Cut to left-to-right tracking shot across "collage," four images pinned to wall. The first is a photo of a man staring spectrally at the camera accompanied by the title,* How I Was Broken by the KGB. *#2 is a page of text titled* About Men. *A small colored drawing of a man's upper torso and head is inserted on the left. The upper portion of the head is cropped to eliminate the eyes and forehead. A large tear seems to be rolling down the cheek. #3 is a*

cigar ad. A handsome well-heeled Anglo-Saxon man holds a large cigar and sits in a lush meadow behind two pedigreed dogs. The phrase The sweet smell of success *appears in the left-hand corner. #4 is a horrible color photo of decapitated corpses and several heads, victims of a Salvadoran death-squad murder.*

Camera comes to rest on image #4.

like the utterances of poets and holy men. In post-revolutionary Russia, not telling your partner about another sexual relationship was sufficient grounds for the partner to press charges for fraud.

Dissolve to right-to-left tracking shot past collage during first part of the following dialogue.

J.D. # 1 (*V-O*): (*cough*) I mean (*cough*), are all these from the N.Y. Times magazine?

Trisha (*V-O*): Only the first three.

J.D. #1: The first three . . . right . . . although the other ones are different.

Trisha: From Mother Jones.

J.D. #1: Yeah . . . well, that makes sense . . . you wouldn't, uh, expect to see that in, I mean the N.Y. Times Magazine is a, is a kind of beacon of reaction, you know, it's always, I mean I'm quite surprised I didn't read that because I must have somehow missed that week. Normally I read it carefully . . . um, the one of Victor Krasin is a bit unclear to me cause I didn't, I don't know the story . . . I mean the thing that interests me is, obviously it's a story about the meeting with Andropov during the time he was head of the KGB and it's, uh, it reminded me of (*cough*) if Reagan had been assassinated at that time, you would have had the same situation in both major countries of the world, having an ex-head of the secret police as, uh, chief of state . . . Andropov and Bush.

And this one is, um, is kind of strange, I mean what struck me as strange was when the wife says, "Please come, father" and you suddenly get this doubletake on, on patriarchy, from the, uh, author.

Trisha (*reading*): ". . . by a wife's terrified cry for help. 'Please come, Father. My husband just put his fist through the wall.' " Uh, yeh. He's a priest.

J.D. #1: I mean it's strangely, it's written from the position of

CU of image #4 (Salvadoran corpses).

uh, father. It's a sort of unpolitical piece. It's not really about sexual politics . . . Uh, and it sees emotion as something purely, sort of completely, self-directed, right? You would only want to cry because, if something happens to you personally, right?

Black and white shots: CU of four-year-old girl looking at camera, another Artists' Call meeting in a small room of Jon Hendricks' house.

Trisha: In the family.

J.D. #1: In the family maybe or, with your peer group. And, um, it's completely emotionally cut off from say, what's happening in, uh, Salvadore. That's not, uh, that's not the kind of emotion which they're talking about at all . . . although strangely enough it has a reference to decapitation in it . . . with Sidney Carton and Thomas More. More had his head chopped off, Carton was guillotined.

CU of image #2 (About Men). *The spectator can read what Trisha reads.*

Trisha: Oh my God . . . (*reading*) "Admittedly there's a place for the debonaire, masculine cover-up of pain. Thomas More blessing his executioner; Sidney Carton calmly setting a life-time of ducks in a row before going to the guillotine . . ." Oh my god, I hadn't picked up on that. . . .

Camera booms down past image #1 to reveal Artists' Call poster below it.

"Life-time of ducks"? . . . No sooner had I extricated myself from the four-year stint with Jack, than I received an eviction notice to vacate my studio. Sheer coincidence, nothing personal. Just the usual Manhattan housing story. Get rid of the first and second wave of artist-

Field of poured concrete structures (Donald Judd sculptures).

gentrifiers. Triple the rent. Get in a new tenant who will have mobilized sufficiently upwards to afford over $1000 a month for a small loft. An all too familiar story in Manhattan real-life real estate . . . only this time it would come with more than the usual quota of bitter twists.

Board of Estimate hearing on "Artists-Homeowners' Program." A "Loi-saidista" is speaking.

Diana Adorno: It's not that we are against artists; it's that we have no places to put them. And I am outraged, because these people are American citizens; they have come here to work. They pay their taxes and they've paid their dues. They have come here to look for a better living which they have been promised by this country. And I think . . . we are not against artists' housing; we have said that they can have the empty schools; they can have the empty storefronts. There are many of them on the Lower East Side. But I think that . . . to give this money, which is the last money, the last Federal Government money that could come in to help these families, I think you people are stealing, and if you were to see . . . I invite you all to come into these people's homes, you need to see these children sleeping on the floor. Velma, who came in, two disabled children in a four-room apartment. She forgot to mention that her daughter has had pneumonia . . . twice because she's sleeping on the floor.

Collage: CU of hands pinning up a new image (#5), ad from a medical journal for estrogen-replacement therapy, including a photo of a tired middle-aged woman.

Trisha (*V-O*): Dear Abby, I've found *Playboy* magazines in my boyfriend's apartment. Shouldn't sex with me be enough for him? After all, we see each other almost every night. Available. Dear Available, don't question men's desires. Mind your own business and stay available. Dear Abby,

J.D. #2 (*V-O*): Yeh . . .

Trisha: Is it bad manners or downright hostile if a guy jerks off while he's in your bed? Puzzled.

J.D. #2 (*V-O*): No, I'm not free today . . .

Trisha: Dear Puzzled, anyone who behaves like that is a jerk. Why don't middle class couples have separate bedrooms so they can jerk or not jerk as they please?

> *MCU: J.D. #2 (Larry Loonin) perched on edge of table talking on phone.*

J.D. #2: *You* know my schedule . . . Sorry . . . yeh, I'm alone . . . she's gone . . . out, moved out . . . Laura, I can't talk now. I have a class this morning . . . There's no

> *Camera begins to dolly past him toward the collage.*

doubt in *my* mind. Countries like Argentina and Brazil will have to reduce their military expenditures to meet IMF demand and avoid social problems . . . A precedent? If only! Laura, let me go. I'll talk to you later . . . Yeh.

> *Images #4 and #5.*

Trisha (*V-O*): The ovaries of the seven-month-old fetus contain almost a million egg cells. From then on the ova constantly decrease in number without replenishment. The only other cells that do this are those of the brain. The ovaries themselves

> *Wide shot, from above, of the empty study. Dellers #1 and #2 alternate entering and exiting in progressive stages of dress, collecting papers and books in a briefcase, pausing to peruse notes, drink orange juice, etc.*

stop functioning altogether long before the rest of the body. With the advances of medicine the human female has increasingly outlived the functioning of her ovaries and, as a consequence, her reproductive potential. In contrast, at the turn of the century, although the cessation of menstruation occurred during a woman's 40's, her life expectancy was only 49 years, which meant that menopause was in all probability an event that took place shortly before her death. The same technological advances that have contributed to a dramatically extended life span for many of us, have also led, if indirectly, to the possibility that the female body may be poorly programmed for its newly realized life expectancy. The drastic reduction in estrogen and progesterone production by the ovaries as they close down can have an extreme and negative effect on a woman's health in later life. Is it fair to say, therefore, that for one-third of a woman's life cycle her body is malfunctioning? The currency of this view in western culture with its frequent accompaniment of despair, is upheld and offset

MS: Jack Deller #1, now fully dressed, pauses to adjust headphones.

Cut to busy downtown street. J.D. #2, wearing headphones, is walking behind two young women.

by privileges associated with being a fertile young woman. But these privileges, we cannot forget, are paid for with the agreement that they will be lost at the coming of menopause.

Five more shots of streets, now with J.D. #1 appearing to tune out, or overhear, fragments of conversation.

Woman #1: Did you know that the male fetus gets an erection?

Woman #2: No! I'm sick!

Woman #3 to #4: He had the gall to ask me, "How did you get to be so smart?" So I said, "By sleeping with smart men." But I don't recommend that form of education. The tuition is too high.

Man #1 to Woman #5: Only gays and women get emotionally involved in love. I mean, only a gay man would be so devastated by his lover walking out on him.

Woman #6 to #7: She told me that women don't get hassled on the streets of Managua.

Woman #8 to #9: A feminist is a man who's found a new way to meet broads. (*They both laugh.*)

J.D. #1 in coffee shop. He is reading The New York Times. *A plate of left-over ham and eggs and a cup of coffee are on the table. He appears to be eavesdropping on conversation of two women in adjacent booth behind him.*

Woman A: He thinks if he were gay, his male partner wouldn't mind doing all the housework. Now that women are trying to get out from under, men have this idea that gays are taking the place of old-fashioned house-fraus.

Woman B: But I was really being straight with him, and I thought I was straight in my own mind about it. If he didn't want to have sex, OK, and if he did, great. I don't care if he's involved with another woman; I'm not tr . . .

Woman A: But last week you *did* care, when you thought he was breaking up with her.

Woman B: I'm not trying to pin him down or anything . . . just get him into bed. . . . It wasn't as if I had to lasso him to get him up there again . . . The trouble is I really like the guy, I like being with him.

Woman A: He reminds me of Robert. You *know* the kind of guy he is and think you can handle him, stay on top of things . . .

*Lecture. Deller #1 and #2 alternate reading at a rostrum in a classroom
which doubles as a newly renovated loft condominium. During the lecture
the camera "works" the room, wheeling around the 10 students to explore
the bath/laundry room, the spanking new kitchen separated from a dress-
ing/bathroom by a curved glass wall.*

[The sound quality of the lecture keeps changing and intermittently the talk of the
crew is heard through a microphone on the traveling dolly. Occasionally the crew
conversation all but obliterates the lecture.]

Cameraman: Would you lean to your right a little bit . . . no, your right.

J.D. #1: That is her right . . . Are we rolling? . . . To back up a bit, in our culture
we have various places, various precise and specific verbal activities that one enters
into, one forms almost a kind of contractual relationship in terms of the kind of
libidinal and psychical economies that are at play. Certainly that site, that primal
scene theorized by Freudian psychoanalysis, is one of those and in fact, according to
that theory a primordial one, a fundamental one.

Other places clearly are in spoken discourse. There's a particular ethos that is co-
extensive with any linguistic activity, any verbal activity. Even the most banal
everyday conversation. There are greater and lesser degrees of formalization within
that, and every situation only allows certain eruptions and certain spontaneities of
language along a relatively determinate axis. In its precise formulations, it's really
quite concrete. It does determine who speaks the truth, who has the authority, the
risk, the obligation to speak the truth, and who has the authority to act upon that
formation of speaking. And what seems to me to be very important in this is that two
things are brought to bear on each other, two particular, two forms of a kind of ethos:
that which is cinematic, which constitutes the disposition of the voice and represents
precise verbal activities, precise social interactions and then, that which is almost the
emblematic activity, which is the double presentation of that because one is, one
believes, at the exterior of that ethos, and one believes in the efficacy of that speech,
be it a man to a woman, women with each other, men with each other, a court-room
situation or whatever.

And what seems to me to be at play here is a really quite transgressive, a really
quite important irony—and as you know, irony is a very destructive and constitutive
play. It introduces a difference into something we had ordinarily considered to be
sealed over, intact, coherent. And it does so via the intervention of the cinematic
apparatus; it does so via the intervention of certain formalisms that are a part of our
cinematic literacy. And yet what happens is, at the same time you have this beautiful
doubled figure, a deconstruction of the cinematic, the cinematic register and a
deconstruction of what is taken to be the object or the representamen of that cinematic
register. So what is represented within that cinematic play, because of the formal
cuttings and placements of that cinematic gaze, also deconstructs that cinematic gaze
which in turn deconstructs that precise verbal activity. So you have that doubled irony
and that doubled play of dialectic happening in there, which I think is really quite
profound, you know (*laugh*).

J.D. #2: We asked Foucault in an interview that I did with him just recently—
"Because you have refused to engage in polemics of any sort concerning your work
or your position on things, except for the correction of matters of fact, why is this?"
And he had a very clear and concise and well-formulated answer for that. He said,
"Because the pattern of political discourse abnegates true discussion and degenerates
into a series of denunciations or a claiming of positions or a casting of epithets, or at
least constitutes a grid to which work is placed rather than a true taking up of
discussion and a true taking up of the work—that is the reason why I don't engage in
polemics because when I don't engage in these polemics and when these polemics are
used against me, I don't participate in discussion because there is not a real discussion, it is only polemics." And he goes on to say that in this situation where, for
example, in thinking about, for example, in talking about nuclear limitations, about
limited nuclear strike capacities, that in a political field where the pattern of discourse
is such where only polemics are at play and the pattern of discourse is such that
difference is recognized only as opposition and not as difference, and that difference
is repressed, that in fact you don't have any true discussion, disallows even a
discussion that will potentially solve all those problems.

Female student (*holding a very bright light which is directed, third-degree-like, at
J.D. #1*): What can be said about this subject constituted as a gaping mouth, a hole, a
lack, a set of needs, desires. These are, this in itself is constant and seems almost
innate. What is this need to find something totally stable, universal, continuous in
human experience that is constantly being overturned by the theories and philoso-
phies of the 20th century? One, the knowledge, and the chasm, it seems—ongoing,
constant—if not contradiction, gap, between knowledge and the particular man-
ifestations of these drives and needs and lacks.

J.D. #1: True. In other words you're saying, the essential, the ineluctable difference
between knowledge and "knower," in a sense.

Student: Between knowledge and behavior, between knowledge and desire.

J.D. #1: Well, I think that one way of approaching that is to consider that, again, in
very close alignment with Freudian theory, and also in fact, Lacan's re-reading of
Freud, is to constantly reproduce within the Freudian discourse the most radical
lesson, in fact a lesson that, according to Lacan, that Freud went to great ends to
repress or abnegate by entering into more meta-psychological or cultural discourses.
But this radicality is really precisely this problem that we're talking about, that. . . .
To use by analogy, an example, and this goes back to our discussion on materiality of
language: when you ask a very simple question and, because we consider language to
be 1) immediately accessible, native speakers, with those differences, know the
language, speak it, it's considered to be an innate human capacity, and something that
is species specifi:. Man is a speaking animal, homo loquens, and no other is, and all
of that.

But when you begin to ask a very simple question, which is the question posed by
structural linguistics, where, if this language is the case, where does it exist? Because

it seems clear that on a purely material basis no group of native speakers at any given time ever speak at any one moment the entire corpus of the language. Because it always is a potentia, the language is always a structure. A structure that has a certain systematicity, that has certain material instanciations, certain material specificities, specific speech-acts, specific in communicative discourse. But where is and what is that structure which is such to allow those instances, and which is to allow for a— both a regularity and a difference, which establishes identity within that regularity for language. Where does this language exist? Does it exist as a material structure in the human brain? Well, that seems to me to be rather unlikely because from biology we know that that's not the case. We can't find it, simply. Does it exist as some sort of collective epi-phenomena for any group of native speakers? No, that seems unlikely too. That may apply for certain jargons or certain ideolects or socialects, but to account for—

Male student (*holding the light*): But something exists in the brain that makes language possible.

J.D. #1: Sure, but it exists as potentia. Because in fact when, and Piaget was quite good on this and Noam Chomsky as well. Noam Chomsky takes it in two different directions. When you deal with how is it possible, with what we learn from cognitive psychology and what we learn from infant studies in learning, for example, how is it possible that in such an incredibly short amount of time infants become mobile and not only, and competent speakers in their language. This is a problem we see most reflected currently in this problem of artificial intelligence. How is this infant capable of learning in such a remarkably short time, such an incredibly huge—he really doesn't use all of it, but having that capacity to generate the novelty, that capacity to speak and to say something new, to communicate. And we can't get a machine to come anywhere close to a fraction of that, and we understand the complexity of that. And so how can we then account for a biological analogue which would contain, I mean it really becomes a somewhat retrogressive notion: Is there a structure within the brain which is manifest to allow us to speak everything that we can say? No, that seems really to be unlikely and no, we haven't found any such organ. We haven't found any such structure in the brain. Everything that we've found in neuro-physiology really goes against that. In fact, the only theory that really still attempts to do that is this theory proposed by Carl Pribram (he's at Stanford now). And he wrote a book called *Languages of the Brain,* which is now unfortunately out of print, but within which he proposes, on purely neuro-physiological grounds, proposes a theory of the way that the brain processes information as being most akin to a holographic process. So that's really one place where there's an attempt to establish a biological grounding for that. But as you see, we immediately end up talking at a meta-discursive level, because clearly the brain is not a hologram. It becomes, really, an analogy that more clearly explains the way things appear to work. But this problem is still: if language is material, and we know that and in fact in our society from late antiquity on, words have been considered to be substantive. Words have been considered to be material. They're real. You can speak, and your speech—you yell "look out" and somebody looks out. There's that kind of, they affect matter, and so therefore must partake in that materiality themselves. And that materiality is then subject to analysis.

But when you deal with the systematicity, and I think this is the real insight for structuralism, when you deal with systematicity you begin to be unable to account for that materiality except in its specific instanciations, which is the problem of "langue" and "parole." Of language as language system, and parole as individual speech acts within a language system. Because of course, a language system is never at any one point constituted of those individual and material speech acts. Because that would just be a cacophony and not account for its capacity to move, to play, to put together, to take apart. I don't know if that answers your question, but it does sort of address some of the problems.

Female student: It does take care of a whole area. I have here, the old dichotomies: heredity/environment, biology/culture.

J.D. #1: Hmm. I think those are still real problems. Because in fact, in discussion with Foucault recently, we were talking about precisely this; we were talking about psychoanalysis, and because it was really just a personal conversation, it was full of a lot of really very interesting anecdotes. One was about Foucault's relationship with Ludwig Binswanger, who had studied with Freud and also studied with Edmund Husserl, a phenomenologist. But one interesting thing that Foucault said is that, you know, the problem with the Freudian unconscious is that it has no history. And in fact, you do find this coming up as a problem with Lacan. Lacan, in many of his polemics, counterposes his analysis to a, for example, precisely to ego-psychology, which would base itself on . . . in fact this answers another one of your questions. That essentially the ego is that thing which represses the eruption of speech, the kind of inner speech that comes out in the pre-conscious, unconscious system. And that act, that function of repression is that thing which renders the ego—to itself, in its relationship to itself—a stability. It is that thing which forms—there's a difference here, of course, between ego and self. And so Lacan of course attacks the notion of the ego psychologist by saying that essentially you're the ones who are attempting to substantiate a ghost. Because that ego really is only an ego in the play of the signifying chain, in the eruptions of, say, desire and lack. And in that play, repression is that thing which constitutes the ego as a coherence to one's self. So what Lacan does is he counterposes that analysis to the ego-psychologist and then claims that instead of categorizing according to a medical and therapeutical model, which is really a physiognomic model, or that categorizes according to this dysfunction, this disorder, this condition, this syndrome, and so on and so on, that in fact one must take into consideration the specificities of human subjectivities, their own histories, their own aggressions, their own traumas, and all that, to be perfectly consistent with the Freudian theory.

> *Camera has by now backed the whole length of the loft away from the podium and is positioned in the empty kitchen area, focused on J.D. #1 a half-block away.*

Trisha (*V-O*): You know, this expression "class struggle". . . .

J.D. #2 (*V-O*): Now, from the outside,

> *Camera begins to dolly forward through a narrow corridor, flanked on one side by a curving glass-brick wall and on the other by a long dressing table. We move toward a glistening bathtub. At some point the camera reverses its direction and dollies slowly backward.*

there's a problem with that because, of course, Lacan, in attacking the taxonomic and hierarchical ordering of psychoanalytic functions, proposes a generality, a general ground, in an odd way very close to the Husserlian transcendental subjectivity. He proposes that ground out of which the subject is, with its play of forces and desires, constantly coming into being and constantly fading away of course. But that whole play of identity and difference, that whole play of coming into being, comes into being only because of difference from what it's not, comes into being only in contradistinction to the other, which, of course, it's not. That "not". . . .

Trisha (*V-O*): This expression "class struggle" that everyone groans at because it calls up more of that Marxist rhetoric and everyone is so sure it has nothing to do with life in America. "Maybe," we say, "MAYBE class struggle is applicable to El Salvador or Guatemala, but America is a different situation." In Guatemala the war against Communism is in actuality a war against the poor. Here in America the war against the poor does not yet have to be masked as a war against Communism.

J.D. #2 (*V-O*): . . . . the subject and process. *But,* the problem is that Lacan, in doing that, reconstitutes a generality that is much more closely aligned to a kind of an essentialism, much more closely aligned to, in one sense, a kind of humanism, and so Foucault's injunction, saying the Freudian unconscious has no history, is true.

> *Cut to tracking around kitchen.*

Because it addresses the fact that Lacan is proposing such a generality and that whole domain between the general basis, the general ground out of which subjectivity comes into being and the material processes which constitute that subjectivity as a particular modality, a particular nodal point, or a particular monad; there's a huge gap there: the gap of the social and the historical. A huge problem with time and temporality in Lacan's process. And so when Foucault says the Freudian unconscious is without history he's quite accurate and quite right, I think.

> *Glass-brick wall fills frame.*

Trisha (*V-O*): In Guatemala the army goes looking for Communists, finds peasants, burns their homes, forces them into the hills, hunts them down in helicopters. Those who give themselves up—mostly the elderly, women and children, and the sick—these are put into strategic hamlets. That's the term they use. Strategic hamlet: an area of

> *Black-and-white photo of empty beds set up in rows in an armory/shelter for the homeless.*

deliberate population relocation, control, and containment. Lately the language has been disturbing my American sleep. The urban poor of America, where do *they* go when they are displaced

> *Camera dollies down a corridor between rows of beds in another shelter.*

from their homes and neighborhoods? Where are *their* strategic hamlets? In New York City the Department of Housing, Preservation, and Development has been accused of saying, "This agency is not set up to address the question of what is to be done with the poor." Without disappearing them, will the housing policies of New York City make the poor

> *Cut to interior of Jack's study. A window washer opens window and clambers out on ledge.*

disappear? Or, like the proverbial State, will they simply wither away?

> *Phone rings. Cut to reverse angle. J.D. #1 removes his headset and answers phone.*

J.D. #1: Hello.

Jackie (*She has a very heavy French accent*): Hello Jack. How have you been?

J.D. #1: Jackie! Fine. (*He is surprised, somewhat guarded.*)

Jackie: Jack, one reason I call is, do you have the transcript of the interview from last year? Rosenthal wanted to see it and . . .

J.D.: Didn't I mail it back to you?

Jackie: I thought you did, but I have looked everywhere . . .

> *Cut to black-and-white shot of Jon Hendricks on phone. He is talking about "the poster," layout, printing, etc. The sequence is quite brief and is replaced by Jack Deller in his study as before.*

J.D.: I'll have to ask my T.A., but I'm pretty sure I gave it to her to mail.

Jackie: I would appreciate that. I cannot find it. And the other reason I am calling you is I would like to see you very much. Are you free on Tuesday afternoons like you used to be?

J.D.: No, I'm not.

Jackie: Ah, no more Tuesdays (*nervous laughter*).

J.D.: It's not what you think. I've been going to a shrink.

Jackie: How interesting. I never thought you, uh, what kind?

J.D.: Are you going to the party for *Con-Stance* tomorrow night?

Jackie: For who?

J.D.: *De Con-Stance.* The magazine.

Jackie: Oh. The magazine. I thought someone named Constance . . . Who is giving the party?

J.D.: DeeDee Costello. Ordinarily I wouldn't go anywhere near the woman, but, *you* know . . . it's a good cause.

Jackie: Ah, yes. She is OK. She put her money, how you say it, she put her money where her mouth is. I had not intended to go, but if you will be there . . .

J.D.: Yeh, I'll be there. I don't know for how long, but I'll be there.

Jackie: Then I will see you tomorrow evening, Jack. Ciao.

J.D.: Bye.

> *He hangs up phone, stands up, fishes a crumpled piece of paper from a pocket, reads it, thumbs through a small address book or calendar, looks at his watch, removes his coat, hangs it on back of chair. Camera follows him to couch, where he collects some newspapers, then places them on a stack of film cans before leaving room. Deller #2 enters with a young woman carrying a briefcase, motions to her to remove her jacket and make herself at home, which she proceeds to do. From the moment J.D. #1 had removed his jacket we have been hearing the following V-O:*

Jon Hendricks: . . . It's to reach outside of our own community, outside of the committed community . . . It's wonderful to have things in the *Village Voice* or in the *Amsterdam News* or *Art and Artists* or whatever it might be, that's fine, that's good, and we have to work at that as well, but it's also imperative that we reach beyond that, out into the mass media, out into the national press, and beyond that into the European press, the South American press, Asian press if we can, in whatever ways possible, because that reverberates back in, it shows people over there that we aren't just sitting around like dodoes, that we *are* saying something, we are thinking something, and it also makes an embarrassment for *our* country, says something in the press over there that artists are dissatisfied, we're dissident artists here in the United States, like they have dissident artists over there. So strategically, as a strategy, that's the most important thing we can do.

> *J.D. #2 and the graduate student continue to engage in what at first appears to be a normal tutorial (totally without sound), conversing, reading, exchanging pages of a manuscript that she takes from her bag. During the following V-O, however, "something else" gradually emerges: the beginning of a seduction is indicated both by the "moves" of the characters and by the increasingly "noirish" quality of the lighting. Trisha's V-O is heard during this scene.*

Trisha (*V-O*): He didn't usually defend his infidelities in a doctrinaire fashion. You would hardly expect him to come out against monogamy, his having lived a legalized version of it for 20 years with my predecessor. But on occasion he would enumerate the ways in which marriage is used in bourgeois society to enslave women. ("*All societies,*" I would reply.) The issue usually boiled down to the simple fact that he had to be free, it was his right, his emotional necessity, and he would not tolerate interference by something so bourgeois as my feelings of betrayal. Even in his most ardent moments of feminist partisanship, however, he didn't try to push me toward a problematic equality. He never said, "Be free like me." Such equality, we both agreed, was too much of an abstraction, promising as liberation nothing more than mutual domination rather than an end to it. He was too smart for that. No, if he offered anything approaching a substantial defense it was that he was a mass of contradictions and what else could one expect under Capitalism? "Consistency is the hypocrisy of repressed bourgeois liberals," he would say. "And 'Capitalist Society,' " I would scream back, "is a specious label to be used as a smokescreen by deceitful spouses." He would groan and throw up his hands at my impossible liberal humanism.

Sometimes, fresh from reading Fredric Jameson or Russell Jacoby, I could play his game at equal cross purposes. "Consumption of goods in the economic sphere runs parallel with sexual consumption in the personal. The womanizer needs a new model to replace the old. The new model, though shoddier than the old, diverts attention from one's boredom, or emptiness, or terror, or whatever, and helps to manufacture, however fleeting, an illusion of rekindled youth and perpetual novelty, in a word, 'happiness.' "

By this time I would be barreling along like a Mack truck. "Emotional depression is a functional component of the marketing system that engenders our consumptions. The marketing of Coca Cola and Cuisinarts goes hand-in-hand with the marketing of being in love again and anti-depressant drugs and is symptomatic of a social order that requires the constant turning over of products and personal intimacies alike in the dual creation of depressive/inflationary emotional and economic cycles."

I knew I was getting carried away. But suggesting that my rivals were like shoddy goods gave me guilty satisfaction, while allowing me to consummate the argument with the horrific idea that the planned obsolescence of social relations had finally come to pass in western society.

> *By this time the lighting is very "noirish." The student faces the camera, the upper part of her face is in shadow. J.D. #2 stands behind her, his hands on her shoulders. The ambience—and their delivery of the following lines—is extremely intense.*

Graduate student: I guess I'll just never understand how the "subject-in-process" is incompatible with the civil libertarian's "person with inalienable rights."

J.D.: You mean "reconcilable," don't you?

Student: Both . . . incompatible and reconcilable.

J.D.: It's the difference between the meaning of reality as a theory-at-one's disposal and the meaning of reality as a human action. As subjects we may be "in process," but we must still act as citizens. In other words, to quote Luis Buñuel, "It's possible to have the whole story of Oedipus playing in your head and still behave properly at the table."

Slow fade-out.

Cut to Dellers #1 and #2 in street as before.

Man #2: All your great men did it: Freud with his sister-in-law, Marx with his maid, Brecht with his acolytes, Wittgenstein with his

Woman #10: What about Althusser?

Woman #11 to **#12:** Living with contradictions is easy. It's living with uncertainty that's the killer.

Man #3 to **Woman #13:** How can you be angry with me? I'm simply a product of social forces beyond my control.

Woman #14: So his shrink says to him, "If you're going to fool around with other women, you'd better become a better liar." And goddammit, he did!

Woman #15: Did what?

Woman #16 to **#17:** I don't want a man who's my equal. I want a man who knows more than me. I want a man I can learn from.

Man #4 to **Woman #18:** Well, just because I like to look at pictures of erections doesn't mean I'm homosexual.

Woman #19 to **#20:** "You can always tell how a woman feels about herself just by looking at her legs." Can you imagine anyone saying something like that? I could've killed 'im.

Man #5 to **Woman #21:** I'll give you an example: There's this American Indian myth about a man going around with a big stick to plug up a devouring vagina . . . But you know, the bottom line is, women really *do* want to devour men.

Jack Deller #1 at therapy session. The film being projected behind him is a slow-motion section from "Watermotor," the Trisha Brown/Babette Mangolte dance film.

J.D. #1: When I married her I said to myself, "This is serious business. She has a daughter. We will be a family." I felt very adult.

But can a man not be genuinely in love with more than one woman? Especially a man who expects nothing but the privilege of loving them? And caring for them when he can, and always being devoted and kind? I am not an average man. There is nothing predatory in me. I am much more of a giver than a receiver. I don't think the sexual act is in itself so terribly important, but I do think compassion and tenderness are vastly important. My former sister-in-law used to say I was the most wonderful husband a woman ever had. But isn't it just because I loved my first wife so much that after she died I loved all gracious and tender women. . . . I suppose that a man who was married for almost 21 years to a woman he adored becomes in a sense a lover of all women, and is forever seeking, even though he doesn't know it, for something he has lost.

> *Scene from "Double Indemnity" is projected (MOS) with Barbara Stanwyck and Fred MacMurray.*

J.D. #1: You can never cheapen a woman. No man of my sort thinks of her exactly as she thinks of herself. After all her body is to her a familiar thing; but to some men it is always a sort of shrine. Women are very subtle in these things. For hundreds and hundreds of years they had to please men with their looks, their charm, etc. Inevitably it must have left somewhere in their minds a deep intelligence about sex, because once that was all they had. Women have to be treated with great tenderness and consideration—

Stanwyck: You're right, I never loved you, Walter . . .

J.D. #1: —because they are women.

Stanwyck: I'm rotten to the heart; I always was, until now . . . when I couldn't fire that second shot . . .

MacMurray: Forget it, baby, I'm not buying.

Stanwyck: I don't want you to buy, just hold me . . .

> *CU of face of J.D. #2.*

MacMurray (*V-O*): Goodbye, baby. [Music swells.]

J.D. #2: I have never known a woman who in any way disgusted me or made me feel cheap, just as I never to my knowledge made a woman feel cheap. Sometimes, afterwards, they would burst into sobs and tears, and that would frighten me terribly, until they told me it was purely an emotional reaction, and not because they were ashamed. God, how little any man can know about women.

> *Camera zooms slowly back. A climactic sequence from "Night of the Living Dead" begins to unfold wherein a daughter stabs her mother to death, a brother murders his sister, etc. The soundtrack, which at this point consists of music and shrieking, is heard as background. In the course of the following voices-over we find ourselves in a movie house with an audience of about fifty people, an audience that becomes progressively more agitated and unruly to the point of violence.*

Trisha (*V-O*): Mmm . . . family life . . . How odd that it's sometimes so hard to think clearly about my family, or what passed for a family—Jack, Alicia, myself . . . Now other people's families, like my brother's, are another matter . . .

[Phone rings.]

Donald (*V-O*): Hi, Trisha, how are you?

Trisha (*V-O*): Donald! Thinking of the devil. Um, how—am—I? Well, considering my incisional hernia, my edema, my cystic breasts, my uterine fibroids, my absorption problems, my blind loop syndrome, my non-symptomatic gall stones, my varicose veins, and my deteriorating cervical disc, I guess I'm doing OK. How are *you*?

Donald: Barbara and I went to see Eustache's *Mother and the Whore* last night.

Trisha: Oh yeh? What'd you think?

Donald: We talked about it for over an hour afterwards. It made me extremely uneasy. You know, usually Barbara holds *my* hand during movies. This time I held onto *hers*. Jean Pierre Leaud's character was too close for comfort.

Trisha: Donald, you're too damn hard on yourself. As far as behavior goes there's nothing in *your* life that resembles his in that movie.

Donald: Oh *I* know that. Like he never washed the dishes because it would give him too much satisfaction. I love to clean up and I do it because it gives me *lots* of satisfaction. No, I'm not talking about the obvious things, like when he acts like a bad child. Remember where he walks across the bed with his shoes on? God, wasn't that awful? . . . if you know how dirty Paris streets are. No, I'm talking about the way he's always *acting,* I mean "putting on an act," and what's really going on is his terror, which he never confronts, and which he's always running away from.

Trisha: What are *you* afraid of?

Donald: (*pause*) I guess what everyone else is afraid of . . .

Trisha: You didn't answer my . . .

Barbara (*V-O*): Yes, you know, I didn't think much about the film immediately after, but later when we talked . . .

Trisha: Oh, hi Barbara, how long have *you* been on the extension?

Barbara: I don't understand the title. It's so superficial.

Trisha: But that's the key to the whole thing: *The Mother and the Whore*. Donald, there's this book you'd be interested in, by Dorothy Dinnerstein, and another by Nancy Chodorow . . .

Barbara: Oh don't give him any more books to read . . .

Donald: *Bar*bara!

Trisha: The issues the film raises are the same ones *I'm* going to be dealing with, but I don't want to create a man you love to hate.

Barbara: What's his name again . . . Jack . . .?

Trisha: Deller, a euphemism for "Tell her."

Barbara: Why not use Teller, Jack Teller?

Trisha: Too close to the father of the hydrogen bomb.

Donald: By why *not* bring in that association? The H-Bomb is as relevant to the sexual problem as . . .

Barbara: I'm going to say goodbye now, Trisha. Take care.

Trisha: Bye, Barbara. That's what I was trying to tell you about those books. The trauma for the infant in having to give up that first sense of harmony with the mother is much greater for the male than for the female and results in both the mother-whore syndrome and the H-bomb. Men spend their lives alternating between punishing and seeking mothering from women and carry their rage and terror out of the family realm and into the public.

Barbara: Why the name "Jack"?

Trisha: Barbara, you're still there. Well, it's about good old Anglo-Saxon rhymes: The House that Jack built; Jack Sprat could eat no fat; Little Jack Horner sat in a corner; Jack and Jill went up the hill; Jack be nimble, Jack be quick . . .

Donald: Get in and out with your big fat prick!

Trisha: Hey, did you make that up?

Barbara: Of course he did.

Trisha: Maybe I will call him Jack Teller.

Barbara: Just don't send him any more books.

Trisha: Barbara, I'm going to hop on the next 747 and come out there and kill you with an ax!

> *Cut to series of travelling shots: past boarded-up buildings on East 8th Street covered with graffiti, through large loft spaces in various stages of ruin or renovation, through the loft of Michael Snow's "Wavelength," along a sidewalk full of workers loading trucks.*

Trisha (*V-O*): Paris streets, 747's, books to buy, innermost terrors to confront. These are but a few of the amenities that form a rampart from which at a safe distance I have followed the struggles of others: Pre-revolutionary Russian women, Rosa Luxemburg, American anarchists of the 20's and 30's. Spanish Civil War, Cuba, and now Central America.

Paris streets, 747's, books to read, innermost terrors to confront. These are some amenities that cushion those struggles closer to home: Vietnam War protests, Abortion Rights, ERA. But then the wars moved even closer. The great Manhattan Real Estate Purge reached my doorstep. I was being evicted. I allied myself with others of my class who found themselves in a similar predicament. Almost overnight

Board of Estimate hearing as before. An artist (Diana Meckley) is at the podium.

we met the enemy. And it was us.

Diana Meckley: . . . and if I made $50,000 a year I doubt if I would have spent a year and a half working to get this housing. I'd probably be sitting on a beach in the Caribbean! Do you think I'd put up with this? I am here because I'm desperate. The jig is up . . . In the past many artists, through their own initiative and ingenuity, solved their need for combined living and work space by renovating previously commercial lofts. Ultimately as a result of skyrocketing rents and lack of protection many artists were forced out of their homes. We all know this. For those who have been able to stay in their lofts, the recently enacted loft law and loft board are a step toward establishing artists' rights as tenants, but it may prove impossible for many artists—myself included—to absorb the financial burden of bringing their landlords' buildings up to code. In the past several years I have joined the ranks of thousands, if not tens of thousands, of artists and other loft dwellers for whom litigation, lack of services, and innumerable meetings, in short: a tremendous amount of time and money spent, have become a way of life, along with some very real physical discomforts. At this point, resourcefulness, which artists are noted for, may not be able to solve their housing problems. Without further recognition of, and assistance in regard to this issue, many artists will be forced to pursue the only course left open to them, and that is to leave New York.

Sequence of travelling shots: past store windows on both sides of West Broadway between Canal and Houston Streets. Late afternoon and early evening.

Trisha (*V-O*): Here's another instance of disappearance: A hardware store used to occupy these premises. It sold things that people needed. Who needs *this* stuff? Just look at this junk. I ask you: Who needs it?! So godammit, what's to be done? I'll tell you: Organize in your community. When leases run out on old established businesses and the landlord triples or quadruples the rent, let the landlords know that the community will boycott any new business that tries to come in here. Get the present occupants to post signs in their windows that the neighborhood supports them and will not patronize their successors. . . . ENOUGH OF THIS NONSENSE!

[Tumultuous applause.]

CU of Jon Hendricks seated midst audience at Board of Estimate hearing. Swish pan to man speaking at the podium.

Chino Garcia: What I would like to say is that one of the main objections to this project is secondary displacement. No private landlord that we know of . . . has rented any space in the last year to any Hispanic or black person in our community. That is one of the most disgusting things. . . .

[Tumultuous applause.]

I would like to close this by saying that if you are responsible and conscious human beings, please vote against this Artist/Ownership project. Vote in favor of the artists and community residents that really need the services. Thank you.

[Applause. Pan to audience. Cut to new speaker at podium.]

Ivan Karp: Why should artists, why should anybody who has the spirit, the liveliness, the willingness, the expansive energy to live in the midst of this turbulent city, not be allowed to live in any part of this city, no matter what his income? Why discriminate against someone who's capable of earning $50,000 a year? [hoots and whistles] I didn't interrupt you, don't you dare interrupt me. There is no powerful justification for supporting one particular racial or ethnic group in a particular part of this city. Artists are by their nature an integrated race of people. And they want to function in any part of the city they can function. And we must allow, because we are a community of creative people and artists, for people outside of this city to come and share the lifeblood of this city no matter what their income happens to be.

[Hoots and hollers. Pan to audience, then to Karp.]

Board Member: (*V-O*): Mr. Karp, there's a question up here.

Cut to

Proxy for Carol Bellamy (*V-O*): . . . you describe artists earning $50,000 a year who would like to come back to the Lower East Side. They're more than welcome back to the Lower East Side. The question, I believe, is whether the city ought to subsidize. . . .

[Tumultuous applause.]

Cut to

Ivan Karp: I don't think there is any dispute, there's no dispute in cultural circles that the visual arts in the United States since the Second World War are the most significant contribution to world culture, TO WORLD CULTURE, since the Second World War, the American visual arts. [Hoots and hollers. A board member calls for quiet.] . . . other forces of greater energy that are viable are the most significant contribution to world culture have been the American visual arts, and I won't have any contestation of that. In any event, in order to sustain this pulsing life-blood, this creative force which has meant so much to world culture, and WHICH WILL BE THE SIGNIFICANT MEMORY

Camera tilts up to plaster eagle perched above the Board of Estimate.

Karp (*shouting*): OF OUR CIVILIZATION, AS IT ALWAYS IS. THE ARTS, ARCHITECTURE, VISUAL ART, ALL THE ARTS. WHAT IS REMEMBERED OF ANY CULTURE THAT

Karp's voice is replaced by Trisha's as the camera tilts down. Shots of segments of the audience are interspersed with shots of gold-framed 19th century portraits and the crystal chandeliers that illuminate the hall.

Trisha (*V-O*): The language troubles my New York sleep: Dislocate, displace, disappear. Relocate, replace, reappear. Property is profit and not shelter. Property is money and not comfort. Property is speculation and not home.

The last shot in the series is a long slow zoom from a portrait to a wide framing of the entire audience.

Evening. Deller's study. CU of J.D. #1 unloading his briefcase. A copy of Playboy *is removed along with books and papers. As camera dollies back, Deller turns on the answering machine.*

Woman's voice: . . . and I just rolled a joint and I'm calling you now 'cause I'm thinking of you and . . . uh, I figure, let them . . . an' I'm . . . I just had lunch with a woman who had an affair with you awhile back who's now a Lesbian and has a black belt in Karate and it's all these incestuous resonances . . . and all these little themes are resonating around, politics and sexuality, in some kind of profound way that my . . . uh . . . gone state lurches toward synthesis on. And I was thinking of you and I hope I didn't bring you down with my last call . . . it was . . . *I* don't know . . . counterproductive . . .

Camera has dollied back to MS. J.D. turns answering machine off. Cut to CU as he picks up stack of mail and shuffles through it. Most of it consists of appeals for contributions from progressive organizations. Camera again dollies away from him as he goes around to other side of table, sits down, looks up a number in phone book, starts to dial phone, changes his mind, lights a cigarette, snuffs it out, picks up Playboy, *walks to another chair positioned in front of bookcase, sits, flips pages of magazine. Cut to long shot of Deller in chair with his back to camera. Low angle. CU of legs in pants walking in from left. A woman kneels so as to position her face sideways in front of camera. Her lips are painted a fiery red. Removing her glasses, she says*

Will all menstruating women please leave the theatre?

Then leaves frame. Camera dollies toward, then over, Deller. We get a brief glimpse of the Playboy *centerfold open in his lap.*

Trisha (*V-O*): OK, here we go; I can't avoid this any longer. It's one theory, OK? . . . "In our culture a woman is sexually desirable only as long as her sexuality can also inspire fear. For the heterosexual male, woman is dangerous because she menstruates. The mystery and power of the menses evoke

Full-frame clip from Gilda. *Rita Hayworth and George Macready on bed. No sound.*

in him the fear of castration. Man's loss of sexual interest in the menopausal, or no longer menstruating, woman goes hand in hand with the waning of his terror of her. Because she no longer has the potential to harm him, she no longer has the power to make him afraid. Anger and contempt now replace fear."

And how about this (I mean, some of us have to do this dirty work, right?): "I shall be bold.

> *Cut to Deller's study as before. Chair is now empty.*

Sex for most heterosexual men is by definition an enactment of power, the kind of power over a woman that is intended to demean her whether or not she engages with that aspect of it. Most women prefer not to acknowledge this intent of their partners. Those of us who have lived with the same man over a protracted period of time may recognize the relation between our eroticism and our desire to please, but must disavow the nastier implications of our mate's

> *Cut to J.D. #1 in therapy session. A scene from* Dangerous *is on screen (Franchot Tone and Bette Davis).*

complementary dominance, which exists irrespective of the specific sexual practices, i.e., who is on top, sadomasochism, etc." Maybe I am being brutal. "Demean" may be too strong a word. OK, "control," "keep her in her place" rather than demean. In any case, it can be safely said that the sexual act is the crucial site where a primary social contract is enforced and the imbalance of dominance and compliance is perpetuated. . . . Good grief! and here I've been thinking all these years that sex was fun.

Bette Davis: You can go now?

Franchot Tone: Yes.

Davis: You must, because if you stay it'll be too late. . . . I love you. You may never love me, but you'll find you'll always come back to me. And each time you return it'll cost you more and more until you've spent your career, your ambitions, your dreams. Oh, I'm bad for people. I don't mean to be but I can't help myself. So I'm being generous to you, darling, kind . . . kinder than I've ever been to anybody before. But I can't be much longer. So go. Leave me. You can leave me, can't you?

Tone: I don't know . . . I've got to find out.

> *Cut to clip from* In a Lonely Place. *The action rushes by pell mell. It has been shot off of a VTR in its "scanning mode." This is followed by the same footage at normal speed. Humphrey Bogart describes a murder scenario to his detective friend and the latter's wife. There is no sound. J.D.'s monologue is simultaneous.*

J.D. #1: When I was a young man and very innocent I lived in a pension on the Boule Miche in Paris and was very happy wandering around, with very little money, but a sort of starry-eyed love of everything I saw. The only thing that upset me was the whores at the door of the apartment building if I happened to be out a little late. And I so innocent that I didn't realize that here were two girls at the pension that couldn't keep their feet off mine and were offering themselves to my innocence and I never even knew it. I knew so little about women then. I know almost too much now. And yet I have for a moment failed to realize that they face hazards in life which a man does not face, and therefore should be given a special tenderness and consideration . . . I have never seduced a virgin nor intruded upon a valid marriage. I think this feeling which I have about women, and which women obviously do not feel about themselves . . . There is nothing to argue about here, so far as I am concerned. If a woman gives herself to me, for one night or for much longer, I regard it as a delicate, almost a sacred gift, and although I am, I suppose, subconsciously aware that she gets something out of it too, I always think of myself as the recipient of a royal favor. . . . Women are so damned vulnerable to all sorts of hurts.

> *The detective's grip has slowly tightened around his wife's neck until she suddenly struggles free.*
>
> *Another clip from* In a Lonely Place*: Gloria Grahame in police station with Bogart. No sound.*

J.D. #1: I had been married so long and so happily that after the slow torture of my wife's death it seemed at first treason to look at another woman, and then suddenly I seemed to be in love with all women. I had no idea what I had to give them that they gave so much to me. The most strict and puritanical woman I had ever met went to bed with me a week after I met her. The strange thing was that such affairs as I had, never ended. There was never any bitterness or boredom. I love them all still and they seem to love me.

> *Clip from* Dead Reckoning*: Lisabeth Scott and Humphrey Bogart. No sound.*

But I could not live alone. It destroyed me. Therefore I could not be completely faithful to any woman who couldn't share my life, but I didn't regard this as infidelity, because after all sex is only a rather minor part of love, delicious as it is when it's right. I really didn't want to get married again because my heart was in too many places and because a wife would never have more than a part of me. So you see, this last marriage was very ill-advised from the start.

Bogart: My bet's on you, kid. If I'm wrong about you this time, I'm dead.

Scott: You're not wrong about me, Rick. I'll be your girl. I'll be anything you want me to be.

> *Cut to wall collage: CU of* About Men *from* The N.Y. Times Sunday Magazine. *This installment is titled "Keeping the Lid On."*

Woman's voice (*Yvonne Rainer*): My first reaction is simply to this "About Men" column, which I have always, I've always despised since they started it. Um, where they give a column for women which is in the Thursday Home section of the paper called "Hers," and then when they decide that some attention should be paid to men, they give it, ah, prominent placement in the, the Sunday Magazine section. Also I don't see why it's the same thing. I don't see why there should be an "About Men" column. I think it's obscene. Ah, and so now we're treated to these columns about men's sensitivity. So here we have, um, a priest, writing about how men, um, aren't sensitive enough, and how they've been educated by their fathers, um, to be stoic, and they're therefore cut off from their emotions and the toll this takes on them.

Trisha (*V-O*): You don't agree with that?

Y.R.: Um, I think that that may be true, but, ah, for me it's the sort of wimpiest version of why men should change. It's, it's again that they themselves will benefit, as opposed to how the rest of us *suffer* from the way that men are. This column's all about how the *man* suffers. Um, you know, it's again, it's again, it's this, this KGB article. Would this be written as an article about how the torturer suffers by having to perform torture on people? How he has been cut off from his emotions? I'm very suspicious of this kind of "About Men" column. Again, it's the, it's the, it's the absolute focus on the individual. Totally without context. Um, it's a, it's an asocial, apolitical, ahistorical, totally psychological and individualistic approach to the problem. And then we see what the conclusion is. We see that the sweet smell of success doesn't happen overnight. Um, a man who earns his first million knows what it takes to make it in this world. He knows that what it takes to make it in this world is this being cut off from his emotions . . . Is this manliness with which you should encounter the KGB, and with which he smokes his cigar and strokes his two dogs which are, uh, pointedly hunting dogs . . . um, they're not, it's not a sheepdog that you see here. It's a, it's a hound that's trained to hunt things down, um, even here, the sweet smell of success, well that film that's uh, being quoted in the phrase, is about the toll that is taken on people trying to achieve that kind of success. Ah, but that's not what we see here. Here the phrase has been inverted and we see the rewards and profits that accrue.

Trisha: Would you say that this left hand message is critical of this right hand here?

Shot of double page spread: "About Men" and Macanudo cigar ad.

Y.R.: Uh, no. I would say this layout, which knows that the right hand side of the page has much greater effect than the left hand side of the page, has an ad here that effectively contradicts and subsumes these wimpy priestly statements on the left hand side of the page. Um, especially if you consider that within this society the priest is not seen as a real man anyway.

Trisha: And yet you say it's given more prominence than a similar, uh, comparable column by a woman . . .

Y.R.: Right. Which is put in the house, home pages of the daily edition. Um, and I'm sure this person is also paid more for writing this for the Sunday *Times Magazine* than the women who are paid to write for the Thursday Home Section, among the newest sofas or whatever.

CU of cigar ad and photo of Salvadoran corpses.

Trisha (*V-O*): Is it so obvious? What do you think is obvious?

J.D. #1 (*V-O*): What, you mean that he's a rich

> *Overhead circular pan (b&w) of Artists' Call meeting in Leon Golub's studio. No sound.*

American . . .

Trisha: yeah . . .

J.D. #1: . . . and those are poor Salvadorans . . .

Trisha: yeah . . .

J.D. #1: . . . and he's alive enjoying his millions and they're . . . dead . . .

Trisha: yeah . . .

J.D. #1: um . . .

Trisha: I mean, isn't it important to spell out the political connection?

J.D. #1: But I just did. I *did* spell it out, but it's . . .

> *Return to images #3 and #4 as before.*

it's . . . just . . . obvious.

> *CU of cigar ad.*

J.D. #1: I forgot. I didn't realize at first of course this is a cigar which, aside from being a cigar and a phallic symbol, is also a product of labor. It says it's still made step by step by hand. And, uh, if it's a really good cigar and made like it was a hundred years ago it's got to be made by very cheap labor. I don't think El Salvador has much of a cigar industry, unlike Honduras, which does. But the point is very clear, in order for this guy to have his cigar, even at the income *he* makes, he and his world are going to have to control the labor that are doing things step by step by hand and, uh, when that gets out of control that's when you see these massacres taking place. I don't know where Macanudo's

> *Another tracking shot of Artists' Call meeting.*

[A low indistinguishable murmuring is heard.]

are made. Probably in Jamaica, I think. And in Jamaica the CIA and company managed to thwart a socialist development by manipulating popular terror and the press, etc. and brought down the Manley regime and now they have a comfortable labor supply to make Macanudo cigars.

Trisha (*V-O*): So you think that's a Jamaica cigar?

J.D. #1: I think so. It says Montego. I suspect it's Jamaican. You might want to look it up. In any case, it was. . . . Jamaica was one of that category of countries within which the threat to this guy's hegemony has occurred, a threat that was managed. . . .

[J.D.'s voice fades down to be replaced by the voice of Jon Hendricks in the Artists' Call meeting:]

Jon Hendricks: The problem is we're understaffed.

J.D. #1 (*V-O*): . . . they don't want to go around beheading

Return to images #3 and #4 on wall: cigar ad and corpses.

a bunch of peasants. They would much rather thwart social revolutions by so-called democratic means, uh, which they have succeeded to do in Jamaica. And now they have 199-dollar round-trip plane fares and readers of the NY Times can fly down to Jamaica for cheap vacations where they can come back and say, "Gee,

Camera moves down and to left to reveal J.D. #2 on rowing machine, looking at TV set. The image on the set is visual static.

that place is beautiful and cheap but people seem to hate us down there. Why do they hate us so much?"

Reverse angle, J.D. #2 still rowing.

J.D. #1 (*V-O*): But I'm not ashamed to be a lover of women. The difficult thing to make another person understand is that I have a code, that I adhere to it, and I have always adhered to it. There was a time in my life as a young man when I could have picked up any pretty girl on the street and slept with her that night. (Bragging again, but it's true.) I didn't do it because there has to be something else and a man like me has to be sure he's not hurting anyone, and he can't know that until he knows more about her. There are lots of cheap women, of course, but they never interested me.

Cut to therapy session. J.D. #1 is speaking in sync. A scene from Caught *is on screen: Robert Ryan on analyst's couch. No sound.*

There are women who are inaccessible, and I can tell that in five minutes. I always could. There are women who could be had tomorrow night but not tonight. That I know also. There are women who for one reason or another would give themselves wrongly, and who would feel awful about it the next morning. That also I had to know.

Clash by Night: Robert Ryan and Barbara Stanwyck having a confrontation in the kitchen. No sound.

Trisha (*V-O*): This is where he says, "A man is nothing without a woman."

J.D. #1 (*sync.*): Because one doesn't love in order to hurt or destroy. There were girls who could have been scarred for life by giving way to a normal human impulse, but not by me. If by someone else I couldn't help it. There were girls who didn't care, but for them I didn't care either. I don't know whether it is a talent or a curse, but I always know.

Another clip from Clash by Night: *Stanwyck and Ryan still in kitchen.*

Trisha (*V-O*): Now he's saying, "Tell me what you want me to be and I'll be it."

J.D. #1: I don't know how I know, but I could give you specific instances in which, against all the outward appearances, I knew. Sometimes this haunts me. I feel as though I must be an evil man, that this intuition is given me only to destroy me. But I guess I don't mind being destroyed very much anymore. After all, I was a loving and faithful husband for almost twenty-one years . . . This second time around was a very different story.

> *Stanwyck and Ryan in torrid clinch. Clip fades out.*

> *Cut to street scenes.*

Woman #22 to **#23:** You wouldn't think one woman could marry two insane men in one lifetime!

Woman #24: When we left work today it was still light.

Man #6 to **Woman #25:** Y'know, emotions are produced. They don't just happen.

Woman #25: Do you mean they're synthetic?

Woman #26 to **#27:** You think white women have it any better? Do you know what she told me? She told me that when she was 12 her father . . .

Man #7 to **Woman #28:** Uh-uh. Christ was crucified so that male saints could have periodic bleeding just like women. That's what those stigmata are all about.

Woman #29: . . . only a change at the top.

Woman #30: When are we getting married so I can have your apartment after we get divorced?

Woman #31: Jus' 'cause the world goes 'round is no reason to be seasick.

Woman #32 to **#33:** You expect too much. You want solutions to be immediate and neat instead of gradual and incomplete.

Woman #34 to **#35** (*they are standing next to a public sculpture*): Sometimes it's enough to make you scream for the cultural vice squad.

> *Early evening. Jack Deller #1 in his study. He is standing in front of the wall collage. He holds a glass of vodka-on-ice and alternately drinks, rearranges the images on the wall, and contemplates them. The voice-over is the actual voice of Martha Rosler responding to the collage (in contrast to the enactments heard previously).*

Martha Rosler (*V-O*): Anything that's labeled "About Men" has got to be disgusting anyway . . . I mean that's sort of taken for granted by me.

Woman's V-O (*Yvonne Rainer*): Why?

M.R.: Because it's the . . . it suggests that the reason there are things about women is some kind of swindle and that men have to get their licks in too. You know, it kind of suggests again that somehow women have gotten ahead of the game and you have to redress the balance. Again, it's about men catching up with female privilege, in this case the privilege to cry.

And this last entity is very hard to look at or even think about, which is dead bodies and decapitation, this kind of horrendous bloody image of dead people. I think one of them is a woman. People who are clearly of some other country. One guesses El Salvador. And below it is tacked on something that suggests in a rather horrible way that there's a victim, a male victim,

> *Photo of Salvadoran corpses.*

six months old in Guatemala, the scene of the worst human rights record in the world. People are being killed all the time simply for wanting a chance to exist . . . for no reason at all. Certainly you don't kill six-month-old babies, if this is a dead person, or a refugee. You don't drive six-month-olds away for their political beliefs, so this is a kind of ultimate terror which, of course, represents the indiscriminate destruction of life and pur-

> *Cut to MCU of J.D. as before.*

pose. Uhm . . . put next to a legend that says a man who earns his first million knows what it takes to make it in this world and seeing people who obviously don't have what it takes to make it in this world, uhm, sort of gives the lie to the idea that it . . . it suggests that it comes from inside you, what it takes to make it in this world, whereas something that shows the impossibility of making it when you begin as a peasant in Central America, shows the impossibility of that. . . . It's really hard to look at this picture . . . It's really awful . . .

Y.R.: Do you want to stop?

M.R.: I guess so.

Y.R.: I have one more image to put up.

[Sound of footsteps.]

M.R.: Oh. OK. So we find the image of another head. This time a woman of middle age of our culture, I guess middle age. A woman between 40 and 55 who is portrayed as nothing *but* an inner life, as a disorder.

> *CU of ad for estrogen replacement therapy from medical journal.*

(*reading*): "Nervous, anxious, irritable, fatigued, restless nights." And the person who's being addressed is clearly a doctor. "While you're calming her down with a tranquilizer, treat what may be her real problem with conjugated estrogens." . . . So, this is a woman as hysteric reduced to what hysteria is, which is supposedly, etymologically, a disorder of the uterus. So, whereas two pictures over we have this guy who is on top of the world, and one more over is the notion of the man who can't feel. We have the female problem, which is not to be masculine at all, or

Cut to MCU of J.D. #1 as before.

enough, that is, not to have any control and to be a bundle of raging hormones. Now it's in the light of that, it seems that what men want is an ability to feel without the necessity of the hormones that are imposed on us poor victim women. So here's a woman who is not portrayed in relation to any status except that what we see of her suggests a solidly middle class woman just because of the tastefulness of her hairdo and the cleanliness and tastefulness of the bit of collar that shows where she's smilingly restored to happiness as a result of taking something called conjugated estrogens, which is a really ironic name. I never heard of conjugated estrogens, but the notion of the relationship between the conjugal or the marital or the sexual and estrogens is funny . . . So, she's a victim of menopause. So, we start with a victim. In the middle of our tableau we have someone who is most assuredly not a victim and we progress to other victims. But victims of opposite things. In one case biology, in another case the state . . . and in the case of the man who can't feel, of course, they're victims of society, but as I said, there is something so clear in the text that suggests that they may be victimized by a lack of feeling but it's just the tragedy of place, a true tragedy. The tragedy of being highly placed and having some unfortunate thing befall you, as opposed to the ignominious death of Guatemalan or Salvadoran peasants, or the ignominious state of being the victim of your own biological disease, because women are clearly defined by being perpetually diseased.

Y.R.: The tragedy of being a woman or the inevitability of . . .

[Phone rings.]

M.R.: . . . of the tragedy of being a woman . . . and the necessity

Cut to J.D. #1 answering phone.

J.D. #1: Yeh.

M.R.: of being drugged as a way of handling the problem.

J.D. #1: Yeh, I'm going . . . Lousy . . . Around 10 . . . See ya.

Cut to J.D. again in front of wall.

Trisha (*V-O*): Following a community board meeting which resulted in a vote in our favor we were nearly attacked by our incensed opposition. The police had to escort us out of the hall. The next morning I read about a

Cut to series of shots of Donald Judd sculpture field.

collision of continents many millions of years ago, a confrontation of such impact that great masses of land crumpled into jagged piles miles high. One day Africa piled into North America. Tomorrow America will ram into China, thrusting Hawaii and Japan high on her shores like a fleet of inner tubes.

"Are you more important than old people, poor people, blacks, and Hispanics?" . . . The larger scheme of things offers a momentary refuge from contesting voices.

Long corridor stretching away from camera, a closed door at its end. Muffled sounds of large party can be heard. Deller #1 emerges from elevator at right. He knocks. DeeDee Costello opens the door while still talking to someone off-camera. A glass is in her hand.

[Cacophony of party in full swing blasts through the open door.]

DeeDee Costello: If Mayor Koch would give them the subways as silos for MX missiles, maybe *then* we'd get some money from Washington to improve the service! Jack Deller! come on in.

Deller enters the blue-tinted space. Door slams behind them. This shot (the empty corridor) lasts throughout the following V-O dialogue.

Trisha: What?! She hasn't been in the subway in 20 years!

Man: Ha! Free enterprise. How can there be free enterprise when the State and its military have become the principal controllers of finance capital?

Woman A: You almost sound like a Republican. Would you rather see more *corporate* control?

Man: No, of course not. I'm talking about the prediction that by 1988 for every $100 of civilian expenditure the U.S. will be allotting $37 in working capital to the military. It's absolutely appalling. It means nothing less than the continued industrial deterioration of this country on a scale unprecedented in history.

J.D. #1: Wait a minute. That ratio can't be right. If it's 33% right now for the military, how can . . .

Man: Oh hello, Jack. No, that's GNP for 1979 you're talking about. And by 1988 *that* figure will be up to 47%. My reckoning is based on a pattern of performance during the 70's. Now, I'll *tell* you what I want . . . (*his voice fades out.*)

Woman B: Assuming the probability of resistance to oppressive institutions being transformed—if successful—into equally oppressive institutions, do you see hope in *any* form of resistance?

Jackie: The only successful form of resistance is through art.

Woman B: But everyone can't make art.

Jackie: They must, at some level.

Woman C: On the way back I sat next to this guy on the train who started to talk about how he had just come back from Las Vegas where he had gone in with some real estate developers. He said, "Everyone's jumping with joy out there waiting for the MX to be approved by Congress." So I said, "Sounds like you're going to make a killing."

Woman D: My Buddhist friend said, "In the universal mind nothing is ever lost." And sure enough, on retracing my steps, I found my glasses.

Jackie: People in America think I am a Marxist!

Woman B: Because they can't understand how you could have written what you've written *without* being one.

Jackie: Yes, in relation to Marxist writing and ideas, I am a Marxist, but not in relation to any existing institutions. Though Marxism is exhausted as a political tradition, it is still one of the richest sources of ideas about modern society.

Woman D: I was treating this seven-year-old girl. After several sessions, the parents, who are Catholic, came to me and said they had decided to discontinue therapy. They said they preferred to put their problems in the hands of God. They simply refused to see the child's difficulties as symptomatic.

J.D. #1: In the universal mind nothing is ever symptomatic.

1st Man: . . . I want less managerialism in favor of workplace democracy. And, of course, a massive reversal of the arms race so that capital can be converted to the repair of our decaying infrastructure. Hey Jack, where're you going?

J.D.: Excuse me.

[Sound of door slamming.]

> *CU of finger jabbing at elevator button, followed by MCU of J.D. #1 leaning back against wall of corridor. He looks toward the camera as the ensuing dialogue begins. Cut to three-shot: Deller in background looking at a couple in the foreground. The man is looming in a sexually aggressive manner over a young woman who seems to be pressing herself into the wall to escape his advances. They both hold glasses.*

Man: I couldn't believe my ears. This guy was actually saying that he didn't see what all the fuss about rape was about. He said he doubted if most women would mind being raped. And *then* he said—and this is the kicker—"After all, the vagina is only an orifice like any other."

> *Cut to CU of J.D. #1 rushing toward camera.*

J.D.: Why didn't ya tell 'im, "How'd ya like it if I stuck my finger

> *Reverse angle: J.D. lunges at man and sticks his finger in his ear.*

in your ear?"

Man (*retreating in disbelief*): Hey! *I* didn't say it.

> *CU of J.D.'s finger on elevator button.*

Jackie (*V-O*): Jack! Are you

> *MCU of Jackie standing at end of corridor. She is wearing a knee-length black and gold lamé dress, very decolleté.*

leaving already?

Cut to images #4 and #5 of wall collage: the Salvadoran corpses and the estrogen-replacement ad.

Trisha (*V-O*): The woman who has stopped bleeding and the corpses that have stopped bleeding. Eros and Thanatos have come and gone. The myths take us far afield, to a place from which we must struggle to return. The images refer to realities that are connected by certain terms: sadism/colonization; social and political terror/cultural and sexual terror; machismo/phallocentrism; the military-police fraternity/the medical fraternity; suppression of resistance to economic domination/suppression of resistance to ideological domination.

> *Corridor. Jackie and Jack Deller #1 are doing a "minimalist song and dance" of seduction, ambivalence, attraction and withdrawal—via exchanges of gaze, gesture, and moves, all of which run parallel with their recited texts, neither "discourse" dominating the other, neither the verbal nor the visceral.*

J.D. #1: The formula "They have the power" may have its value politically; it does not do for an historical analysis. Power is not possessed, it acts in the very body and over the whole surface of the social field according to a system of relays, modes of connection, transmission, distribution, etc. Power acts through the smallest elements; the family, sexual relations, neighborhoods, etc. As far as we go in the social network, we always see power as something which "runs through" it, that acts, that brings effects. However that is not always true. Power becomes effective or not, that is, it is always a definite form of momentary and constantly reproduced encounters among a definite number of individuals. Power can thus not be possessed because it is

> *Audience at Board of Estimate hearing. They start to applaud (low volume).*

always "in play," because it risks itself. Power is won like a battle and lost in just the same way. At the heart of power is a war-like relation and not one of appropriation.

[Volume of applause rises. As applause dies out the voice of the proxy for the Borough President of Brooklyn can be heard.]

Brooklyn (*V-O*): If our goal is to revitalize this part of the

> *Cut to MCU of proxy.*

Lower East Side, then all we have to do, from what I see, is let private enterprise do what it already is doing. We can better use our limited funds elsewhere. I vote no.

[Enthusiastic applause. A voice says "President of the Council."]

> *Cut to proxy for Carol Bellamy.*

C.B.: . . . a revised plan for artists' housing which takes into account the limits of our city budget, the needs of our low income artists, and the needs of greater minority participation. I vote no.

[Tumultuous applause. Cut to Andrew Stein, the Borough President of Manhattan.]

A.S.: . . . the government only has, due to federal cutbacks, very little resources, and I think that we have to deal with people who need the most help first to the best of our ability, and that's why I am voting no. [Applause.]

Cut to CU of proxy for Borough President of Queens.

Queens: The Borough President of Queens votes no. However, the Borough President of Queens would also welcome the opportunity to explore with the Mayor and the Housing Agency the possibility of instituting in Queens, housing for artists.

[Four seconds of dead soundtrack.]

Cut to corridor as before.

Jackie: What is happening when women must work so hard in distinguishing the penis and the phallus? What is going on when the privileged areas of a marxist theory become "the subject" on the one hand and "language" on the other?

In one sense, it is easy to see the immediate value of this, since constructing a theory of the subject involves trying to work on two legendary disaster-and-devastation zones: one being the outcome of a pugnaciously practical feminism actively hostile to any reflection, confiding itself trustfully to the tender care of sociology, ignoring the claims of economy, and proceeding from the attempt to pit all women against all men at all times, to the discovery that the main enemy,

> *Cut to "Session." Jack Deller #2 is the patient talking (MOS) to the off-screen "doctor." A scene from Ophuls' Caught is on the screen: Barbara Bel Geddes and James Mason are sitting at a bar. Another woman has come up behind them and asked Mason something. The clip is MOS.*

when not in The Head, was other women; the other being the failures of an economistic marxism which not only failed to account for subjective contradictions and the appeals of bourgeois ideology, but could not even begin to account for its own remarkable failure to appeal.

Cut to corridor.

J.D. #1: Power is never totally on one side. Just as there are not those who "have" power, neither are there, on the other hand, those who do *not* have it. The relation to power is not contained in the schema of passivity-activity. Clearly there is within the social field "a class" which, looked at strategically, takes up a privileged place and can assert itself, score up victories and can achieve an effect of superior power for its own benefit. But power is never monolithic. It is never completely controlled from one point of view.

Cut to image #4 and #5 of wall collage as before.

Trisha (*V-O*): While you're treating her hormonal problem, Brother Doctor, keep her under control with tranquillizers, pity, and contempt. While you appear to be dealing with the problems of your country, President Duarte, keep your people under control with torture and random murder. "But pity and contempt are not torture and murder," you will say. And I will tell you, "Slavery is slavery wherever people cannot change the conditions of their lives."

Corridor as before.

J.D. #1: At every moment power is in play in small individual parts.

Jackie: Only the naive humanist feminist thinks she can change something by changing her consciousness. The rigorous feminist plumbs the hidden depths of subjectivity, studies its construction in language, follows the diffusing implications of Benveniste's empty instance through to its fulfillment elsewhere, winds through the labyrinth to find not a monster but a new position of the subject.

Leaving aside the transfer of some theorists from armchair to couch, one awkward consequence of the freudo-marxist marriage presided over by language, is to open up an inviting space for marxist and feminist labors which can only be defined by the systematic evacuation of certain questions—political, economic, and above all, historical questions. It then becomes a point of departure for "theory" to insist on the presence of humanism, etc., in feminist discourses and practices. The immediate disadvantage of this is not that it can lead to a delirious enumeration of theoretical errors and dangers, though these do diversify delightfully in the site of the hapless subject: apart from the old favorites idealism, humanism, and empiricism, there can be essentialism, moralism, ahistoricism,

Session as before: J.D. #2, continuation of the same scene from Caught.

unification, centralization, necessitation, globalization, and totalization. The immediate disadvantage is that "the" subject looms up even more hugely as problem and as formulation, ensuring that there is no escape from "the" subject as an effective concept in the analysis of political struggles, and, in the process, largely depriving that analysis of any way of distinguishing between strategies of power and tactics of resistance, between statements in common (Right to Life, Right to Choose, for example) on the one hand, and antagonistic discourses on the other.

Corridor. Jackie and J.D. #1 are locked in a tight embrace.

Theory as watchdog is a poor creature: not because it is nasty or destructive, but because for attacking the analysis of confrontations, it simply has no teeth.

Reverse angle. Deller releases Jackie, pushes her away from him.

J.D. #1: Power cannot be described as something localized in the state apparatuses. Perhaps it is even inadequate to say that the state apparatuses are the stake in an internal or external struggle. The state apparatus is a concentrated form—an auxiliary structure—the instrument of a system of powers, which goes far beyond it, so that, looked at in practical terms, neither the control nor the destruction of the state apparatus can suffice to bring about the disappearance or the change of a definite type of power.

Power is not caught in the alternatives: force or ideology. In fact every point in the exercise of power is at the same time a site where knowledge is formed.

Cut to black-and-white shot of Artists' Call meeting. Jon Hendricks is in the foreground.

Jon Hendricks: I know the power of co-option of politicians, and also the magnetism of . . .

Leon Golub: They may co-opt, but they can also get you ten times more public recognition at the same time . . .

Doug Ashford: We don't have to have a big debate . . . They *are* invited and we're not offering them a forum. . . .

J.D. #1 (*V-O*): And conversely,

Cut back to corridor.

every established piece of knowledge permits and assures the exercise of power. Put otherwise, there is no opposition between what is done and what is said.

High angle. Jackie moves away from Deller as she talks.

Jackie: Passing from the realm of the theory of the subject to the shifty spaces of feminine writing is like emerging from a horror movie to a costume ball. The world of "theorization" is a grim one, haunted by mad scientists breeding monsters through hybridization, by the haunted ghosts of a hundred isms, and the massive shadow of the subject surging up at every turn. Feminine writing lures

Continuation of scene from Caught, *now full-frame. Mason and Bel Geddes leave the bar and move onto the dance floor. It is very crowded, and they are repeatedly jostled as they try to dance.*

with an invitation to license, gaiety, laughter, desire, and dissolution, a fluid exchange of partners of indefinite identity. All that custom requires is infinite variety, infinite disguise. Only overalls are distinctly out of place [dance music fades up]; this is the world of "style." Women are not welcome here garbed in the durable gear of men; men, instead, get up in drag.

James Mason throws back his head and chortles:

James Mason: I'm having such a wonderful time.

Cut to "Dream sequence," a series of shots that operate in-and-out of phase with the voice-over. The location is Deller's study, now garishly lit in pinks, purples, greens. The furniture is strewn about higgledy-piggledy, the sofa and desk up-ended. The ironing board reappears in some of the shots. The sequence is as follows:

1. *A woman (Yvonne Rainer), dressed in white frilly apron, removes dishes from a corrugated tub in which is floating a plastic duck. She throws dishes to the floor one at a time.*
2. *CU of dishes breaking as they hit the floor.*

3. *CU of interior of old-fashioned wooden ice box. A hand reaches in and removes a painted decoy duck.*
4. *J.D. #1 throws duck into water of tub and manoeuvers YR into a tango kiss.*
5. *Cat sitting on floor in the middle of debris from desk.*
6. *YR and J.D. #1 move a table filled with assortment of kitchen paraphernalia, including three red balls that roll to floor.*
7. *J.D. #1 tussles with two men (Ben Speth and Larry Justice). A woman (Nancy Salzer) passes behind them with the decoy duck on her head.*
8. *Camera circles the bed. J.D. #1 and YR struggle for possession of a pink moth-eaten blanket. She is wearing a mask, crudely-drawn features on grey cardboard.*
9. *J.D. #1 and YR in bed, propped on elbows. He is talking to her (MOS).*
10. *CU of one-eyed cat in YR's lap. She is petting it.*
11. *MCU of YR peering from behind screen. Only one of her eyes is visible.*
12. *MCU of YR saying (in sync) the last line of the dream.*

Jackie (*V-O continuing over first shot of dream sequence*): Lacan reigns here not as law-giver, but as queen.

Woman's *V-O (YR)*: Hey! What's this? I must be dreaming. There's my mother and she's only 48 years old. Still in her apron.

My God, what's *Jack* doing in here? And there's the old dog and cat. Dreams mix everything up. Those animals had barely been born then. I should wake up from this. But who are all these people? Oh no, I can't believe it—my mother's telling that terrible joke from that movie about the guy with the duck sitting on his head who goes to a psychiatrist. The psychiatrist says, "Well, what can I do for *you?*" and the duck says, "Get this guy off my ass."

What? What is going on here?! That's me in the bed. He and *I* shouldn't be making love. Jack and *Mama* are supposed to be married in this dream, not Jack and me. But there's my mother standing by the door. Mama, get out of there. What's that he's saying? "I've always been what?" And now he's coming with a big long Oh. And no, I don't believe it. Mama is watching.

Now what is he saying? Something like "I've always been . . . committed"? That's it, "committed to you." LIAR!! How odd that he should be expressing his love on the back stairs. I haven't been in a house with back stairs since I was a kid. And Mama's carrying *my* one-eyed cat. This is too much. Wake up, wake up. I don't want to hear her. Mama, shut up, shut up!

MCU of YR facing the camera. She speaks in sync:

Y.R.: I don't mind one bit that you two are carrying on. Jack and I stopped having sex ten years ago.

Corridor. Jackie leans against wall. J.D. #1 moves toward her, leans his elbow against the wall and nuzzles her neck as she speaks.

Jackie: Each performance has its code, however, and the naive feminist blunders in at her peril.

Jump cut to Jackie in gray coveralls.

The audience gathers to watch her slip on a central shibboleth, the language of psychoanalysis. In Frankenstein's castle, the penalty for careless definition is swift but clean dismemberment: in the shimmering world of feminine impersonation, a worse fate awaits the woman with the wrong style of argument—she is exposed for the straight that she is, stripped bare to reveal (to her shame and surprise) that she is only equipped with a phallus.

J.D. disengages himself, looks at her, then rolls away to lean against wall. At this point they are both standing on left side of frame.

In either case, however, there is no forgiveness for not knowing what you do

Reverse angle. Jackie and J.D. now stand on right side of frame, J.D. in the foreground, Jackie half hidden behind him.

when you speak.

J.D. #1: The penal system is an example of the perfectly carried through and calculated strategies of power. No analysis can give an adequate account of the prison so long as it is posed only in terms of economics.

If, on the contrary, we pose

A young woman emerges from door at end of corridor and enters an adjacent bathroom. (A mirror on the inside of the door fleetingly reveals washbasin and toilet.)

the problem on the level of power-knowlege, we then must speak properly of the disciplinary system, that is, of a society equipped with an apparatus whose form is sequestration, whose aim is the constitution of labor-power and whose instrument is the acquisition of discipline or habits as social norms.

Until the 18th century we had a society in which power took the visible form of hierarchy and sovereignty. This power pursued its operation through a set of demar- cations, of ceremonies. Since the

Dissolve. Jackie turns to face camera, leaning her elbow on wall. Her clothing changes from coveralls to lamé dress.

19th century, the discourse that will now accompany the disciplinary power is that which grounds, analyses, and specifies the norm in order to make it prescriptive. The discourse of the king can disappear

Woman emerges from the bathroom and stands looking toward them. Jackie turns her back to camera and stares at other woman.

and be replaced by the discourse of him who sets forth the norm, of him who engages in surveillance, who undertakes to distinguish

Black and white shot: Artists' Call meeting, beginning with CU of Lucy Lippard laughing, then a pan to Kate Linker and Audrey Zimmerman.

[Indistinct murmur of voices can be heard under J.D.'s voice.]

the normal from the abnormal: that is, through the discourse of the teacher, the judge, the doctor, the psychiatrist, and above all,

Corridor as before. Young woman has re-entered the party through door at the far end.

the discourse of the psychoanalyst.

Dissolve to what appears to be a new space, perhaps the space of the party that Deller had originally entered. The light is dark blue. Deller is holding a drink, standing on the right side of the frame while Jackie faces him on the left.

[The "party walla" is again heard.]

Jackie: If a girl takes her eyes off Lacan and Derrida long enough to look . . .

J.D. #1: In Foucault's later work, one discovers to what degree medicine becomes one of the main foci for changes in configurations of power. We see how the control of epidemics and the reorganization of the hospital contribute to the implantation of discipline, and public health policies become one of the great sources of bio-power. To see this in operation we have only to look at the use of hysterectomy for population control, drug experimentation on prisoners, and sequestration of political dissidents in mental hospitals. Eventually, medicine was to play an important part in modern racisms.

Disciplinary and punitive methods are not simply consequences of legislation or indicators of social structure. Rather, they are part of a diffuse, yet autonomous, network that has gradually subordinated and colonized the legal institutions and social sciences for the purpose of imposing order and control rather than forbidding, protecting, or healing.

Cut to new shot (same location): Jackie and J.D. #1 seen from the waist up, facing the camera.

Jackie: Can the structure of a brain inhibited and weakened by thousands of years of patriarchal oppression be modified by sudden and rapid social change? Shall we invite the men to flaunt and fling and giggle with the girls? Shall we make the priests tremble by showing them our "sexts"? Shall we create a culture of disruption and revelation, savagely ingenuous and unsusceptible to the teasing of pricks? Shall we join the sext show (sex you have said we are, sex we will be)? Shall we cling—or return, as the case may be—to our simplistic view of class and sex, our binary vision of power, our imperative utopianism? Shall we disgrace and disqualify ourselves beyond the construction sites of theory, stretch binary schemes to their limits, work at the Unspeakable, refuse the everyday but wheel around for an extraordinary future, disgrace ourselves with Valerie Solanis when she says, "Life in this society being, at best, an utter bore and no aspect of society being at all relevant to women, there remains to civic-minded, responsible, thrill-seeking females only to overthrow the government, eliminate the money system, institute complete automation, and destroy the male sex"?

Trisha (*V-O*): If a girl takes her eyes off Lacan and Derrida long enough to look, she may discover

> *Coffee shop. Camera dollies backwards as before. In the first booth is a man reading a paper; in the middle are two women conversing; in the front booth sits J.D. #1, eavesdropping. This time his headset is on the table. It is late at night.*

she is the invisible man.

1st Woman: How can any self-respecting feminist be anything *but* "male-identified"? No matter how much we empathize or express solidarity with each other, we've got to identify with . . . well, if not men then with the idea of men, with their power in the world, what some people would call . . . the phallus.

2nd Woman: Kristeva says that in order to place woman within its symbolic order Christianity demands that while living or thinking of herself as a virgin impregnated by the Word, she lives and thinks of herself as a male homosexual.

1st Woman: Yeh, all that means is that she's royally screwed! We could make up a variation of our own . . . Let's see: "I submitted as if I were a man who thought he was a woman, to a man who looks and acts like a man but would rather be a woman."

> *J.D. gets up and leaves.*

2nd Woman: I guess, in a manner of speaking, we are *all* men. The only difference is that those of us with ovaries wear women's clothing.

1st Woman: That reminds me of something I read: Man is a human being with a pair of testes attached, while woman is a pair of ovaries with a human being attached. (*laughter*)

[They continue to talk (*MOS*).]

Trisha (*V-O*): Lately I've been thinking yet again: I can't live without men, but I can live without a man. I've had this thought before, but this time the idea is not colored by stigma, or despair, or finality. I know there will sometimes be excruciating sadness. But I also know something is different now. Something in the direction of unwomanliness. Not a new woman, not non-woman or misanthrope, or anti-woman, and not non-practicing Lesbian. Maybe unwoman is also the wrong term. A-woman is closer. A-womanly. A-womanliness.

[Voices from Artists' Call meeting are heard.]

Woman: It should be made very clear that this is not a protest march, that it be called a procession . . .

Man: We're calling it a procession.

> *Cut to very grainy (Super-8 to 16mm to optical print to two more generations) color CU of Audrey Zimmerman, who speaks more-or-less in sync.*

A.Z.: . . . uh, two nights, February 10 and February 24th, which will be films about Central America by women, and then the second night it will be films by Latino women about Central America . . . They're getting some films up from Central America. We'll ask to see previews of fuller programs . . . later in the year . . .

> *Freeze—frame of A.Z. Her hand is over her mouth.*

Y.R. (*V-O*): If this were an art work, how would you critique it?

> *Cut to J.D. #1 rearranging images of collage.*

Martha Rosler (*V-O*): I would feel I was being tricked into trying to deal with things that have become incommensurable, as though they weren't incommensurable. That I was being told that the myths of civility at home and the problems of daily life are only a veneer over the truth that the state destroys people. It's as though I'm being told that when dealing with the ultimate, my worries about how to live my life in America are not important. As soon as I am presented by an image of dead bodies, which is in a situation that I know without a doubt my own government is responsible for, I am made to be a complicit party . . . and yet the concerns of the other elements are not nothing. It *is* a matter of interest whether men are or are not presented as hard surfaces that exude the smell of success from their very physical appearance. It *does* matter what this man is complaining about, which is a problem, which is that masculinity is defined as uncaringness and unthinkingness and unfeelingness. It does matter because it does determine how we conduct our foreign policy. It isn't only a matter of economic interest, but how we choose to pursue that interest. If we're willing to grind up other people because we can't be bothered to feel about them then it does matter. But this image is so strong that I can't . . . I can only wince and it makes it really difficult to think about the other stuff once I get to this.

> *Cut to black. Credits rise from bottom of frame.*

> *Selected Credits:*
> *Jack Deller #1*   William Raymond
> *Jack Deller #2*   Larry Loonin
> *(a middle-aged*
> *professor)*

Trisha's Voice *(his estranged wife)*	Trisha Brown

Jackie
  (one of Deller's
  former lovers)
	Jackie Raynal

Graduate Student	Thyrza Goodeve
DeeDee Costello	Iris Owens
Window Washer	Antonino D'Agostaro
Trisha's Body	Kate Flax
Women in	Anne Friedberg, Ruth Mullen, Amy Schewel,
Coffee Shop	Fronza Woods, Sabrina Hamilton
Woman in Corridor	Melody London
Speakers at Board	Robb Storr, Norman Siegal, Diana
of Estimate Hearing	Adorno, Chino Garcia, Ivan Karp, Diana Meckley
Speakers at Artists'	Daniel Flores Ascencio, Jon Hendricks,
Call Meeting	Leon Golub, Doug Ashford, Audrey Zimmerman, Lucy Lippard
Collage Voices	William Raymond, Martha Rosler, Trisha Brown, Yvonne Rainer
Party Voices	Ryan Cutrona, Edith Becker, Jackie Raynal, Fronza Woods, Caroline McGee, Sabrina Hamilton
Telephone Voices	Gary Rosenblatt, Ruth Gray, Edith Becker

DIRECTOR: Yvonne Rainer

DIRECTOR OF PHOTOGRAPHY: Mark Daniels

ADDITIONAL CINEMATOGRAPHY: Emilio Rodriguez, John Murphy, Michel Negroponte, Elliott Caplan

VIDEO: Jacki Ochs

SOUND RECORDIST: Helene Kaplan

ASSISTANT DIRECTOR: Christine Le Goff

PRODUCTION MANAGER: Edith Becker

CASTING DIRECTORS: Larry Loonin, Nancy Salzer

ASSISTANT CAMERA: Wayne De La Roche

GAFFER: Ben Speth

KEY GRIP: Larry Justice

2ND ASSISTANT DIRECTOR: Michael Taylor

2ND ELECTRIC: John O'Toole

EDITORS: Yvonne Rainer, Christine LeGoff

SUPER-8 EDITOR: Marjorie Keller

Script compiled from the speech and writing of the following people:

Raymond Chandler, Michel Foucault, Russell Jacoby, Fredric Jameson, Joel Kovel, Julia Kristeva, Meaghan Morris, Paul Patton, Mark Rappaport, Yvonne

Rainer, B. Ruby Rich, Martha Rosler, Paula Weideger, Peter Wollen, Tom
Zummer.

Sculpture Field	Donald Judd
Music	"Penguin Cafe Single," Penguin Cafe Orchestra
Film Clips	*Un Chien Andalou* (Luis Bunuel)
	Dark Victory (Edmund Goulding)
	Otherwise Unexplained Fires (Hollis Frampton)
	Watermotor (Trisha Brown and Babette Mangolte)
	Double Indemnity (Billy Wilder)
	Night of the Living Dead (George Romero)
	Gilda (Michael Curtiz)
	Dangerous (Alfred E. Green)
	Wavelength (Michael Snow)
	In a Lonely Place (Nicholas Ray)
	Dead Reckoning (John Cromwell)
	Clash by Night (Fritz Lang)
	Caught (Max Ophuls)

Special thanks to Steering Committee of Artists' Call Against U.S.
   Intervention in Central America and No More Nice Girls

Financed in part by grants from the New York State Council on the Arts and
the National Endowment for the Arts.

© 1985 Yvonne Rainer

IN MEMORIAM
Hollis Frampton
1936–1984

Filmography

1972	*Lives of Performers*	16mm, b/w, sound, 90 minutes
1974	*Film About a Woman Who . . .*	16mm, b/w, sound, 105 minutes
1976	*Kristina Talking Pictures*	16mm, color & b/w, sound, 90 minutes
1980	*Journeys from Berlin/1971*	16mm, color & b/w, sound, 125 minutes
1985	*The Man Who Envied Women*	16mm, color & b/w, sound, 125 minutes

All the above films are distributed by
First Run/Icarus Features
153 Waverly Place
New York, New York 10014   Tel: (212) 243–0600

Bibliography

Compiled by Patricia White

Anderson, Jack. "Yvonne Rainer: The Puritan as Hedonist." *Ballet Review*, vol. 2, no. 5 (1969), pp. 31–37.

Arthur, Paul. "Desire for Allegory: The Whitney Biennials." *Motion Picture*, vol. 2, no. 1 (Fall 1987).

Baecque, Antoine de. "Yvonne Rainer: Le style, c'est l'emotion." *Cahiers du Cinema*, no. 369 (March 1985), pp. 41–42.

Banes, Sally. "The Aesthetics of Denial." *Terpsichore in Sneakers: Post-Modern Dance*. Boston: Houghton Mifflin Company, 1980, pp. 41–54.

———. "Lives of Performers: Annette Michelson Discusses Acting in *Journeys From Berlin*." *Millennium Film Journal*, nos. 7, 8, 9 (Fall 1980–Winter 1981), pp. 69–84.

Bassan, R. "Forme et ideologie chez Yvonne Rainer." *Revue du Cinema*, no. 357 (January 1981), pp. 129–30.

Blumenthal, Lyn. "On Art and Artists: Yvonne Rainer." *Profile*, vol. 4, no. 5 (1984).

Borden, Lizzie. "Trisha Brown and Yvonne Rainer." *Artforum*, vol. 11, no. 10 (June 1973).

———. "Yvonne Rainer: 'This is a story about a woman who . . .' Theater for the New City." *Artforum*, vol. 11, no. 10 (June 1973), pp. 80–81.

Buckley, T. "The Screen: 'Journeys from Berlin/1971.'" *New York Times*, February 11, 1980, p. C16.

Bruno, Giuliana. "La mela di Adamo." *Filmcritica* vol. 37, no. 365–66 (June–July 1986), pp. 361–62.

Camera Obscura Collective. "Yvonne Rainer: An Introduction." *Camera Obscura*, no. 1 (Fall 1976), pp. 53–70.

———. "Appendix: Rainer's Descriptions of Her Films." *Camera Obscura*, no. 1 (Fall 1976), pp. 71–75.

———. "Yvonne Rainer: Interview." *Camera Obscura*, no. 1 (Fall 1976), pp. 76–96.

Carroll, Noel. "Interview with a Woman who . . ." *Millennium Film Journal*, nos. 7, 8, 9 (Fall 1980–Winter 1981), pp. 37–68.

Castle, Frederick. "Occurrences: To Go to Show Them." *Art News*, vol. 67, no. 4 (Summer 1968), pp. 34–35.

Chin, Daryl. "Add Some More Cornstarch; or, The Plot Thickens: Yvonne Rainer's *Work 1961–73*." *Dance Scope*, vol. 9, no. 2 (Spring 1975), pp. 50–64.

Christie, Ian. "Lives of Performers." *Monthly Film Bulletin*, vol. 44, no. 520 (May 1977), p. 101.

Coco, William, and A. J. Gunawardana. "Responses to India: An Interview with Yvonne Rainer." *The Drama Review*, vol. 15 (T–50, Spring 1971), pp. 139–42.

Copeland, Roger. "Toward a Sexual Politics of Contemporary Dance." *Contact Quarterly*, vol. 7, nos. 3–4 (Spring–Summer 1982), pp. 45–51.

Copeland, Roger, and Marshall Cohen. *What Is Dance?* Oxford: Oxford University Press, 1983.

Dawson, Jan. "A World Beyond Freud." *Sight and Sound*, vol. 49, no. 3 (Summer 1980), pp. 196–97.

De Lauretis, Teresa. *Alice Doesn't: Feminism, Semiotics, Cinema*. Bloomington: Indiana University Press, 1984.

———. "Strategies of Coherence: Narrative Cinema, Feminist Poetics, and Yvonne Rainer." In *Technologies of Gender: Essays on Theory, Film, and Fiction*. Bloomington and Indianapolis: Indiana University Press, 1987, pp. 107–26.

DeMichiel, Helen. "Rainer's Manhattan." *Afterimage*, vol. 13, no. 15 (December 1985), pp. 19–20.

Devins, S. "The Man Who Envied Women." *Variety*, October 2, 1985, p. 13.

Field, Simon. "The State of Things." *Monthly Film Bulletin*, vol. 54, no. 636 (January 1987), pp. 4–6.

Foster, Susan Leigh. *Reading Dancing: Bodies and Subjects in Contemporary American Dance*. Berkeley: University of California Press, 1986.

Goldberg, Marianne. "The Body, Discourse, and *The Man Who Envied Women*." *Women and Performance*, vol. 3, no. 2 (1988), pp. 97–102.

Goldberg, RoseLee. *Performance: Live Art 1909 to the Present*. New York: Harry N. Abrams, Inc., 1979.

Goodman, Saul. "Yvonne Rainer: Brief Biography." *Dance Magazine*, vol. 39 (December 1965), pp. 110–11.

Hecht, Robin Silver. "Reflections on the Career of Yvonne Rainer and the Value of Minimal Dance." *Dance Scope*, vol. 8 (Fall–Winter 1973–74), pp. 12–25.

Hoberman, James. "All About Yvonne." *Village Voice*, February 11, 1980, p. 47.

———. "Explorations: Our Movies, Ourselves." *American Film*, vol. 7, no. 1 (October 1981), p. 34.

———. "Film: The Purple Rose of Soho." *Village Voice*, April 8, 1986, p. 64.

Howell, John. "Ca Va? Pas Mal." *Art-Rite*, no. 8 (Winter 1975).

———. Review of *Work 1961–73*. *Art in America*, vol. 63 (May–June 1975), pp. 18–21.

Hulton, Peter, ed. *Fiction, Character and Narrative: Yvonne Rainer*. Devon, England: Department of Theatre, Dartington College of the Arts, Theatre papers, 2d ser., no. 7, 1978.

Jayamanne, Laleen, with Geeta Kapur and Yvonne Rainer. "Discussing Modernity, 'Third World,' and *The Man Who Envied Women*." *Art and Text*, vol. 23, no. 4 (March–May 1987), pp. 41–51.

Johnston, Jill. "Judson 1964: End of an Era." *Ballet Review*, vol. 1, no. 6 (1967), pp. 7–13.

———. "The New American Modern Dance." In *The New American Arts*, edited by Richard Kostelanetz. New York: Collier Books, 1965, pp. 162–93.

———. "Rainer's Muscle." In *Marmalade Me*. New York: E. P. Dutton, 1971, pp. 36–40.

Jowitt, Deborah. "Two Choreographers." *Artscanada*, vol. 32 (March 1975), pp. 46–47.

Kaplan, E. Ann. *Women and Film: Both Sides of the Camera*. New York: Methuen, 1983.

King, Kenneth. "Toward a Trans-Literal and Trans-Technical Dance-Theater." *The New Art, a Critical Anthology*, edited by Gregory Battcock. New York: E. P. Dutton, rev. ed., 1973, pp. 119–26.

Kleinhans, Chuck. "Lives of Performers." *Women and Film*, vol. 1, nos. 5–6 (Winter 1974–75), pp. 52–54.

Koch, Stephen. "Performance: A Conversation." *Artforum*, vol. 11, no. 4 (December 1972), pp. 53–58.

Kruger, Barbara. "'Difference: On Representation and Sexuality' (film program), the New Museum/The Public Theater." *Artforum*, vol. 23 (April 1985), pp. 94–95.

———. "Yvonne Rainer; The Man Who Envied Women." *Artforum*, vol. 24 (Summer 1986), p. 124.

Kuhn, Annette. *Women's Pictures: Feminism and Cinema*. London and Boston: Routledge and Kegan Paul, 1982.

Lardeau, Yann. "Yvonne Rainer, Journeys from Berlin/1971." *Cahiers du Cinéma*, no. 316 (October, 1980), p. x.

Levin, David Michael. "The Embodiment of Performance." *Salmagundi,* nos. 31–32 (Fall–Winter 1975–76), pp. 120–42.

Lippard, Lucy R. "Talking Pictures, Silent Words/Yvonne Rainer's Recent Movies." *Art in America,* vol. 65, no. 3 (May–June 1977), pp. 86–90.

———. "Yvonne Rainer on Feminism and Her Film." *The Feminist Art Journal,* vol. 4, no. 2 (Summer 1975), pp. 5–11. Reprinted in *From the Center.* New York: E. P. Dutton, 1976, pp. 265–79.

Livet, Anne. *Contemporary Dance.* New York: Abbeville Press, 1978.

MacDonald, Scott. "Text as Image in Some Recent North American Avant-Garde Films." *Afterimage,* vol. 13 (March 1986), pp. 9–20.

McDonagh, Don. "Yvonne Rainer/Why Does It Have To Be That Way?" In *The Rise and Fall and Rise of Modern Dance.* New York: Outerbridge and Dienstfrey, 1970.

———. "Yvonne Rainer." *The Complete Guide to Modern Dance.* New York: Doubleday, 1976, pp. 445–48.

Mekas, Jonas. "Interview with Yvonne Rainer." *Village Voice,* April 25, 1974, p. 77.

———. "Yvonne Rainer's A Film about a woman who . . ." *Village Voice,* December 23, 1974, pp. 94–97.

Mellencamp, Patricia. "Images of Language and Indiscreet Dialogue: *The Man Who Envied Women.*" *Screen,* vol. 28 no. 2 (Spring 1987), pp. 87–101.

Michelson, Annette. "Yvonne Rainer, Part I: The Dancer and the Dance." *Artforum,* vol. 12, no. 5 (January 1974), pp. 57–63.

———. "Yvonne Rainer, Part 2: Lives of Performers." *Artforum,* vol. 12, no. 6 (February 1974), pp. 30–35.

Mueller, J. "Yvonne Rainer's 'Trio A.'" *Dancemagazine,* vol. 53, no. 3 (March 1979), pp. 42–43.

Mulvey, Laura. "Feminism, Film and the Avant Garde." *Framework,* no. 10 (Spring 1979), pp. 3–10.

Nemser, Cindy. "Editorial: Rainer and Rothschild, An Overview." *Feminist Art Journal,* vol. 4, no. 2 (Summer 1975), p. 4.

Pahlow, Colin. "Film About a Woman Who . . ." *Monthly Film Bulletin,* vol. 44, no. 525 (October 1977), pp. 211–12.

Phelan, Peggy. "Spatial Envy: Yvonne Rainer's The Man Who Envied Women." *Motion Picture,* vol. 1, no. 3 (Winter–Spring 1987).

Pontbriand, Chantal. "Interview with Yvonne Rainer." *Parachute* no. 10 (Spring 1978).

Pym, John. "Working Title: Journeys from Berlin/1971." *Monthly Film Bulletin,* vol. 47, no. 558 (July 1980), pp. 140–41.

Rainer, Yvonne. "Annotated Selections From the Filmscript of *Kristina Talking Pictures.*" *No Rose,* vol. 1, no. 3 (Spring 1977).

———. "Beginning with Some Advertisements for Criticisms of Myself, Or Drawing the Dog You May Want to Use to Bite Me With, and Then Going On to Other Matters." *Millennium Film Journal,* no. 6 (Spring 1980), pp. 5–7.

———. "Conversation Following Screening at Cinemateque of Christina [*sic*] Talking Pictures, April 6, 1978." *Cinemanews* 78, nos. 3–4 (1978), pp. 16–17.

———. "Don't Give the Game Away." *Arts,* vol. 41 (April 1967), pp. 44–45.

———. "The Dwarf Syndrome." In *The Dance Has Many Faces,* edited by Walter Sorrell. New York: Columbia University Press, 1966, pp. 244–45.

———. "Film About a Woman Who . . ." (script). *October,* no. 2 (Summer 1976), pp. 39–67.

———. "From an Indian Journal." *The Drama Review,* vol. 15 (T–50, Spring 1971), pp. 132–38. Reprinted in *Work 1961–73,* pp. 173–88.

———. "Incomplete Report of the First Week of the Edinburgh International Film Festival, August 17–30, 1980 and Musings on Several Other Films." *Idiolects* nos. 9–10 (Winter 1980–81), pp. 2–6.

———. "Kristina (For a . . . Opera): Filmscript." *Interfunktionen,* no. 12 (1975), pp. 13–47.

———. "Kristina Talking Pictures" (script). *Afterimage,* no. 7 (Summer 1978), pp. 37–73.

———. Letter to *Artforum,* vol. 12, no. 16 (September 1973), p. 10.

———. "A Likely Story." *Idiolects,* no. 6 (June 1978).

———. "Looking Myself in the Mouth." *October,* no. 17 (Summer 1981), pp. 65–76.

———. "The Man Who Envied Women" (script). *Women and Performance,* vol. 3, no. 2 (1988), pp. 103–60.

———. "More Kicking and Screaming from the Narrative Front/Backwater." *Wide Angle,* vol. 7, nos. 1–2 (Spring 1985), pp. 8–12.

———. "Notes on Deborah Hay." *Ikon,* February 1967.

———. "A Quasi Survey of Some 'Minimalist' Tendencies in the Quantitatively Minimal Dance Activity Midst the Plethora, or an Analysis of Trio A." In *Minimal Art, A Critical Anthology,* edited by Gregory Battcock. New York: E. P. Dutton, 1968, pp. 263–73. Reprinted in *Work 1961–73,* pp. 63–69; and in *Esthetics Contemporary,* edited by Richard Kostelanetz. Buffalo: Prometheus Books, 1989, pp. 315–19.

———. "Some Retrospective Notes on a Dance for 10 People and 12 Mattresses Called 'Parts of Some Sextets' Performed at the Wadsworth Atheneum, Hartford, Connecticut, and Judson Memorial Church, New York, in March 1965." *Tulane Drama Review,* vol. 10, no. 2 (T–30, Winter 1965), pp. 168–78. Reprinted in *Work 1961–73,* pp. 45–51.

———. "Some Ruminations around the Cinematic Antidotes to the Oedipal Net(tles) While Playing with De Lauraedipus Mulvey, or, He May Be Off Screen, But . . ." *The Independent,* vol. 9, no. 3 (April 1986), pp. 22–25.

———. "Thoughts on Women's Cinema: Eating Words, Voicing Struggles." *The Independent,* vol. 10, no. 3 (April 1987), pp. 14–16. Reprinted in *Blasted Allegories: An Anthology of Writings by Contemporary Artists,* edited by Brian Wallis. New York: The New Museum of Contemporary Art; and Cambridge, MA: The MIT Press, 1987, pp. 380–85.

———. *Work 1961–73.* Halifax: Press of the Nova Scotia College of Art and Design; and New York: New York University Press, 1974.

———. "Working Title: Journeys from Berlin/1971" (excerpts from script). *October,* no. 9 (Summer 1979), pp. 81–106.

———. "Yvonne Rainer Interviews Ann Halprin." *Tulane Drama Review,* vol. 10, no. 2 (T–30, Winter 1965), pp. 142–67.

Reynaud, Bérénice. "Chorégraphie et cinéma: entretien avec Yvonne Rainer." *Cahiers du Cinéma* no. 369 (March 1985), pp. 43–45.

———. "Impossible Projections." *Screen,* vol. 28, no. 4 (Autumn 1987), pp. 40–52.

———. "Petit dictionnaire du cinema independent new-yorkais, II." *Cahiers du Cinéma,* no. 340 (October 1982), pp. 35–47.

Rich, B. Ruby. "The Films of Yvonne Rainer." *Chrysalis,* no. 2 (1977), pp. 115–27.

———. "Kristina: For an Introduction . . ." *Afterimage,* no. 7 (Summer 1978), pp. 32–36.

———. *Yvonne Rainer.* Minneapolis: Walker Art Center, 1981.

Rosenbaum, Jonathan. "Aspects of the Avant-Garde: Three Innovators." *American Film,* vol. 3, no. 10 (September 1978), pp. 33–38.

———. "Explorations: The Ambiguities of Yvonne Rainer." *American Film,* vol. 5, no. 5 (March 1980), pp. 68–69.

———. "Regrouping: Reflections on the Edinburgh Festival 1976." *Sight and Sound,* vol. 46, no. 1 (Winter 1976–77), pp. 2–8.

———. "Yvonne Rainer." *Film: The Front Line—1983.* Denver: Arden Press, 1983.

Rosenbaum, Mitchell. "Interview with Yvonne Rainer." *Persistence of Vision,* no. 6 (Summer 1988).

Rosovsky, P. "Journeys from Berlin/1971." *Variety,* February 6, 1980, p. 20.

Sagel, Hildegard. " 'Film About a Woman Who . . .' von Yvonne Rainer: Bemerkungen zur Kamera, Aspekte einer Konstruktion." *Frauen und Film,* no. 10 (December 1976), pp. 44–45.

Sharpe, Willoughby, and Liza Bear. "The Performer as a Persona: An Interview with Yvonne Rainer." *Avalanche,* no. 5 (Summer 1972), pp. 46–52.

Siegel, Marcia. *At the Vanishing Point: A Critic Looks at Dance.* New York: Saturday Review Press, 1972.

Silverman, Kaja. "Dis-Embodying the Female Voice." In *Re-Vision: Essays in Feminist Film Criticism,* edited by Mary Ann Doane, Patricia Mellencamp, and Linda Williams. Frederick, MD: University Publications of America and the American Film Institute, 1984, pp. 131–49.

Storr, Robert. "The Theoretical Come-On." *Art in America,* vol. 74, no. 4 (April 1986), pp. 159–65

Taubin, Amy. "Daughters of Chaos: Feminist and Avant-Garde Filmmakers." *Village Voice,* November 30, 1982, pp. 80–81.

Trend, David. "True Stories." *Afterimage,* vol. 14 (January 1987), pp. 3–4.

Vincendeau, Ginette. " 'The Man Who Envied Women': Yvonne Rainer Discusses Her Film with Ginette Vincendeau and the Créteil Audience," *Screen,* vol. 28, no. 4 (Autumn 1987), pp. 54–56.

Walworth, Dan. "A Conversation with Yvonne Rainer." *Psychcritique,* vol. 2, no. 1 (1987), pp. 1–16.

Wikarska, Carol. "A Film About a Woman Who . . ." *Women and Film,* vol. 2, no. 7 (Summer 1975), p. 86.

Wooster, Ann Sargeant. "Yvonne Rainer's *Journeys from Berlin/1971.*" *The Drama Review,* vol. 24, no. 2 (T–86, June 1980), pp. 101–18.

WATKINS COLLEGE OF ART
The films of Yvonne Rainer
PN 1998.3 .R35 A25 1989

14223